NetWare®
The Macintosh® Connection

Marty Jost

Windcrest®/McGraw-Hill

Appletalk™	Apple Computer, Inc.
CompuServe™	CompuServe Information, Inc.
Ethernet™	Xerox Corp.
HP™	Hewlett-Packard Company
ImageWriter™	Apple Computer, Inc.
LaserWriter™	Apple Computer, Inc.
Norton Utilities™	Peter Norton Computing, Inc.

FIRST EDITION
FIRST PRINTING

Library of Congress Cataloging-in-Publication Data

Jost, Marty.
NetWare : the Macintosh connection / Marty Jost.
p. cm.
Includes index.
ISBN 0-8306-2195-4 (pbk.)
1. Operating systems (Computers) 2. NetWare (Computer file)
I. Title.
QA76.76.063J68 1991
005.7'1369—dc20 91-32239
CIP

TAB Books offers software for sale. For information and a catalog, please contact TAB Software Department, Blue Ridge Summit, PA 17294-0850.

Acquisitions Editor: Stephen Moore
Book Editor: Melanie D. Brewer
Series Design: Jaclyn J. Boone
Cover: Sandra Blair Design and Brent Blair Photography, Harrisburg, PA WT1

Contents

Introduction

This book was written to guide you in implementing and using Novell NetWare to network Macintosh computers. Networking has a reputation of being a complicated discipline, which in many respects it deserves. This book is focused on simplifying the subject.

This book is for current users of Novell networking products for the Macintosh, potential buyers of Novell networking products, and Macintosh network's system administrators. This book brings together a wide range of information concerning the planning, preparation, management, and everyday use of a Macintosh in a Novell network. Those new to computer networking will appreciate this book's practical explanations, and find useful background information that will help them quickly grasp new concepts. Experienced readers will find that sufficient technical information is included to make their reading time well spent.

This book is an extension, not a rehash, of the manuals that come with Novell networking products for the Macintosh. Network users, especially those who work on Macintosh computers, quickly learn the basics of accessing and using obvious features, but sometimes never go much farther than the obvious. People's effectivness with networks is often constrained by the amount they do not know about them. This book is focused on broadening the knowledge of readers, so that they can increase their effectiveness.

This book will address the needs of several categories of readers, with particular topics aimed at the following audience:

- Those who already use NetWare. This book will help current NetWare users use the network more efficiently and extend their understanding of its capabilities.
- Those who have not yet decided what to use for a Local Area Network solution. This book discusses some of the key criteria for designing and implementing a local area network and compares the benefits of NetWare for Macintosh to those of other Macintosh networking products.
- Those with the basic need to connect several Macintosh computers. This book discusses the issues and the features that NetWare provides for Macintosh-only networking
- Those who need to connect both Macintosh computers and IBM or compatible computers. This book addresses the issues of compatibility and data sharing in a mixed computing environment.

If the reader is a user, this book will help develop his or her knowledge, productivity and effectiveness within the networking environment. It will discuss user-specific issues, such as keeping an environment secure.

If the reader is a manager of users, this book will expand his or her understanding of the applications and implementations possible with the network. It will give the manager a look at new ideas, and even examples of how other organizations have used the technology to help accomplish their objectives, such as implementing a company-wide electronic mail system.

If the reader is a supervisor, system integrator, or consultant, this book will help him or her better understand the needs of Macintosh users, and what NetWare has among its administrative capabilities to facilitate meeting their needs. It has sufficient technical content to address important administrative and planning issues, such as backing up data for not only Macintosh users, but all PC users who are NetWare clients.

This book begins with general explanations of networking concepts that are necessary to understand Macintosh networking and the NetWare related material that follows. It also contains tips and explanations about the latest networking applications and technologies that NetWare offers the Macintosh user, along with an appendix of complementary third-party products.

Topics covered by this book include:

- Definitions of networking concepts
- About NetWare
- Macintosh networking basics and NetWare's Macintosh environment

- Designing a NetWare Macintosh network
- Making the connection, and installing software for a Macintosh in a NetWare network
- NetWare for Macintosh user basics and the issues of a mixed PC environment
- NetWare security methods and concepts
- Applying security principles and setting up a NetWare applications environment
- Transferring data between Macintosh and IBM or compatibles

Because many users might need knowledge on a specific topic, and have a limited amount of time to gain it, this book is structured to permit jumping ahead to chapters that are of the most immediate importance. Thus certain concepts are explained at the beginning of more than one section. Although this book does encourage skimming ahead when needed, the reader who takes time to read it all will acquire a great deal of useful information.

Also included at the end of the book is a comprehensive glossary of networking terms for AppleTalk and NetWare networks.

1
Chapter

A networking overview

In a sense, the world of personal computing has reached its limit of achievement. In its original state, the personal computer was a device invented for stand-alone applications and personal productivity. The personal computer was propelled to success by innovative productivity software applications, such as spreadsheets, word processors, and databases that enhanced an individual's ability to write, store, and analyze data.

Other recent trends in the design of computer operating systems, such as the graphical user interface of the Apple Macintosh computer or Microsoft's Windows for DOS computers, also increased the productivity of their users by making the computer easier to use. These innovations were significant at the time of their introductions and have made great contributions to the way people work, but they might have taken personal computing about as far as it can go.

Future productivity gains for personal computer users will not likely come from upgrades to existing personal software tools. The most significant productivity gains for the next few years probably will come from computer software that enhances the way people work with other people. In other words, people will become more productive by using their personal computers to interact and collaboratively process data with other people's personal computers. They will use computers that are networked together to share the data they create, or to operate workgroup software. This kind of computing environment could be called network computing.

Network computing permits the user to transcend the bounds of personal computing, because it enables the computer to do more than it can when it stands alone. A networked computer allows people to share a database, access common peripherals, and send messages to other computers. Network computing consists of tools and applications designed to facilitate collaborative work. The individual is empowered by the ability to work better with other individuals.

This move towards collaboration is ironic when you consider that personal computers gained popularity because of their ability to provide a computing environment apart from the restrictions imposed by the day's existing computer technology of terminals networked to mainframe or minicomputers. Those environments consisted of centralized computing resources that came with a high degree of control over their access by computer professionals who worked in MIS departments. The mainframe environment was intimidating and often labeled with a Big Brother metaphor. Personal computers became popular because they came without the intimidation, and they were individual. They humanized the task of computing. Because a personal computer was a stand-alone device, the user could control his or her own environment.

Now in the network computing age, personal computing is giving way to group computing, where computers are connected together via networks. To make computer networks function properly, some degree of centralized planning and control is neccessary. Some of personal computing's individuality is at risk, but network computing is fundamentally different than computing was in the mainframe and minicomputer environment. The basic machine that people use on a microcomputer network is still a personal computer. In network computing, users retain the abilility to run stand-alone applications for their individual needs, and they gain the ability to work on collaborative applications.

Anatomy of a PC network

Computer networking is not new. Mainframes have used networks of terminals almost from the beginning. Networking to the mainframe via terminals was a

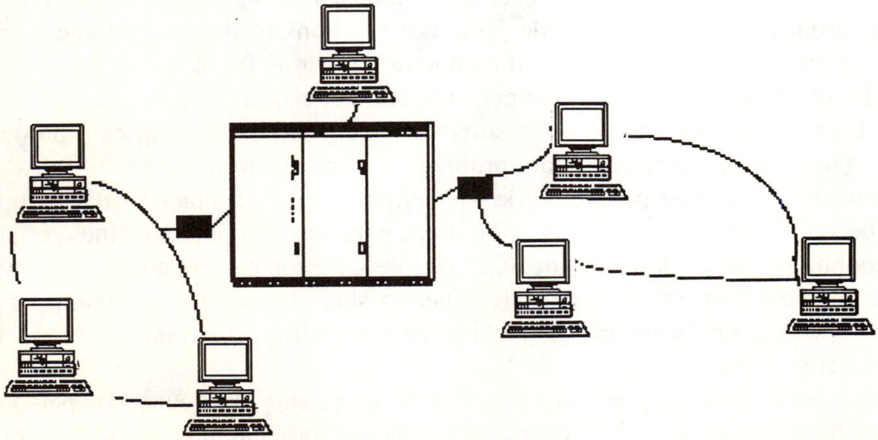

1-1 A mainframe computer and its network of terminals.

way of sharing the cost of the mainframe resource among a group of users. See Figure 1-1. Later minicomputers followed the model of the mainframes, providing a central processing unit and terminals to give users access to it.

Minicomputers were successful in what was originally a mainframe world because they could do much of the same as mainframes at far less cost. Cost has been a major factor in the proliferation of personal computer networks as well. A network of personal computers can achieve frequently the same objective as a mainframe or minicomputer at far less cost.

Although networking is not a new concept, PC networking has introduced a new twist to the concept. In a mainframe and minicomputer network, the terminals at which users worked were *dumb terminals,* with no ability to process data themselves. They simply allowed a user to input and receive data. The processing happened at the central computer. In contrast, the terminals at which people work on a PC network are individual computers. Each PC on a PC network has the ability to do its own processing.

PC networks take many forms. They can consist of only personal computers, or a mixture of personal computers, mainframes, terminals, and minicomputers. This book deals primarily with networks of personal computers, although at times it covers the mixed variety, shown in Figure 1-2.

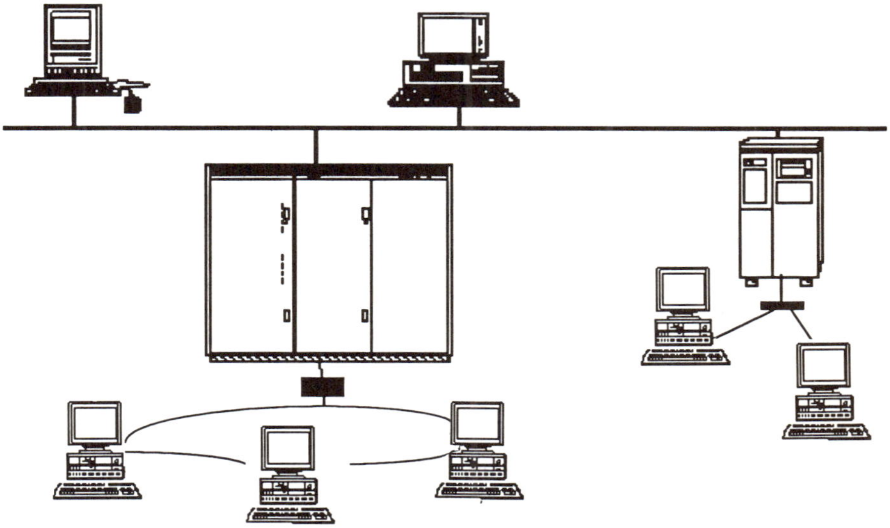

1-2 A mixed computer network.

Networks come in many sizes. A network can be as small as two computers connected to each other in the same room or large enough to consist of thousands of computers distributed across the globe. Consequently, many terms have evolved to describe the variations of networks.

PC LANs

The term *local area network,* or LAN, describes a network of computers connected in the same area. A connected group of computers in the same general area of a building is a good example of a small LAN. A larger network that runs throughout an entire floor or building is also a LAN. Even if a network consists of computers linked between separate buildings at the same site, it still is referred to as a LAN, because the computers are all on the same local network.

The focal point of most PC LANs is called a *server*. In its most passive form, a server is essentially a computer with a large central disk where shared data is stored and printers are connected. In other cases, the server can play an extremely active role not only in storing data, but in managing a network's flow of information and determining the structure of network software applications. The various roles of the server are discussed in more detail later.

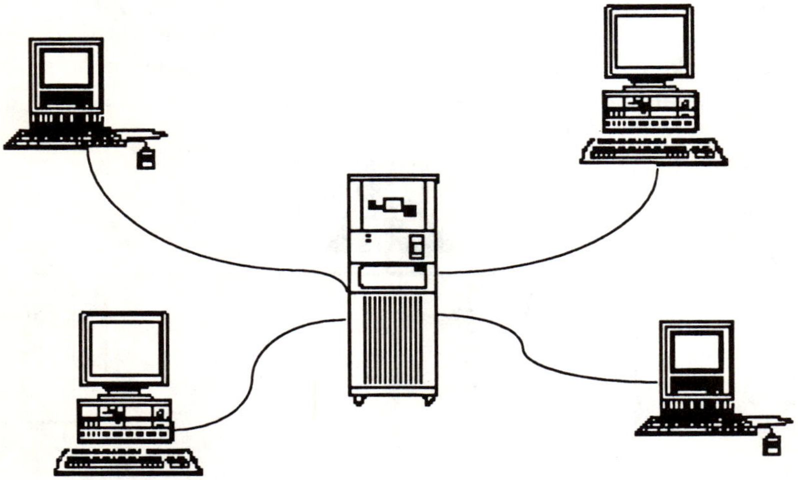

1-3 A LAN file server with client computers.

The computers used by networkers to access the server's resources are referred to as *clients* of the server. The arrangement of client computers connected to the server is called the network *topology*. A circular physical arrangement of clients and servers is called a *ring topology,* an arrangement with a centrally located server is called a *star topology,* and a continuous chain of clients and servers is called a *bus topology*. All of these topologies are diagrammed in Figure 1-4. The names of the ring and star topologies are obvious in their origins. The name bus was chosen because the word *bus* was used historically in computer circles to describe data paths within the computer itself.

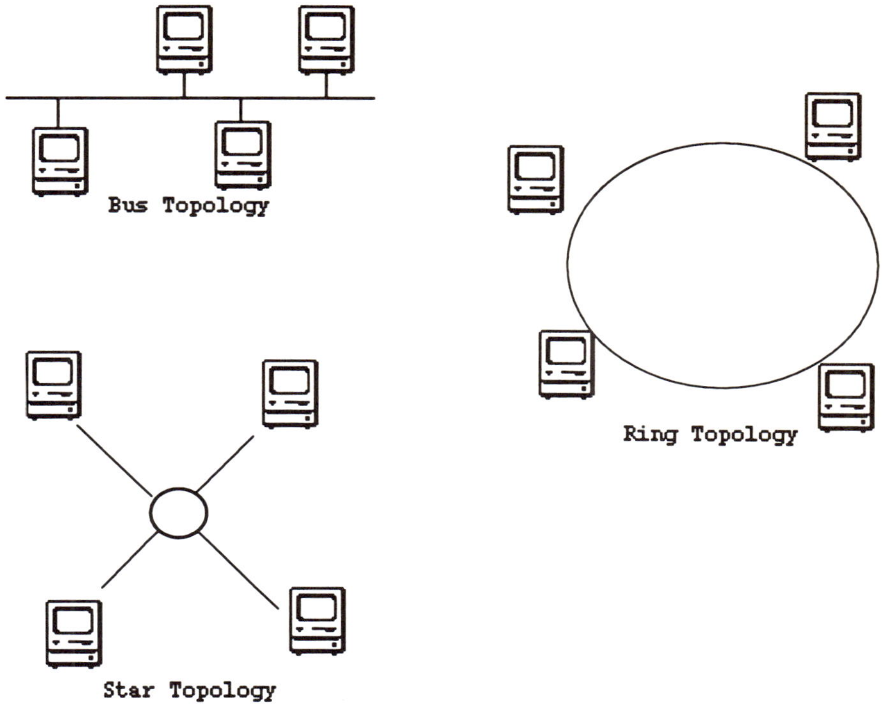

1-4 Common LAN Topologies.

The cabling technology underneath these PC network topologies is highly standardized. Four cabling standards are discussed in this book. They are *LocalTalk, Arcnet, Ethernet,* and *Token Ring*. The standards vary in the kind of wire types and connectors they use to attach the computers, and the data transmission speeds they support. A brief table is included in Figure 1-5 that summarizes their characteristics. Bus networking topologies are supported by LocalTalk, Arcnet and Ethernet, star topologies by Arcnet and ring topologies are supported by Token Ring; however, these are not absolute rules.

	LocalTalk	ARCnet	Ethernet	Token Ring
Speed	low	medium	medium - high	medium - high
Expense	low	medium	medium	high
Topology	bus	bus	bus	ring
Ease of use	easy	moderately easy	moderately easy	difficult

1-5 LAN Transmission Media Comparison.

Most PCs are not manufactured with built-in connections for networks. The Macintosh computer is unique because it is equipped with a built-in connection for LocalTalk cabling, but nothing is built in for the other cabling standards. When networking connections are not built in, they are added usually by inserting a *network interface card* into the computer that has a connection for attaching the computer to the network cable. The card permits the passing of data from the network wire to the computer's microprocessor. Network interface cards are available for all of the previously mentioned cabling types.

Networking protocols

The word *protocol* is frequently used in networking. As the English Language uses the word to describe a form of accepted etiquette among people, networking uses the word to describe an accepted ettiquette between computers. Computers talk to each other over networks through a formal set of accepted protocols. This is how they ensure proper communication.

As an analogy, protocols for computer network communication sessions could be compared to the protocols humans use when they communicate by radio. Broadcasts on police band radios, begin with the speaker identifying himself or herself, stating what needs to be said, and then ending the sentence with the word *over*. Computer network protocols allow a computer to communicate in much the same fashion.

Computers process data in a numerically coded format. Although data appears on the screen in english, or whatever language the program is written in, inside the computer the data is all numeric codes. Much of the data that passes over the wire of a computer network is also in numeric code. When a computer transmits data over a network, the transmissions are sent in data units called *packets*. Within these transmission packets, much like the radio broadcast analogy, are numeric codes containing the identity of the sending computer and the identity of the receiving computer. A computer network transmission also contains an indication of the beginning of the real data, its ending, and when the sending computer is finished so, it is available for receiving. The networking protocol handles these and other details of computer communication.

Preamble	Destination Address	Source Address	Type	Data Field	CRC

1-6 A network data packet (Ethernet Frame Format).

Numerous protocols are used in the world of networking. They were developed over the years for different purposes, and are still used because they do certain things well, or because of their installed bases. For example, Macintosh computers in a Novell NetWare network use a protocol called AppleTalk. AppleTalk was developed by Apple Computer to simplify Macintosh networking and all Macintosh computers are capable of using AppleTalk. Alternatively, DOS personal computers in a Novell NetWare network use in part a protocol called SPX, an acronym for Sequenced Packet Exchange. It was invented by Novell because nothing better existed for the networking of DOS computers.

This book discusses four protocols that Novell announced are supported by NetWare. Those protocols are Apple's AppleTalk, Novell's SPX/IPX, TCP/IP (a standard in the UNIX world), and SNA (a standard developed by IBM that is used to network their computers).

Local, remote, and network devices

Because computers attach to networks you should distinguish between computer resources that are attached to an individual's computer and resources attached to other parts of the network.

One of these distinctions is the difference between a *local* and *remote* resource, which is basically a matter of perspective. Suppose you have a computer with a printer attached to it. To you that printer is a local device. The network you are on has a server with a different printer attached to it. To you that server's printer is remote, as shown in Figure 1-7. To another computer user who does not have any attached printers, both your printer and the one on the server are remote printers. When you are attached to a computer network, you often gain the ability to use remote printers, as well as the local printers attached directly to your computer.

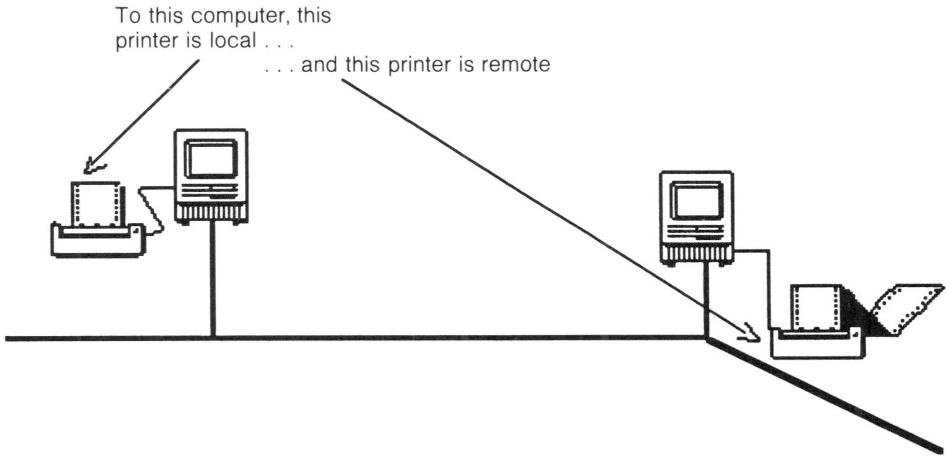

1-7 Local vs. remote resources.

Another type of network resource is a device that attaches directly to the network. An Apple LaserWriter is an example of this kind of device. The Apple LaserWriter has a network connection, a microprocessor that gives it intelligence, and a networking protocol, called Printer Access Protocol, stored in chip memory. This allows it to communicate directly with other users on the network. A device such as the Apple LaserWriter that attaches directly to the network is called a *network printer,* shown in Figure 1-8.

1-8 A network device.

The network printer also would be a remote device to you, however it differs from the remote printer that is attached to the server. To access the one on the server, you would need to go through the server, whereas you could access the network printer directly.

Joining separate LANs, or different networks

Large organizations often begin their forrays into PC LAN networking by letting the computer users in individual departments connect together in a workgroup. Then as pockets of networked computers proliferate, it's fairly common for departmental LANs that have always been separate to connect together. This connection often is done through a device called a *router*.

Routers are devices that link two physically separate LANs together. Some kinds of routers can achieve this link even when the LANs use two different transmission media, such as LocalTalk for one LAN and and Ethernet for the other. This example is depicted in Figure 1-9. A router's function is to pass data from one LAN to the next. Although the transmission media could be different, a router is generally connecting two networks that are much the same, such as this example with two separate PC LANS.

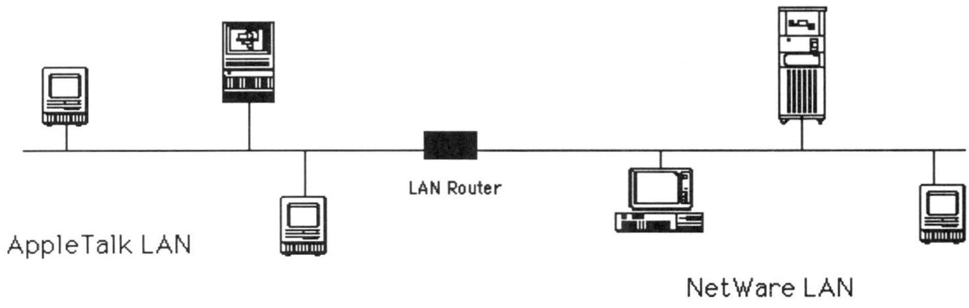

1-9 A router joins two networks together.

Similarly, an organization sometimes needs to connect a PC LAN to some other type of network, such as a network of a mainframe computer and its terminals. This connection is done through a device called a *gateway*. A router joins two networks of the same type of protocols, but a gateway generally connects a network to a different type of network. Joining a PC LAN to a mainframe network that runs on an entirely different set of protocols is an example depicted in Figure 1-10.

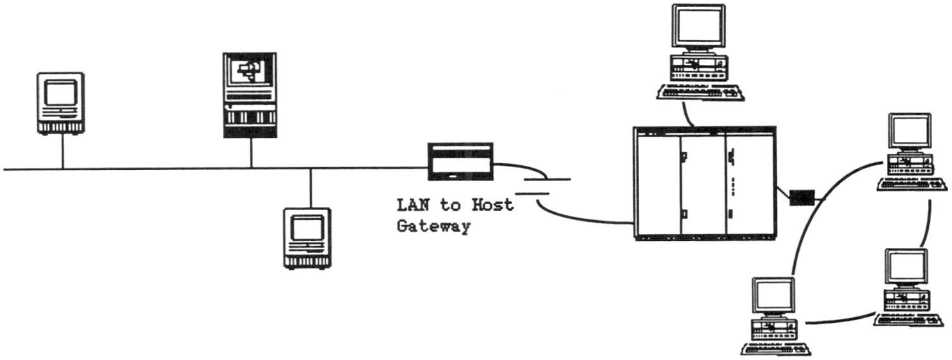

1-10 A LAN Gateway.

As networks grow to encompass more parts of a large organization's campus routers and gateways more frequently are used to join the different computing elements of the organization together.

When a LAN becomes a WAN

At some point the term LAN might become an inappropriate description of a network. That point typically results from geographical distribution or diversity of the network. Networks that span multiple sites within the same city, or span across cities, are termed wide area networks (WANs).

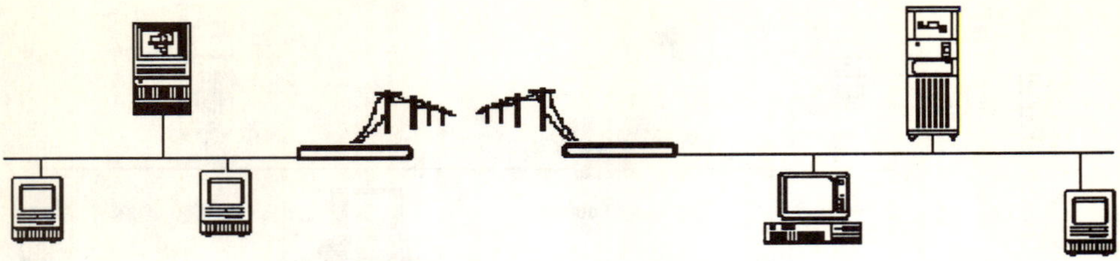

1-11 A Wide Area Network (WAN).

A description of a simple wide area network is a series of LANs interconnected through telephone lines, microwave transmissions, or satellites. These networks are never simple. By the time a network grows to the point that it spans multiple locations, it often contains the computers of many different manufacturers, several mainframe and/or minicomputers, and hundreds of personal computers. These networks are commonly joined by specialized wide-area routers that ensure reliable operation between the network's many parts. These routers often have telecommunications equipment built into them to establish their links. Sometimes they use dedicated telephone lines for a datapath, but some can use microwave or satellite transmission.

Wide area networks are becoming more and more common in modern business and academic organizations. In response, the high end of the Novell NetWare product line has encompassed more technology that accomodates these moves towards enterprise-spanning wide area networks.

The evolving network server model

A network server is the hub of activity on a local area network. As described earlier, one of its roles is to act as a large central disk that stores files for shared use and as a center for shared printer access among the network clients. This is a fairly passive role for the server, and virtually all LANs use a server in some form of this model, where it is called a file server.

Some networking schemes have adapted the file server model to make every computer on the network a potential server. This type of model is called a *peer-to-peer* network, shown in Figure 1-12.

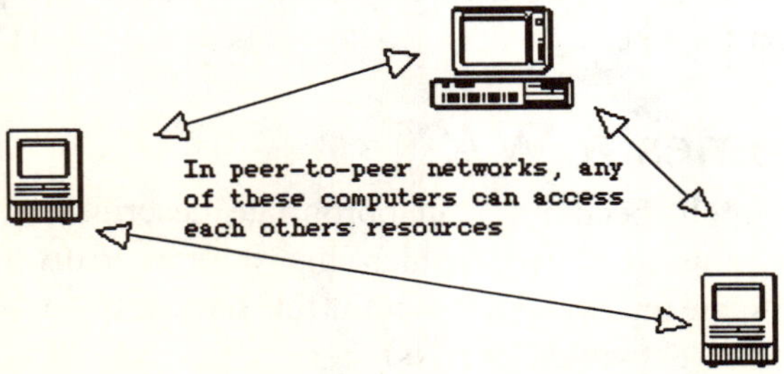

1-12 Peer-to-peer networks.

The peer-to-peer networking model uses *nondedicated* servers. A nondedicated server is a personal computer in a peer-to-peer network that is a server, yet still can be used as a personal computer. The network serving happens in the background. This solution is good for small networks that can't afford to dedicate a computer as a server. Because the server is nondedicated, it can be used for word processing or some other function, even while client computers are accessing its files. In peer-to-peer networks, every computer is equal because each is a potential server; hence, the term peer.

In the Macintosh networking world the nondedicated, peer-to-peer server model was originally popularized by a networking product called TOPS. Later it was implemented by Apple's Claris software division in a product called Public Folder that Claris gave away with most of its major productivity applications. Apple contributed to the nondedicated server market with a product called Personal AppleShare that is included with Apple System 7.0. This will make every Macintosh computer a potential peer-to-peer networking participant with other Macintosh computers in an AppleTalk networking environment.

Nondedicated file servers work fine in low-demand networking environments. However when the size of a workgroup grows beyond a handful of users, or the needs of the network users become more than a casual file sharing and include multiuser applications, however, servers can't function in the background like nondedicated servers are designed to do and still deliver the performance that networking clients expect. Heavy client access to a nondedicated server would bog down the computer.

For networks of moderate or large size, a strictly peer-to-peer networking configuration with nondedicated servers is not practical. Dedicated servers have become the norm for networks that need their servers for serious applications, as shown in Figure 1-13. This might even become the case for small networks in the future. Network servers are playing a much broader role in the services they provide to network users because servers are being expected to do more and more work. For example, network servers are becoming the center of electronic

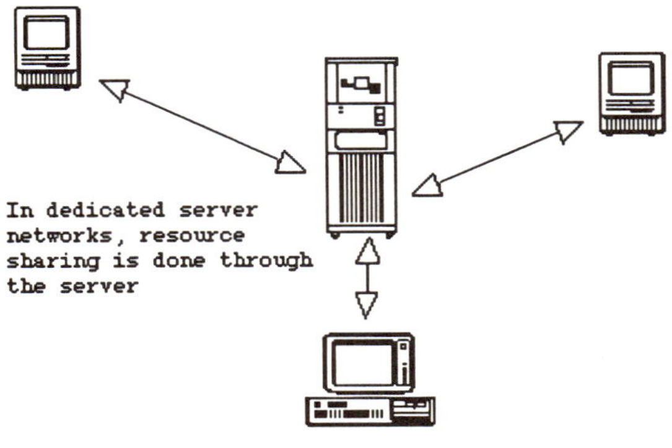

1-13 A dedicated server network.

mail systems that organizations, large and small, are using to enhance personal communication. In facilitating services such as E-mail, even small network servers are growing out of their nondedicated file server role.

Servers also are taking on more critical roles in integrating applications such as E-mail works into wide area networks, as shown in Figure 1-14. Server-based technology is emerging to allow any computer user on a network to locate and communicate with any other computer anywhere in the world. Part of this function in a network environment is fulfilled by a group of programs called *directory services*. Directory services consists of a database that most often is distributed and synchronized among a group of network servers. The directory services of a network provides a system for managing the users on large networks and the ways they can communicate with each other. Directory services will be a major step toward making computer networks as ubiquitous as telephone networks.

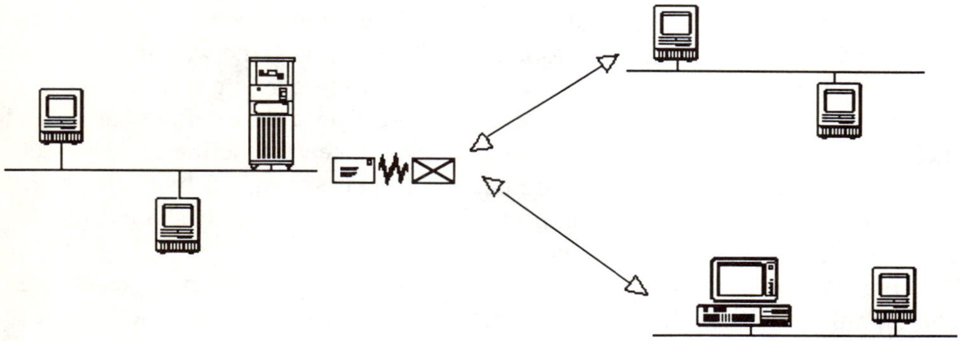

1-14 Servers are being used as hubs for wide area applications such as electronic mail.

Networking dissimilar computers

Today's local area networks must not only connect desktop computers across diverse geographical layouts, they must connect diverse types of desktop computers. The four primary standards of desktop computers that will be discussed are Macintosh computers, DOS and Windows computers, OS/2 computers, and UNIX computers. These computer standards are identified by the operating systems because in a Novell Netware environment, the computers' operating systems determine the application programs they can run and the kinds of files and networking protocols they use.

Many organizations own more than one type of desktop computer and want them to be able to talk to each other. For example, a company might have Macintosh computers for word processing and desktop publishing as well as a number of DOS or Windows computers that other people use for accounting and finance tasks. A truly functional LAN for this type of organization must be able to address the needs of all these computer users. Network servers offer the potential to provide this connectivity.

Various networking vendors have offered solutions that address connections to multiple types of computers. In the Macintosh networking arena prior to Novell NetWare, this connection generally required all types of computers to be standardized on the same networking protocol. For example, TOPS and AppleShare network server products required AppleTalk to be used on all the network nodes, even if some nodes were DOS computers. Similarly in the world of UNIX computers, solutions generally required that TCP/IP be used by all the clients.

The alternative that has been pioneered by Novell with its NetWare network computing solutions allows the server to communicate in multiple networking protocols. This design allows servers to connect to networking clients in the protocol that is optimal for the clients. For example, Macintosh computers probably would prefer to use AppleTalk because the protocols that NetWare supports are AppleTalk, SPX/IPX, and TCP/IP. Figure 1-15 shows a diagram of the standard protocol environments of the four primary desktop networking standards.

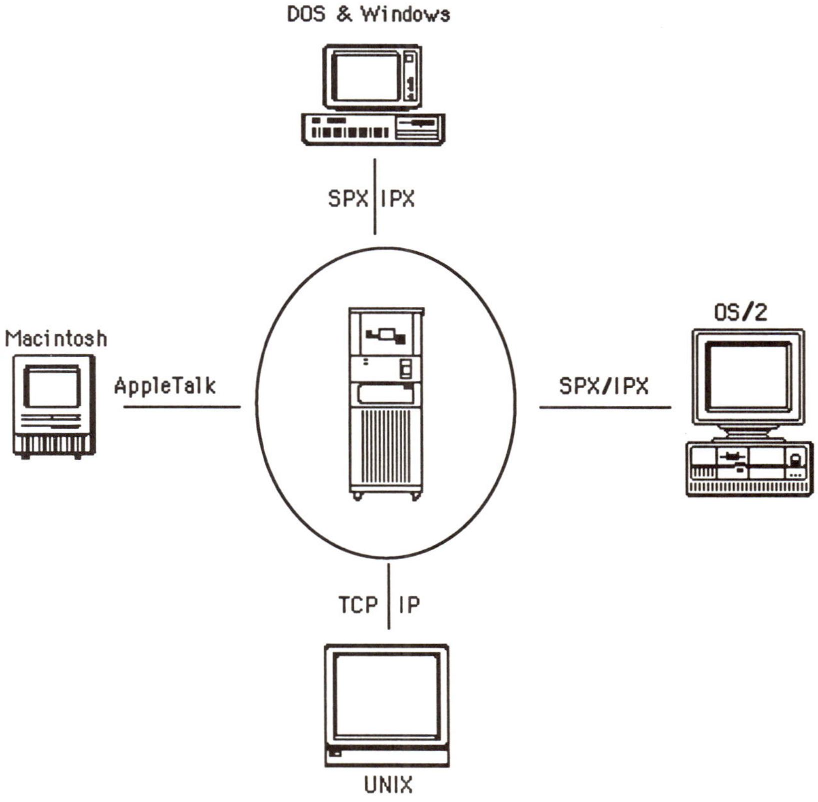

1-15 Novell NetWare supports multiple desktop clients in their native environments.

In addition to providing basic cross-platform connectivity, organizations also can be helped by a network server's ability to provide consolidated services to its users. For example, five sets of services seem to be almost universally needed by all types of desktop networking clients: services for sharing files with other users, sharing network printers, communicating with other users through methods such as electronic mail, accessing stored databases of information, and acting as a part of mainframe and mincomputer networks.

Figure 1-16 shows a network server acting as the hub for all of the previously-mentioned services. These services can be provided on a network without centralizing them through a network server, however, the centralization through the server makes it easier to manage the network and usually is more cost effective because the single point of access that a server provides eliminates duplication of resources.

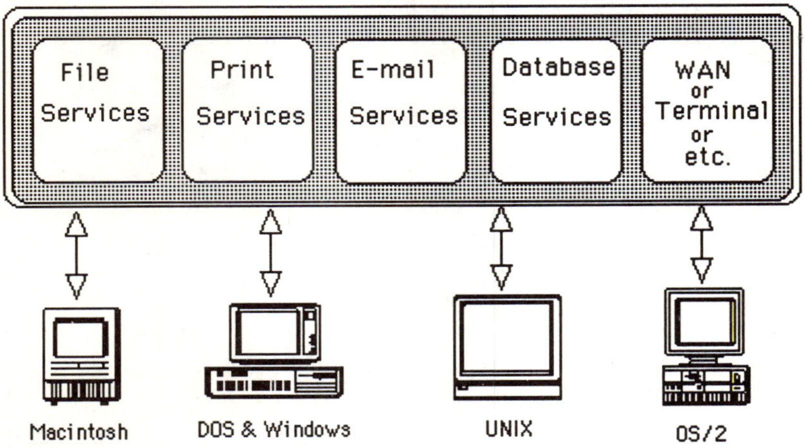

1-16 Network users most often require 5 primary network services.

NetWare

Novell's NetWare is a family of server-based software products that provide all of the five key services for Macintosh networking clients, either directly or through some combination of Novell products and the products of other software manufacturers that work with Novell NetWare. These services are most often available to DOS, Windows, OS/2, and UNIX clients too.

Although client computers for Netware servers can be any of the above, the servers are computers that follow the basic design of the IBM PC and use microprocessor chips from Intel. There are also versions of NetWare that run on mainframe computers, and minicomputers, such as Prime, Data General, and NCR, but the mainstay NetWare product is for the Intel chip set.

The NetWare network operating system

The NetWare operating system product consists of two versions. At the time of this writing, the latest member of the product line is NetWare v3.11. Because Novell typically updates NetWare at least once a year, for the remainder of this book NetWare v3.11 and its inevitable descendents will be referred to as NetWare v3.X, so that the name carries some longevity. NetWare v3.X was written to take advantage of the features provided by computers with Intel 80386 or 80486 microprocessors. It will not work on servers with 80286 processors. The other product in the line is NetWare version 2.2, which hereafter will be referred to as NetWare v2.X. NetWare v2.X is the traditional line of NetWare that will work on 80286, 80386, or 80486 servers.

Several fundamental design differences exist between NetWare v2.X and NetWare v3.X. They stem primarily from the capabilities of the 386 and 486 chips that the 286 chip does not have. NetWare v2.X is designed around capabilities common to all the Intel chip family including the 80286. It is a 16-bit operating system that adresses up to 16 Mbytes of memory and two Gbytes of disk storage.

NetWare 3.X is a 32-bit operating system that address up to four Gigabytes (billions of bytes) of memory and 32 Terabytes (trillions of bytes) of disk storage. The Intel 386 and 486 chips permit more addressable memory and feature a more effective memory management method than the 286 chip. NetWare v3.X leverages this technology advance, and can manage its memory and processes in a dynamic fashion that makes administration easier. NetWare v3.X also is more configurable than Netware 2.X because it can be expanded with new operating system extentions called NetWare Loadable Modules (NLMs). These extensions to NetWare v3.X further enhance its services. Because of these design differences, NetWare v2.X is probably best suited for workgroup networking, while NetWare v3.X is better suited for high-performance applications and organization wide connectivity.

NetWare for Macintosh is an NLM extention to the NetWare operating system that supports Macintosh computers. It does not permit Macintosh computers to be NetWare servers, but rather it permits Macintosh computers to be clients to NetWare servers. The NetWare for Macintosh product line is also divided into two versions. The first product is called NetWare for Macintosh v3.X, and works with NetWare v3.X. The other product is called NetWare for Macintosh v2.X, and works with NetWare v2.X. Most of the differences between NetWare for Macintosh v2.X and NetWare for Macintosh v3.X stem from the functional differences between the operating systems that lie beneath them, NetWare v2.X and NetWare v3.X, respectively.

Despite their differences, however, the two NetWare for Macintosh product lines have many things in common. At the user interface level, they work identically most of the time. As a result, this book presents material in a manner that is independent of NetWare versions, and points out differences between versions if and whenever they are relevant.

NetWare services for Macintosh computers

One of the services provided by NetWare is network file storage. Novell's NetWare for Macintosh product allows your Macintosh computer to store files on a NetWare server. NetWare file services allow you to store files in a shared workspace so all other users can access those files, or it permits you to store files in private workspaces accessible only by you.

NetWare's ability to support DOS, Windows, and other clients in addition to Macintosh enables you to share files not only with other Mac users, but with DOS, Windows, OS/2 and UNIX users as well. An example of how this works is depicted in Figure 1-17.

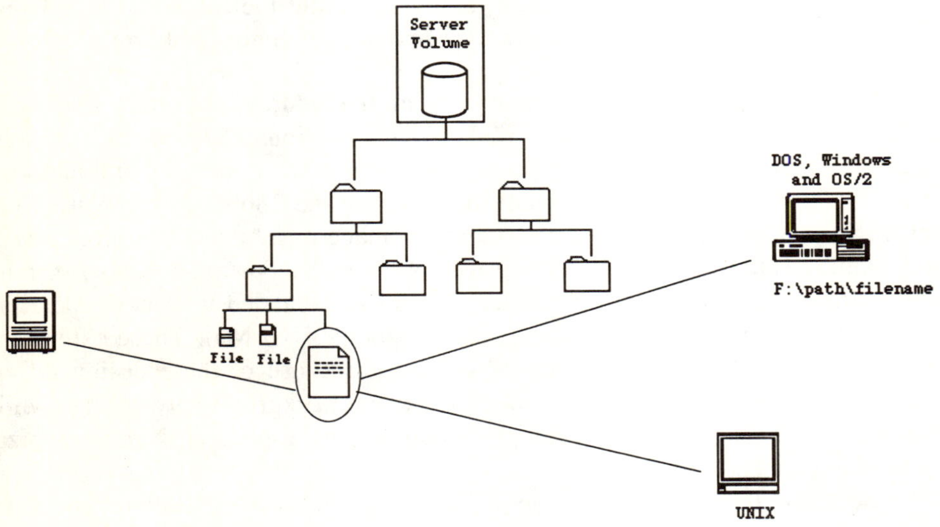

1-17 All NetWare clients can access data equally on a server.

The NetWare and NetWare for Macintosh system for file sharing is flexible and powerful. It enables groups of computer users to pass data back and forth to each other without passing floppy disks. Although it is sophisticated enough to let multiple kinds of computers attach to its file services, these services are not difficult to use. For a Macintosh user it is as simple as accessing a device in the

Macintosh chooser, assuming the user has AppleShare workstation software installed on his or her computer.

The wealth of storage space provided by a NetWare and NetWare for Macintosh server is welcomed by users who have known the frustration of filling up their local floppy disks or hard disks. A NetWare for Macintosh server can be equipped with trillions of bytes of disk space.

NetWare print services

As with file services, NetWare provides Macintosh clients with print services that enhance the printing capabilities of Macintosh computers. The primary benefits come from the access that other client computers gain to Macintosh printers, and also in the access that Macitosh users gain to the printers of other clients. Figure 1-18 shows a diagram of this print integration.

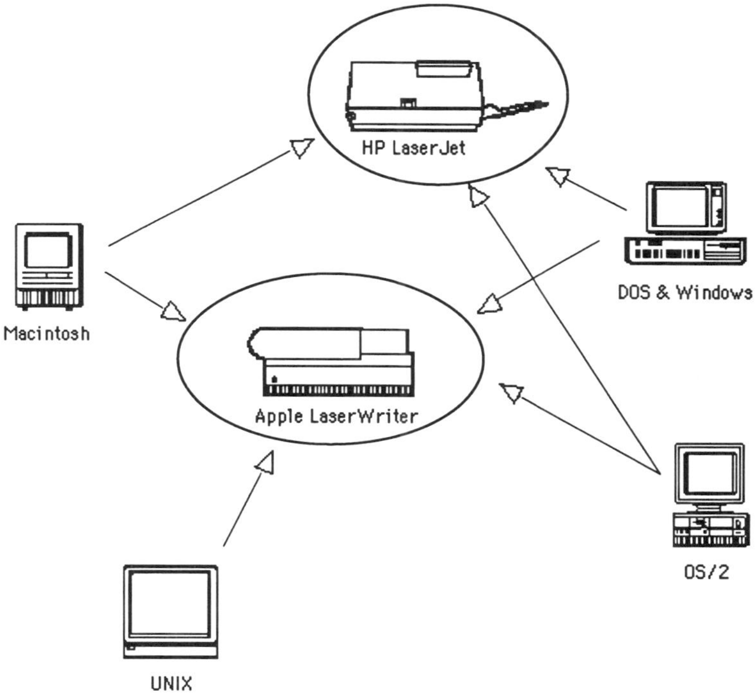

1-18 NetWare for Macintosh allows all NetWare clients to share Apple LaserWriters, and provides a way for Macintosh computers to share HP LaserJets.

NetWare and NetWare for Macintosh allow DOS, Windows, OS/2, and UNIX users to print to Apple LaserWriters. NetWare and NetWare for Macintosh also allow Macintosh computers to print to Hewlett Packard LaserJet and

DeskJet printers that are attached to a NetWare server, or even attached to a DOS client computer. An indepth explanation of how this works is included in chapter 6.

Database access

Perhaps the most visible and critical application that organizations use on desktop computer networks is a database application. In this context, a database application is an application used by multiple clients that stores records of information, such as an accounting program, a list of customers, etc. Many kinds of generic, off-the-shelf database application programs can be used to create these kinds of end-user applications. Many kinds of customized application programs written specifically for a type of business or organization also fall into the category of a database.

Database applications allow users to manage information. On a LAN, as opposed to on a stand-alone desktop computer, a database application is usually designed to provide information to many users at the same time. Therefore, virtually all database application programs and data files are stored on LAN servers where multiple clients have access to them. Because of concurrent attempts to access a networked database program by multiple users, performance on a LAN is an issue of concern to database designers. Novell NetWare for Macintosh is an excellent database platform with superlative performance. NetWare for Macintosh is an ideal host for common third-party Macintosh database

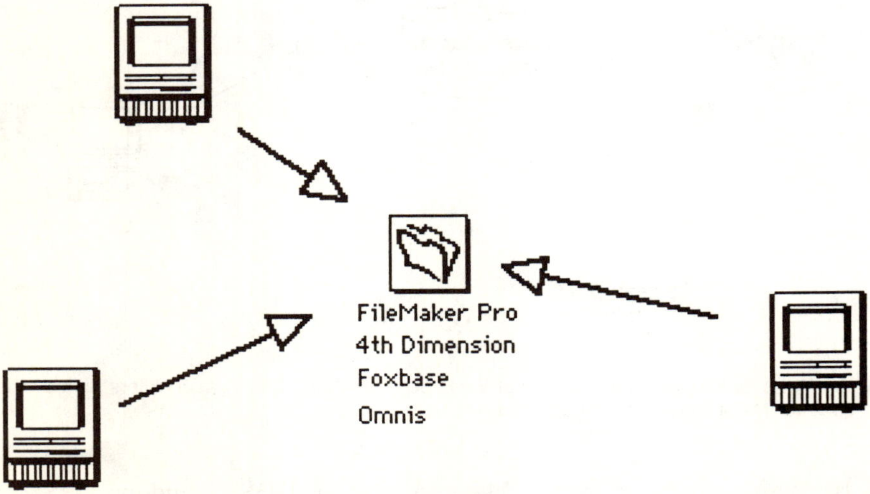

1-19 NetWare supports single, as well as cross-platform, database applications.

application programs, such as ACIUS's 4th Dimension, Claris's FileMaker Pro, FOX Software's FOXbase, and Blythe Software's Omnis.

Although database application design is a fairly mature science, permitting access from multiple kinds of clients is a relatively new expectation. In a world of multiple desktop computer standards, however, multiple desktop access is an important requirement. Cross-platform, file server database access for Macintosh, DOS, and Windows products is available from both FOX Software's FOXbase and Blythe Software's Omnis, which provide popular, basic, and straightforward solutions. These solutions consist of separately available application programs for Macintosh, DOS, and Windows clients that share a common database file.

Client/server database applications

Products have been announced by several leading database software vendors that fulfill the multiple desktop client need with a focus on high speed data transaction processing, including Oracle Corporation and Sybase. Driven by a customer shift away from mainframe and minicomputer based applications to downsized applications running on LANs, these companies are producing products for NetWare networks. These solutions follow an applications model that is called the *client-server* model. The client-server applications model achieves optimal LAN performance by distributing the applications processing burden between both the LAN server and the client.

Novell also has announced the intention to support database applications for cross-platform access in the client-server model through a Novell product called NetWare SQL. The initials SQL stand for *Standard Query Language,* an internationally standardized language for database access that NetWare SQL incorporates. The NetWare SQL solution from Novell will add special value to Macintosh clients by allowing them to access NetWare SQL's data through a related database language for the Macintosh called Data Access Language (DAL).

The Data Access Language is a part of the Macintosh's System 7. and is separately available for Apple System 6.X versions. Therefore DAL gives every Macintosh the ability to access NetWare SQL by issuing DAL commands. The value of the DAL connection to NetWare SQL data is enhanced by DAL commands imbedded in many common Macintosh software applications, including Hypercard 2.0, Excel 3.0, Informix WingZ, Claris' Resolve, and others. The added benefit of DAL support within these applications is that data can be imported easily into the applications, where it is easy to manipulate and analyze, as shown with Microsoft Excel 3.0 in Figure 1-20.

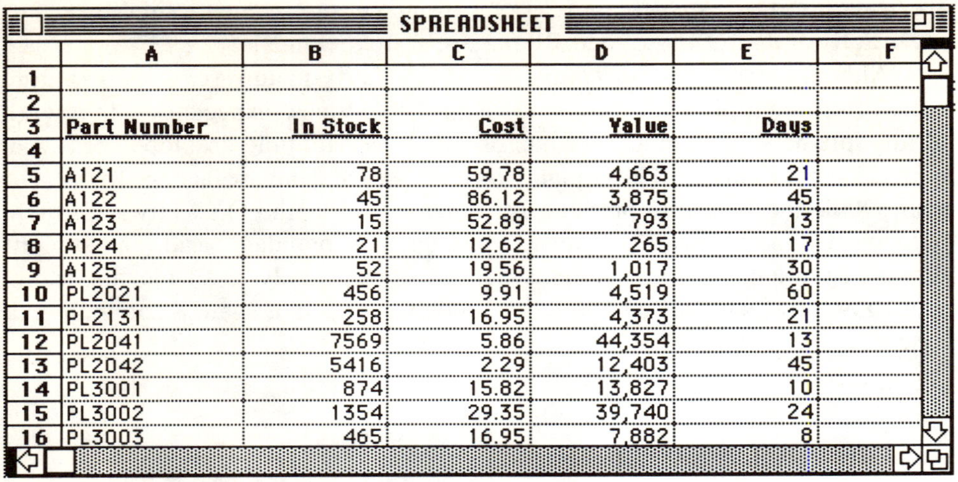

SPREADSHEET

	A	B	C	D	E	F
1						
2						
3	Part Number	In Stock	Cost	Value	Days	
4						
5	A121	78	59.78	4,663	21	
6	A122	45	86.12	3,875	45	
7	A123	15	52.89	793	13	
8	A124	21	12.62	265	17	
9	A125	52	19.56	1,017	30	
10	PL2021	456	9.91	4,519	60	
11	PL2131	258	16.95	4,373	21	
12	PL2041	7569	5.86	44,354	13	
13	PL2042	5416	2.29	12,403	45	
14	PL3001	874	15.82	13,827	10	
15	PL3002	1354	29.35	39,740	24	
16	PL3003	465	16.95	7,882	8	

1-20 DAL allows Microsoft Excel 3.0 to pull data out of a database server and into a spreadsheet.

Accessing mainframe computers

In addition to providing integration with other desktop computers, Novell NetWare has a couple of products that allow Macintosh users of a NetWare server to go through the server to gain access to IBM mainframe computers. This Novell solution is called NetWare for SAA, which consists of software that runs on a server, and an application program to be run on the Macintosh client that allows the Macintosh to emulate an IBM 3270 mainframe terminal. SAA is an acronym from IBM's networking terminology language and stands for *System Applications Architecture*. SAA is IBM's set of standards for connecting to, and designing applications for, IBM computers. Figure 1-21 shows a layout of how a NetWare for SAA configuration would work.

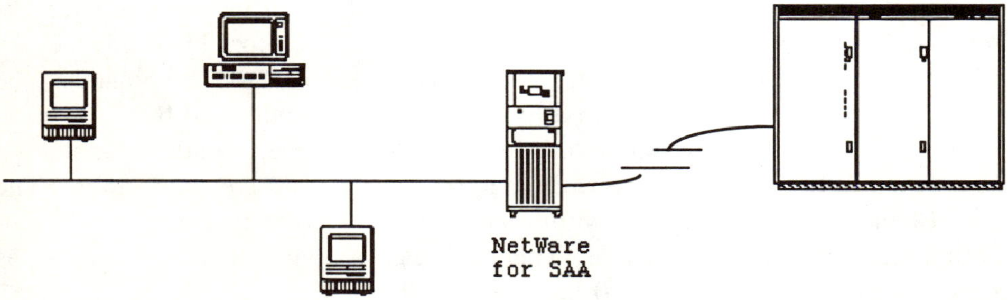

1-21: NetWare for SAA allows Macintosh computers to act as terminals to IBM mainframes.

Some vendors of communications products sell alternative solutions for Macintosh mainframe access. One popular product uses a hardware card in the Macintosh that makes the connection to the mainframe. With this kind of solution, however, the computer would need an additional network interface for NetWare server access. NetWare for SAA is different in that it allows the Macintosh to get to the mainframe computer through the same network connection used to get to files and printers on the server. If preferred, NetWare for SAA also can be installed on a server dedicated for its communications.

By emulating an IBM mainframe terminal, Macintosh users can gain access to the mainframe based applications they need. By allowing the Macintosh to emulate a terminal, users can avoid having both a Macintosh computer and a mainframe terminal on their desk. Figure 1-22 shows the screen of a Macintosh computer running an IBM mainframe session in Novell's NetWare LAN 3270 LAN Workstation for Macintosh application program.

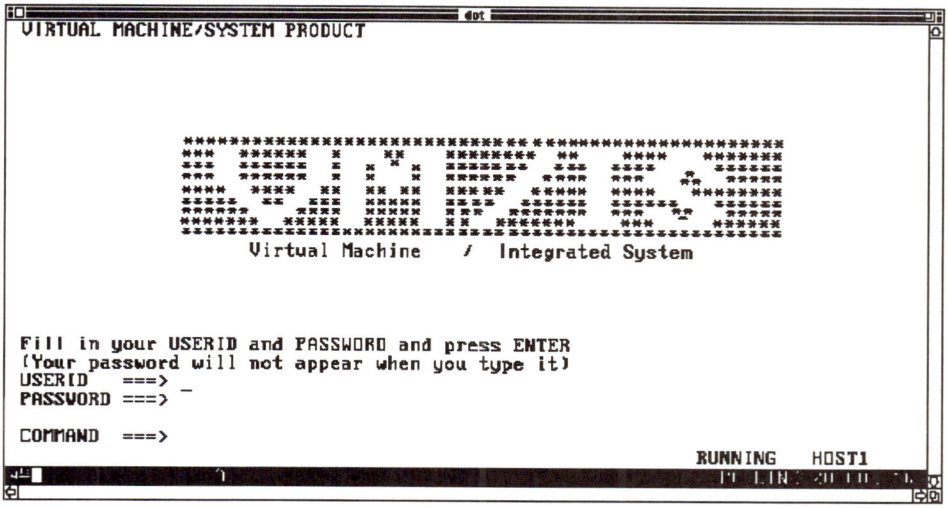

1-22 The NetWare LAN workstation 3270 for Macintosh interface.

In 3270 emulation mode, a Macintosh can download files to its hard disk for local use, or have a terminal's view of the massive amount of data stored on most mainframe disks. When accessing mainframe applications from NetWare LAN 3270 for Macintosh, users can cut and paste data from their mainframe application into another Macintosh application program.

Electronic mail packages

Electronic Mail software is software that generally runs on a networked server, allows users to send messages to other users, allows users to send files to other users, and permits the messages to be sent whether or not the recipient is logged into the network. The ability to eventually pass messages to users who are not currently logged in is called *store and forward* technology, and all serious E-mail applications use it.

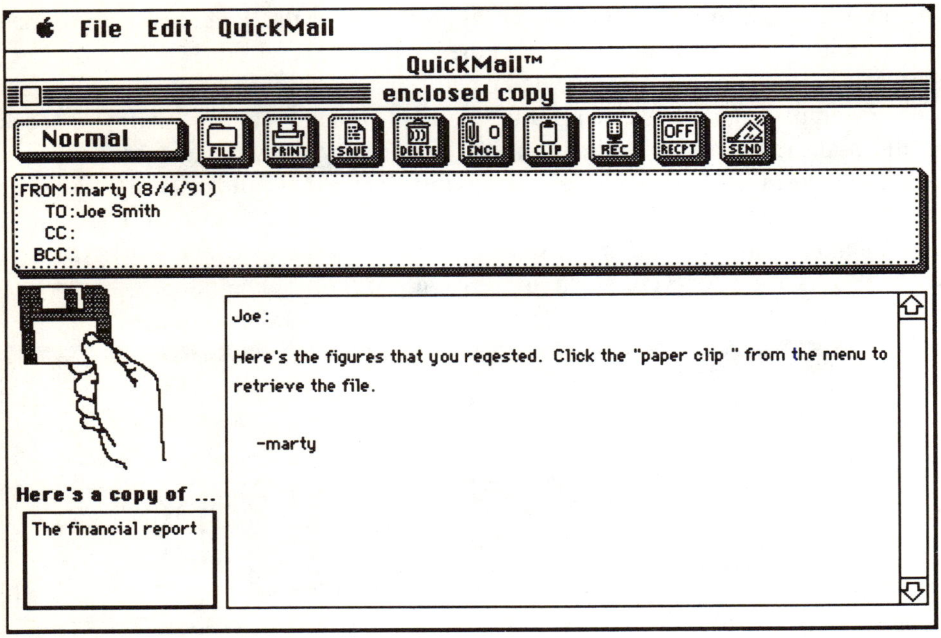

1-23 Macintosh mail packages, such as Quickmail, allow users to send electronic messages easily.

Electronic mail is a good productivity enhancer. For users with computers on their desktops, it provides a convenient way to express ideas to others and make requests, even when the recipient of the communication is not available to listen. It also is a means for documenting your communications. Without leaving your chair, electronic mail will let you type your business and send it to another party. The recipient of the message can react to it and send back word without you having to speak to them. In today's harried business environments, E-mail can save users a lot of time and phone tag.

In broad terms, E-mail packages generally provide client application software that allows users to compose and send messages to special message and mail system files located on a server. These files store messages, keep track of the mail systems users, and perform mail routing to the addressees. Within that description are two types of designs: Macintosh mail packages whose message files rest on a NetWare server, and those that are written to work only on Macintosh servers.

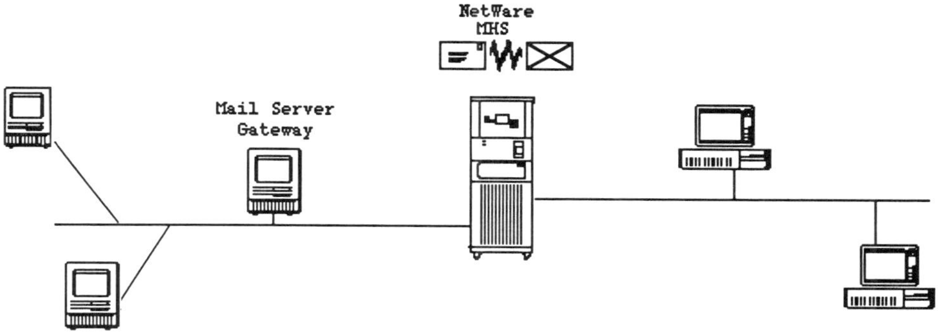

1-24 NetWare MHS allows mail packages to be gatewayed to each other.

The two most popular Macintosh E-mail software packages are the previously mentioned Quickmail from CE SoftWare and Microsoft's Microsoft Mail. These mail packages require message and system files to be stored on a Macintosh server because a mail server based application program that manages the messages depends on the Macintosh operating system. NetWare allows this type of Macintosh mail package to exchange messages with DOS, Windows, and other client mail applications through a store and forward technology called the NetWare Message Handling Service (MHS). NetWare MHS allows any kind of E-mail program to exchange messages with other E-mail programs. With MHS on NetWare, an E-mail program with a NetWare MHS gateway might run only on a Macintosh server, but it can send a message to NetWare's MHS, which can pass it on to a DOS or Windows mail package that can read MHS formatted messages. Figure 1-24 shows a conceptualization of this.

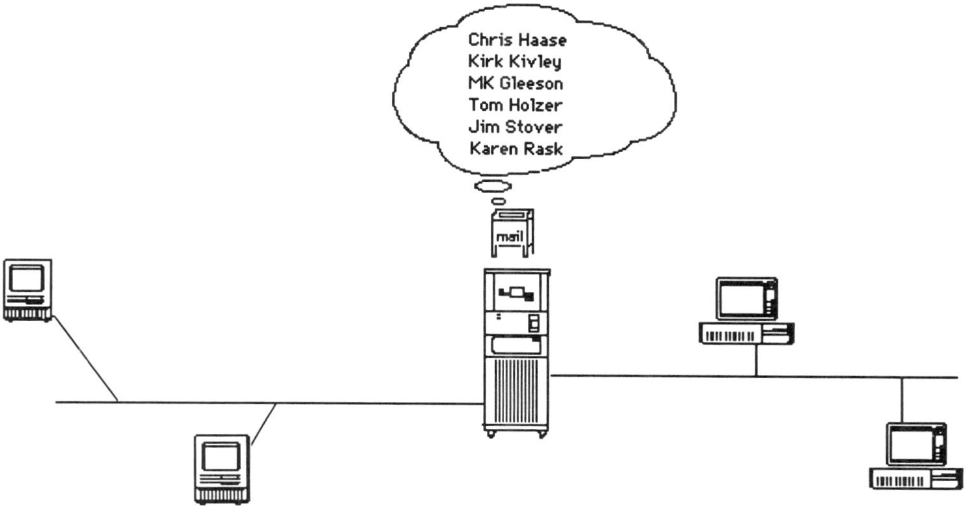

1-25 Single server mail packages share a single list of users and a single message database among their clients.

NetWare MHS is not required for Macintosh mail packages that store messages on NetWare servers, however, NetWare is still a key component in the store and forward capability of the mail system. As long as the server is running, the E-mail message and system software will accept, store and route messages. Two of the most popular Electronic mail packages that work this way are Lotus's cc:Mail and Sitka's Inbox. These packages provide a single-server, one-vendor mail solution for Macintosh, DOS and Windows. This is shown in Figure 1-25.

There are some advantages to the single-server, one-vendor mail packages, and other advantages to gatewayed server solutions. Single-server packages require less administration than gateway solutions, because the latter requires the management of multiple user lists. For example, if a solution used an MHS gateway to exchange messages between a mail application that ran only on a Macintosh server and a mail application that ran in another client environment, two user lists must be managed: one for the Macintosh mail users, and one for the other mail users. The single-server application has only one list of users to manage. Some Macintosh server mail packages have great feature sets, however, and many organizations find the additional management required to gateway them to other clients well worth the effort for the gain in functionality.

2
Chapter

The NetWare Network operating system

This book has focused thus far on the basic terms and concepts of networking, PC local area networks, and application services for NetWare LANs. This chapter discusses some of the more technical and nontechnical issues that network users are concerned with. It also explains how the design and functionality of the NetWare network operating system addresses these issues.

The issue of performance

One generalization always seems to be true of PC LAN and WAN users. They are frustrated by networks that are slow. When users attach to a networks they want their computers to work just as fast as they did when they were not attached. If their computers are slowed down, they are dissatisfied.

Performance on a network is dependent on four factors: the various network server's ability to respond to the activities of multiple network clients, the server's ability to write and read data from the disk with speed, the ability of the network's cabling and interfaces to pass data in volume and with speed, and the human factor—how, and how often, the network is used. Each of these factors has a great individual impact, but none of them has as big of an impact as the operating system used on the network server.

PC operating systems

A PC's operating system is software that makes the computer usable. This is true of all personal computer or desktop computer operating systems, whether a Macintosh, an IBM PC clone, or an engineering workstation. Some of the most common desktop computer operating systems are the Macintosh Operating System for Macintosh computers, DOS, Windows (an extention to DOS) or OS/2 for IBM PC compatible computers, and UNIX for engineering workstations. These computer operating systems manage the flow of data between the computer's input devices and its display, its microprocessor and memory, its memory and storage disks, and through its interface card if the computer is on a network. The nature of a personal computer operating system is singular; see Figure 2-1. The personal computer's operating system is meant to service the demands of only one computer—itself.

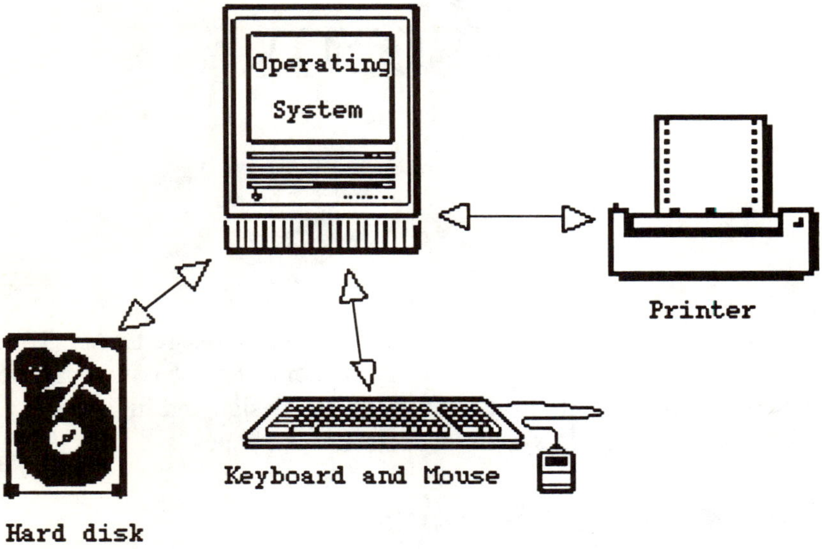

2-1 A computer and its communication with peripherals is controlled by its operating system.

Because a network server is a computer, it also needs an operating system. The requirements of the operating system for a server, however, are different than those of a personal computer. One operating system feature critical to the efficient operation of a network server is *multiuser* support. Multiuser support gives multiple network clients the ability to have some level of control over the server's processor. *Multitasking,* an operating system feature that allows concurrent operations, is also important because the server sometimes must do more than one thing simultaneously.

On top of all of that, a server operating system must be highly efficient in managing network input and output, so it can make the best use of the network server hardware. All the money spent on high-performance hardware means nothing if the operating system running the computer is unable to make the most of it.

Clearly, the needs of the operating system on a network server are much different than the needs of an individual's personal computer. Personal computer operating system manage the transactions of only one user, but the network server must manage the transactions of many users. The personal computer operating system was not designed for meeting the demands that would be placed on it if it were used as a network server.

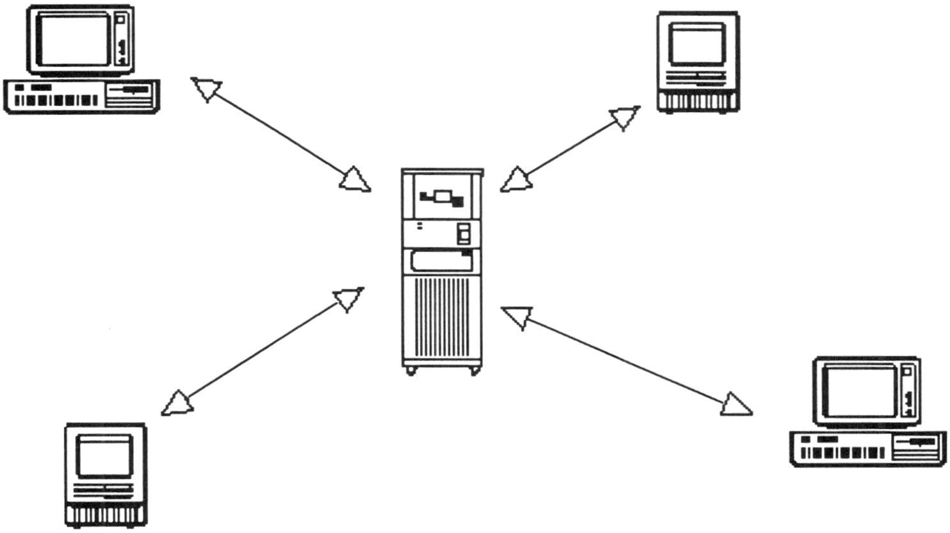

2-2 A network operating system must simultaneously control the activity of multiple clients.

The network operating system

In contrast to a personal computer operating system, Novell NetWare is a network operating system, written from the start for networking. As a true real-time network operating system, NetWare is optimized for sharing, synchronizing, and responding to frequent and often simultaneous client accesses of networking services.

At times NetWare's association with Intel-based computers has created a misunderstanding of what NetWare is, because the machine used for a NetWare server is often a desktop computer exactly like the ones people use to run DOS and OS/2 productivity applications; however the similarity to DOS and OS/2 ends there. NetWare is a specialized operating system for networking. When installed on a desktop or free-standing computer, NetWare transforms the computer into a multitasking, multiuser server that can provide all of the services explained in chapter 1. In low-demand situations it can be nondedicated, but its true potential is best realized as a dedicated server.

2-3 The NetWare network operating system works on many kinds of computers based on Intel microprocessors.

The NetWare network operating system allows each client computer to access the server's disk. To keep the server's shared disk responsive, NetWare was designed with many performance optimized capabilities that ensure the network disk access is not ensure the disk reacts quickly when multiple users attempt simultaneous access. For example, NetWare permits the use of large amounts of server memory as temporary storage for data, so less frequent disk access is required as clients read and write files. This capability, called disk caching, stores frequently accessed data in a memory cache rather than reading it from the disk each time it is requested, as shown in Figure 2-4. Disk caching helps NetWare complete disk transactions faster because reading from memory re-

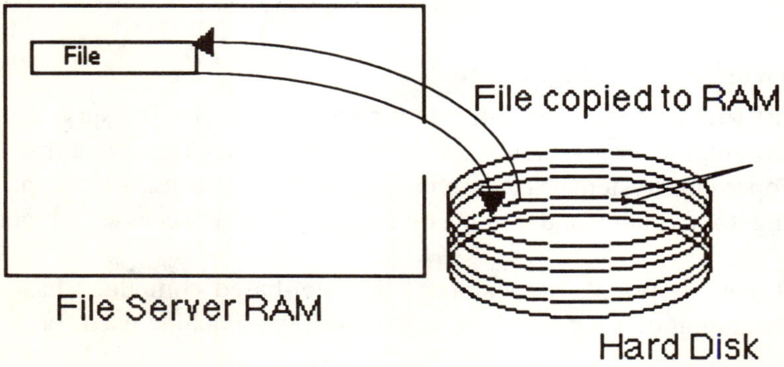

2-4 disk caching helps to speed a NetWare server's disk access.

quires only the movement of electrical current, and no mechanical disk movement. The less mechanical movement, the faster the response. When writing data, the cache permits the operating system to refrain from actually writing to disk until there is a lull in disk activity.

To enhance disk storage technology, the authors of NetWare incorporated some other customized features that allow a NetWare server's disks to operate at their peak. One of these features is file indexing. To explain file indexing with an analogy, a computer disk is essentially a platter with a head that moves about the platter reading and writing to the disk according to a mapping system, like the grid system used by most roadmaps. When you have trouble finding the location of a street, you can look it up by its name in the index of the map. The index speeds your search by giving you the exact grid coordinates for that street. NetWare indexes files in somewhat the same fashion.

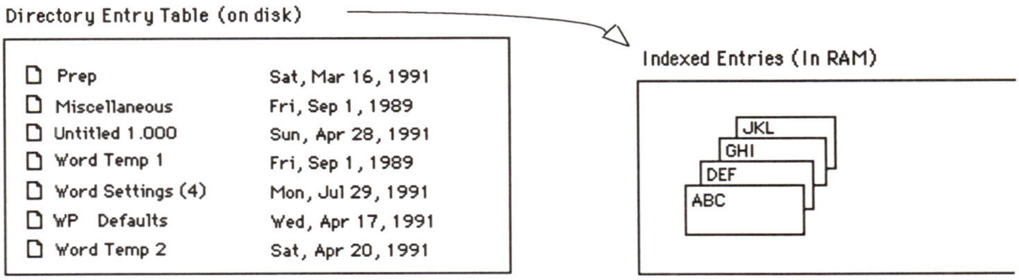

2-5 Netware indexes files to make disk searches more efficient.

To further use the benefits of disk indexing and to get the most out of a PC server's network input/output, NetWare uses a disk access method called *elevator seeking*. Elevator seeking uses a disk read process sorted into an order of priority based on the drive's current head position, shown in Figure 2-6. Rather than jumping around from section to section of the platter, the head reads the next closest sector, even if it is out of order. This technique further reduces disk

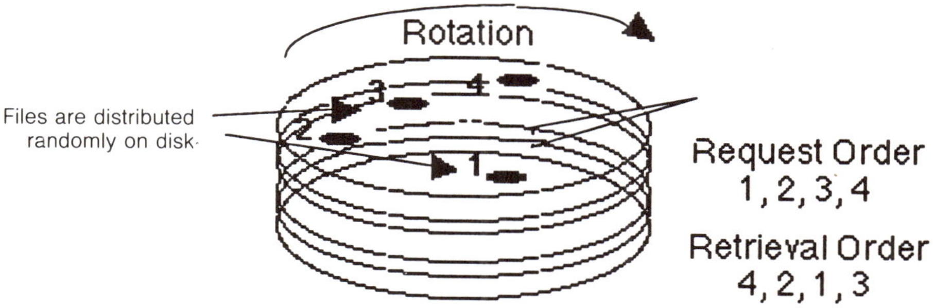

2-6 Elevator seeking selects the most efficient access order, regardless of the order of request.

head movement and results in significantly higher disk throughput under loaded conditions.

These are just a few of the features of NetWare that relate to server file access performance. With a network operating system such as NetWare, the operating system issue of network performance and how it impacts the total performance equation is addressed. NetWare ensures that the operating system software running on the server will be efficient, but all that operating system efficiency is wasted unless the rest of the network can match it. For a network to perform well, the network infrastructure and the server must be powerful enough to take advantage of NetWare's speed.

Hardware and cabling

The server's ability to respond swiftly to NetWare's directions relates to the kind of computer that is used. In NetWare networks, servers must be computers based on the Intel/IBM PC architecture. As a general rule, the faster the disk, the internal data bus, the microprocessor of the computer used as a server, and the amount of memory in the server, the faster the performance.

At one time the most cost effective choice for a server was probably an IBM AT compatible, Intel 80286 based machine. In today's world of ever-lower-priced IBM compatible 80386 and 80486 computers, a reasonable choice for a minimum server configuration might be a basic 386 or 486 desktop model, because they are almost sure to have faster processing speeds. Bear in mind, however, that a machine with a 386 or 486 CPU could provide no advantage in performance if its disk and internal data bus are no faster than a 286 model. A server should be selected not only for a 386 or 486 microprocessor, but also for a data bus and disk fast enough to use the 386's or 486's power. In addition, the server should have at minimum 5 Mb megabytes of memory—generally, the more the better.

If the network server is intended for heavy use, a more specialized high-end server might be warranted. There are two standards for high-end microcomputers, positioned as servers that are fighting it out in the market. Both are based on Intel 386 or 486 microprocessors. They differ most in their internal data buses. One of the standards uses a data bus called MicroChannel. The other uses a bus called EISA (Extended Industry Standard Architecture). IBM is the most visible champion of MicroChannel, and Compaq Computer Corporation is the most visable champion of EISA, but there many clone makers have adapted one or the other of these standards to make fine machines as well.

Performance is clearly an advantage of high-end servers, but they can be expensive. Some of these machines cost well over $10,000, although prices are falling somewhat. If you don't have a vendor preference, your selection process for the right combination of price versus performance might be aided best by gathering and analyzing comparative test data from sources such as computer periodicals. Most libraries have back issues of *PC World, PC Week,* and other periodicals that contain articles rating the relative price/performance merits of various systems.

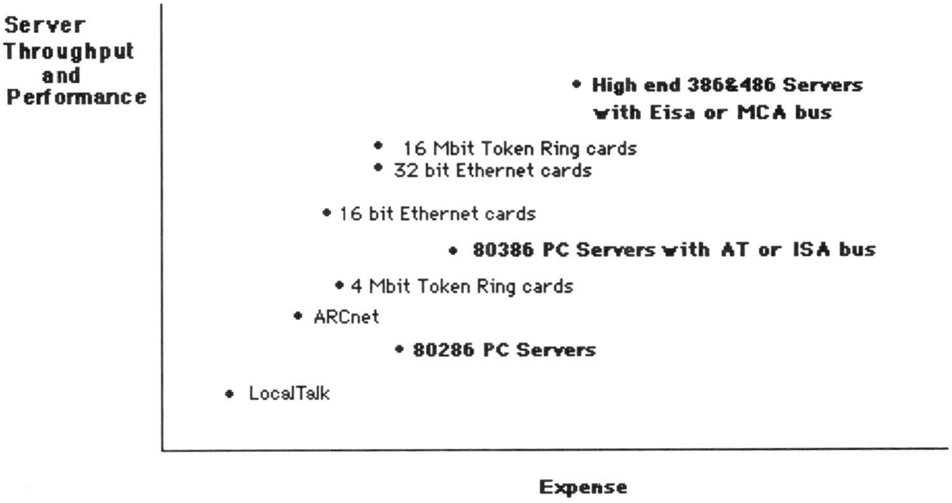

2-7 Server performance is influenced by many factors.

There is also a component of network performance that can be enhanced or inhibited by the interface cards computers use. It is senseless to invest in expensive high-end server hardware and then put a networking card in that server that will not pull data off the network fast enough to make a difference. Today's latest networking card technology features a data bus that has a 32-bit data path to match the data bus path of higher-end 386 and 486 computers. Older card technology was often limited to a 16-bit data bus. If your choice of server technology and performance requirements warrant it, a 32-bit network interface card in the server will make a significant difference. Your network can probably get by with a 32-bit card only in the server. Even if the client computers use only a 16-bit card, they probably still will benefit from the server's gain in performance from the 32-bit card.

The data speed and capacity of the network cabling is another criteria of performance. The standard of measurement for a cabling's speed and capacity is called *bandwidth,* which is measured in bits (units of data) per second. Although bandwidth's bits/second unit of measure implies that it measures speed, it really measures the media's capacity to pass data. This capacity results from a complex relationship between its many characterstics. It is fair to generalize, however, that the greater the bandwidth of the cabling media, the better it is able to speed data quickly over the wire when network usage is low (to a point), and the less susceptable it is to traffic jams when the usage is high. Of the network cabling media that NetWare for Macintosh supports, the one with the lowest bandwidth is LocalTalk. The bandwidth of LocalTalk is about .23 Mbits/second. Ethernet is a much higher capacity media, which tops out at 10 Mbits/second. Arcnet falls somewhere between LocalTalk and Ethernet. Token Ring has a higher potential bandwidth than Ethernet. It can go as high as 16 Mbits/ second, although a 4 Mbits/second version of Token Ring also exists. Even greater bandwidth media have been developed using fibre optic cabling.

Ethernet is often an organization's choice when weighing the need for performance against cost. LocalTalk is always the cheapest for a Macintosh network because the network connection is built into the Macintosh, but Ethernet's performance is dramatically better than LocalTalk. Token Ring can be faster yet, but the network connections are more expensive.

In the Macintosh networking environment there are some AppleTalk protocol considerations that affect performance, particularly on Ethernet networks. The AppleTalk Phase 2 generation of AppleTalk protocols was designed to enhance AppleTalk performance on Ethernet cabling systems, and will significantly outperform AppleTalk Phase 1 on Ethernet. Chapter 4 discusses this issue in greater depth.

Network printing

In networking environments there are inevitably times when more than one user wants to print a document to a shared printer. Network servers resolve this situation through a service called a *print queue*. A print queue is a program that runs on the server to store a print job when it comes in over the network, and then send it on to the printer. The process of storing a user's print job is called *spooling*. The word originates from an analogy of what happens when the print job is accepted into the queue. The job arrives at the queue as a string of characters and the queue metaphorically rolls the string onto a spool to store it.

Print queues facilitate network printing because they can accept a print job from a user even if the printer is actually busy with another user's job; thus, users do not have to wait for the printer to be free. Print queues can accept and store numerous jobs, and send them to the printer one by one as it becomes available. See Figure 2-8.

Many non-NetWare Macintosh networks share Apple LaserWriters without the benefit of print queues. This is made possible by the ability of the Apple LaserWriter to attach directly to the network, and by the ability of a user's Macintosh computer operating system to locally spool its own print jobs. At the printer, jobs are handled on a first-come, first-served basis.

The local spooling, first-come, first-served method works pretty well in networks that have small amounts of printer contention. In high contention environments or large networks, however, it leaves users at the mercy of a system

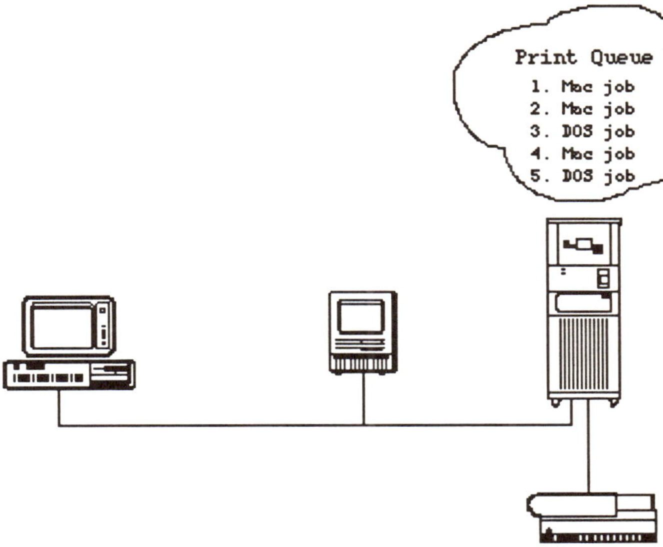

2-8 NetWare print queues allow users to send print jobs to the server for spooling and management.

that can't be manged easily. NetWare for Macintosh print queues can benefit Macintosh users in these environments because when print jobs are stored in print queues, they can be prioritized and tracked. Queues also provide performance benefits. When the queue does the print spooling, rather than the Macintosh operating system, some of the print processing burden is relieved from the Macintosh.

A server's security

A network server is a shared resource. Other network users have access to the server and to potentially the same information, possibly at the same time. Consequently, servers generally implement a set of restrictions that can prevent the inadvertant compromise of information not meant to be seen by others. Servers also implement features that prevent compromises of data that are not accidental.

Security is implemented differently by various server solutions. At minimum, a security system needs the ability to set up individual user accounts with individually set passwords. More sophisticated security systems extend user accounts to user groups, which assign users to broad categories, such as members of the legal department, so that information access can be managed easier.

The best security systems keep audit trails of user logins to track when they occur, where they occur from, and how long the user was logged in. They set limits on how long an account is valid, and how often passwords must be changed. Comprehensive security systems protect the information on a server by providing access protections down to the level of directories and folders or the level of individual files. They also allow files to be restricted to certain characteristics, such as readable—but not writable, or noncopyable.

Finally, data security is important for more than just the information stored on a file server. The network should be secure for data passing over the network wires. For example, although passwords are a good account protection tool, unless they are encrypted as they are passed over the wire, their security is not guaranteed. If they are unencrypted, a cable tap, or even a commonplace network analyzing tool, could decipher them. The same concerns apply to backups of server data. If the backup is done over the network wire from one server to another, it also should be encrypted. Backups done on media, such as magnetic tape, should be encrypted so they are still secure after leaving the server.

NetWare's security system addresses all of these security issues. Starting with the login procedure, NetWare security requires user names and passwords to access the server's information, shown in Figure 2-9. NetWare extends that security with user profiles listing the resources a user has access to, and the rights he or she has while using that resource. NetWare allows restrictions by time, place and frequency for login access, and keeps audit trails of accesses.

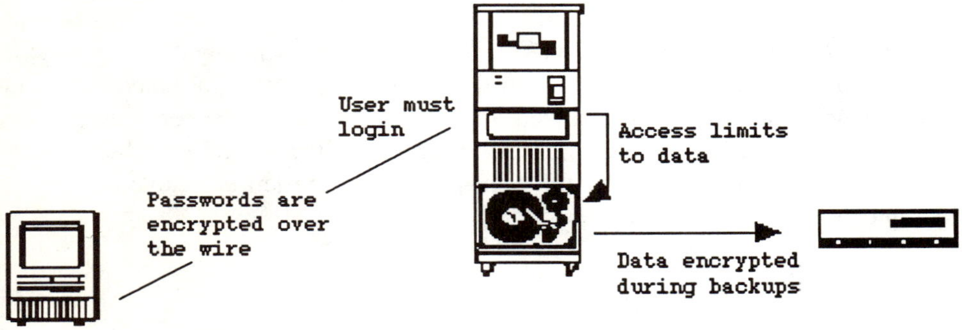

2-9 Some of the security features of NetWare.

The set of access limits are comprehensive and including such restrictions as the inability to see files, write to files, and copy files, so that sensitive information can't be carried away on floppy disks. Other capabilities permit the manager of a network to limit the date, time, and location from which a user can log into the network. To supplement the access protections, Novell added intruder detection and other features that notify supervisors of any unauthorized access attempt.

NetWare stores passwords in encrypted format, so even if would-be intruders acquire physical access to a server, the passwords are secure. NetWare encrypts passwords as it sends them over the network wire as well. Even backups can be sent over the wire and stored on backup media in encrypted format. This further protects all security information that gets backed up in the process.

Reliability

As organizations increase their reliance on networks, the issue of network reliability has become more and more important. An organization that runs its business on a computer network can't afford the prospect of bad data or the possibility of the network going down. This reality has given birth to the concept of fault-tolerant network design.

Fault tolerance

Making a network fault tolerant requires planning to prevent problems like a break in a network wire or the failure of a server's hard disk stopping network activity. Much can be done to minimize the potential of failure. For example, a network wire could be crimped and broken accidentally by someone moving a desk out of an office. This break in the wire would cut off the access to the network of users on that length of wire. If the network were designed to provide an alternate wire path to the network, however, those users would be unaffected. Fault tolerant networks provide redundancy of network resources, and wiring in ways similar to what is shown in Figure 2-10. In practice redundant wiring is often accomplished through the use of commercially available wiring hubs and racks, such as those available from cabletron and synoptics.

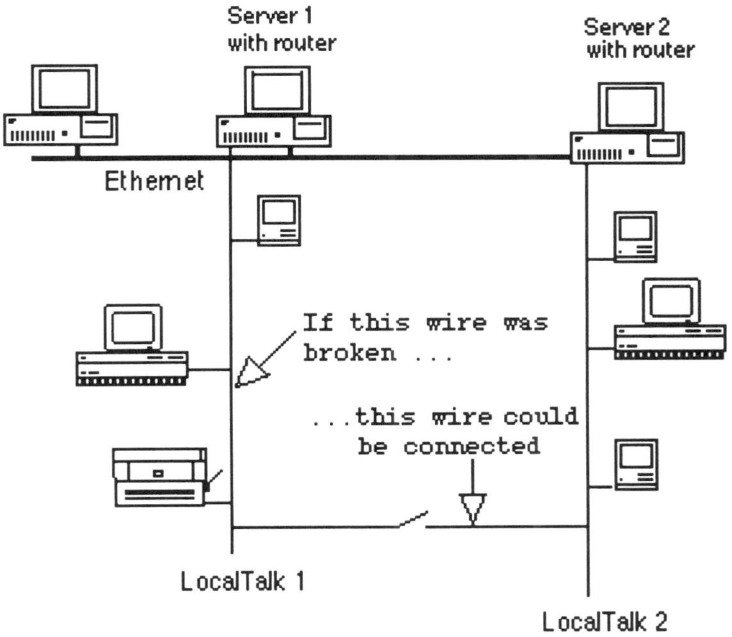

2-10 Fault tolerant network design begins with cabling systems.

In addition to fault-tolerant wiring layouts, business-critical networks also need servers that can be fault tolerant. The hardware of newer *high-end* server products have built-in disk technology that can be made fault tolerant. These high-end servers can be set up so that two of the server's disks act in unison to create redundant data. This kind of configuration is called either disk mirroring or disk duplexing, depending on the method of synchronization. Both data redundancy methods automatically ensure that every time the server writes files to its disk, it is actually writing to two separate disks, thereby making two copies of the information. Disk duplexing requires separate disk controller cards to be installed in the server, whereas disk mirroring permits both disks to be run off of the same controller card, shown in Figure 2-11.

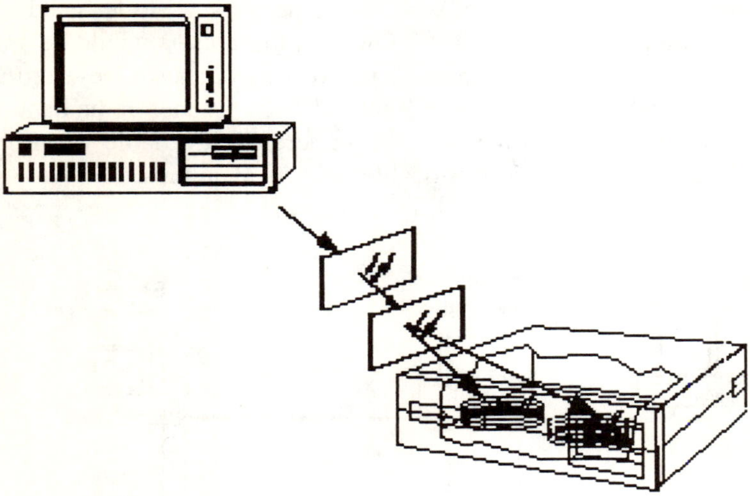

2-11 A PC server with mirrored disks.

Even without high-end, fault-tolerant disk arrays in servers, much can be done to eliminate points of failure. Servers running critical applications always should be attached to a device called an *uninterruptable power source* (UPS), shown in Figure 2-12. A UPS has a battery in it that automatically takes over if electricity fails. Network server software such as Novell NetWare, vastly can improve fault-tolerant protection on a network server if it has the ability to monitor disk defects and UPS devices. To extend the network's fault-tolerance to networking clients, UPS systems should be attached to client computers in addition to servers.

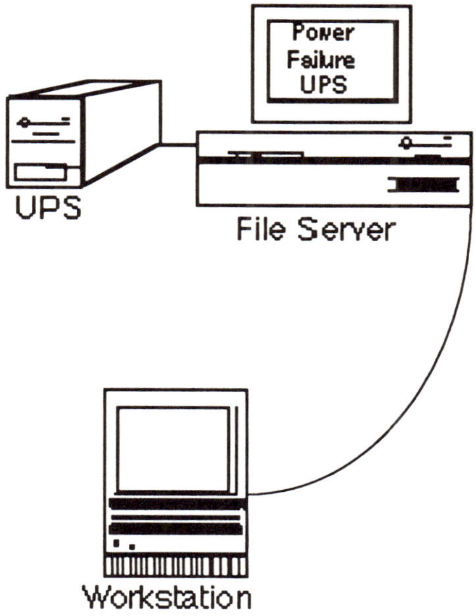

2-12 Uninteruptable power sources can prevent loss of data during power failures.

NetWare does have some of these fault-tolerant features written in to its operating system. For example, NetWare has a feature called UPS monitoring, which safeguards against data loss when a UPS is forced to take over a server's operation because its normal power source fails. Many UPS manufacturers have created units that send alerts to NetWare when they are activated. After receiving the UPS's alert, NetWare notifies all the current users of the power failure, and after a configurable time out will close any open files and shut itself down.

Another fault-tolerant feature called the *Transaction Tracking System* (TTS) works with database application programs to prevent database corruption if system failure occurs while data is being written to disk. This could happen if the server has a UPS, but the client doesn't. If a power failure caused a clients file changes to be written and thus corrupted, NetWare's TTS can restore the database to the state it was in before the failure. TTS automatically rolls back or aborts failed transactions without affecting others that might be, or might have been, in progress.

Data integrity

In addition to network and database fault tolerance, NetWare was designed to provide reliability features that ensure data integrity. One set of these data integrity features monitor how data is stored on a server's disk. Operating systems of every computer ensure that the files on the computer's disk are stored properly.

NetWare has taken data checks to reassuring extremes. Figure 2-13 illustrates how NetWare data write integrity reread and verify to ensure every write to a disk.

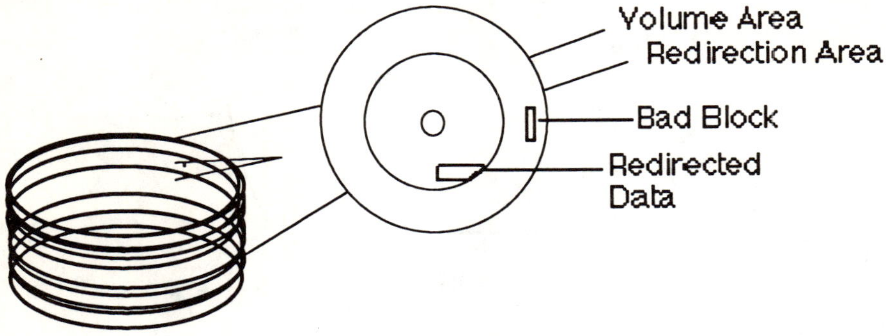

2-13 NetWare verifies that every file is properly written, and hot fixes bad sections of the disk.

Data storage integrity is ensured in several ways. The first is through diligent watching of the storage disk(s) physical condition. NetWare performs media defect detection on the fly. If it notices a bad spot on a disk, NetWare skips over that spot and records its location for future reference. This is depicted in Figure 2-13. Novell calls this process *hot fixing*.

Another data safeguard of NetWare is redundency of *directory tables,* which helps ensure that data written to disk always remains retrievable. Directory Tables are a NetWare disk's map to where files are physically located. When NetWare reads a file from the disk it must first consult the directory table for the location of the file. NetWare automatically duplicates directory tables on the same disk so that data is never rendered unrecoverable should a directory table become damaged.

Resource accounting

NetWare has supporting features and products that permit the allocation and tracking of the network server's resources. For example, NetWare supervisors can preset the amount of disk space a user can have or specify an expiration date for a user's account privileges. NetWare also has features to audit user logins, logouts, and the amount of time connecting them; thus, a NetWare server can be accounted for just like any noncomputer resource an organization invests in and shares among users.

To draw an analogy of how this can be useful, think of the telephone. Organizations have to track the use and cost of its telephone service. An account with the telephone company is generally a shared expense. The organization has one account for monthly service, and the monthly expense is shared by its various users. If the expense must be charged to the organization's various departments, those people responsible for planning and accounting for these expenses need to be able to track the use of each individual. NetWare's accounting features enable a shared network server to be handled much the same way. Users can be charged for the number of documents they print through it, the amount of disk space they use, or other criteria.

Blocks Read Charge Rates

Wednesday
8:00 am To 8:29 am

Rate	Charge	Rate	Charge
1	.01	11	
2	.02	12	
3		13	
4		14	
5		15	
6		16	
7		17	
8		18	
9		19	
10		20	

	Mon	Tue	Wed	Thu	Fri
8:00 am	1	1	1	1	1
9:00 am	1	1	1	1	1
10:00 am	1	1	1	1	1
11:00 am	1	1	1	1	1
12:00 pm	2	2	2	2	2
1:00 pm	2	2	2	2	2
2:00 pm	2	2	2	2	2
3:00 pm	2	2	2	2	2
4:00 pm	2	2	2	2	2
5:00 pm	2	2	2	2	2
6:00 pm	2	2	2	2	2
7:00 pm	2	2	2	2	2
8:00 pm	2	2	2	2	2
9:00 pm	2	2	2	2	2
10:00 pm	2	2	2	2	2
11:00 pm	2	2	2	2	2

2-14: Resource accounting features can track and charge for server use.

Server administration

Keeping networks running requires some management. The amount of management required usually varies with the sophistication of the network. In single-server networks, the management tasks are relatively simple and relate to the administration of the server. Networks that incorporate more than a single server have somewhat more complex needs in addition to server administration.

One of the tasks that all networks must complete is the initial setup of the servers. This first entails installing the NetWare operating system software. That can be done through the disk drives and the keyboard of the server itself. Other required setup tasks include creating user accounts and print queues. NetWare provides tools for these tasks that can be used on client computers, so setup and routine maintenance, such as adding accounts later for new employees, can be conducted from anywhere on the network. Using these tools from a Macintosh computer is discussed at length in following chapters.

Application development tools

NetWare also has a set of tools to allow programmers to write customized applications that take advantage of the many NetWare features outlined in this book. These tools consist of a set of disks and manuals for programming libraries and exposed NetWare APIs (application programer's interface). They permit technically inclined NetWare owners to write their own custom applications that leverage the abilities of NetWare. A list of application programming interfaces and a description of each can be found in Table 2-1.

These APIs also benefit nontechnical NetWare owners because a large community of professional software developers have written commercial applications for NetWare. These applications consist of everything from small business accounting packages to control programs for robotic manufacturing equipment. Novell NetWare is a widely supported standard for networking applications. A catalogue of these applications can be ordered directly from Novell.

Table 2-1 Application programming interfaces.

Bindery

Each NetWare file server maintains a database, called the Bindery, which holds a list of all network objects or entities, including groups, file servers, print queues, etc. Bindery interfaces permit the client application to see, add, delete or otherwise modify this information. The Bindery also implements security on the Novell server.

Connections

Interfaces exist which enable applications to obtain information about connections between network entities and file servers.

File Server Environment

These interfaces allow applications to see and set information concerning file servers. For example, these functions enable or disable log-ins, set data and time, clear existing connections, or determine the nature of disk peripherals, volume blocks, etc.

File System

These calls enable applications to obtain or modify information about NetWare volumes, directories and files, add or delete NetWare trustees, etc. They show a NetWare view of the file system.

Messages

These permit an application to broadcast and receive messages to users logged into the NetWare server regardless of client platform (Macintosh, DOS, Windows, OS/2, etc.).

Queue Management

Applications may create queues for controlling the flow of jobs and services on the network as well as service these queues. Networks may have many different kinds of job servers, including print servers, archive servers, mail servers, etc. By confining requests to network queues, a job server can provide services that are both flexible and efficient.

Synchronization

These services enable applications to coordinate access to shared files as well as any other network resources by providing semaphoring and locking. Locking is extended beyond physical files to include logical locking of resource sets defined by the application.

Transaction Tracking (TTS)

NetWare file servers that enable TTS can track transactions and ensure file integrity by backing out (or erasing) interrupted or partially completed transactions. The NetWare OS provides implicit transaction tracking requiring no coding by the applications programmer. However, explicit tracking may be tailored by the application to meet its exact needs.

3
Chapter

The Macintosh networking environment

The Macintosh operating system includes a built-in networking protocol called AppleTalk, and a built-in networking client software called AppleShare workstation software. These built-in networking attributes give the Macintosh a uniquely simple and intuitive method for networking. This chapter outlines how the Macintosh computer uses the AppleTalk networking protocols and client software to access AppleTalk network services, and how NetWare uses AppleTalk to implement its Macintosh client environment.

Macintosh networking standards

AppleTalk is not the only networking protocol that Novell could have used to allow Macintosh clients to communicate with NetWare servers, but it probably was the most sensible. Macintosh users have it built in to their operating system and most of them have used it from the day they took their Macintosh out of the box, if only to print to Apple LaserWriters. Consequently, those already familiar with the AppleTalk networking environment will recognize many similar conventions when using NetWare from a Macintosh client.

The AppleTalk networking protocols are actually the basis of an entire Macintosh networking environment that consists of technologies for making physical connections, sharing files, using printers, and various other elements. It also includes a standardized interface for interacting with resources.

The most rudimentary part of AppleTalk networking systems are those that make the physical connections to the network. These physical systems along with the protocols of AppleTalk were designed to make Macintosh networks self configuring, so users essentially could attach a Macintosh anywhere into the network and it would work. Users don't necessarily need to know any more about the physical elements of AppleTalk other than how to plug in the network cabling. If you desire to learn, however, chapter 4 provides a more detailed section on AppleTalk network design, and the end of this book contains an appendix that describes the protocol in technical detail.

AppleTalk network filing systems

One of the elements of AppleTalk networking technology that users regularly interact with is a network file system based on a protocol subset of AppleTalk, called AppleTalk Filing Protcol (AFP). The AFP file system of the AppleTalk environment defines how network servers store files, how application programs work with those files, and how client computers access the server's files. The icon designating AFP is depicted in Figure 3-1.

3-1 The AppleShare icon indicates AFP compliance.

Client access to AFP servers is acquired through software in the Macintosh operating system called AppleShare workstation client software. Apple Computer Company, Inc. created its own trademarked brand of dedicated AFP server called AppleShare, which supports the AppleShare workstation client; however, the AppleShare client software works with other AFP servers such as NetWare for Macintosh as well.

All Macintosh computers, beginning with Macintosh System 7.0, will include AFP server software, in addition to client software, that will enable them to be servers in a peer-to-peer networking model. This ability will complement the offerings available through dedicated servers, such as NetWare for Macintosh, by allowing Macintosh users to bypass the server for casual Macintosh to Macintosh file sharing needs. However, Personal AppleShare (as it is called), will not provide the ability to do peer-to-peer file sharing with DOS, Windows, or UNIX computers nor will it be a good applications platform.

AppleTalk network printing systems

Another AppleTalk network technology defines how Macintosh computers use printers on a network. This technology, which gives printers a certain amount of networking intelligence, does not affect printing to local printers (such as the Apple ImageWriter), but it has everything to do with printers such as AppleTalk ImageWriters (an ImageWriter with a network attachment) and the Apple LaserWriter family of printers, which are network-attached laser printers.

AppleTalk network printing uses an AppleTalk subset protocol called Printer Access Protocol (PAP) to establish communication with a networked Apple LaserWriter. PAP controls the communication between Macintoshes and PostScript printers that are attached to AppleTalk networks and maintains a constant dialogue between the LaserWriter and a Macintosh client that is using the LaserWriter. PAP allows the LaserWriter to send its clients messages, such as notification that the LaserWriter is out of paper, shown in Figure 3-2.

Waiting for LaserWriter: 'LaserWriter II NTH', User: Marty Jost

Document: Sample Document, Status: Printer is out of paper

3-2 AppleTalk protocols allow the Apple LaserWriter to maintain a dialogue with its networked users.

Complementing AppleTalk's PAP protocol is a printer driver which is part of a Macintosh clients operating system for a printer language called *PostScript*. The Macintosh uses the PostScript printer language to tell the Apple LaserWriter how to create an image and permits the graphic printing styles for which the Macintosh is known. Some of the PostScript printer language is burned into the ROM chips of the LaserWriter, but some of it is kept in software on the Macintosh client. Figure 3-3 explains the difference between PostScript and nonPostScript printers supported by Macintosh.

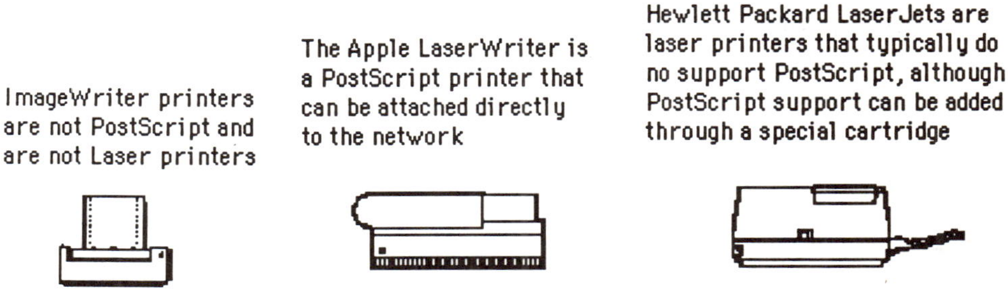

3-3 Common printers in NetWare environments.

In Macintosh System 6.X, PostScript print support is provided by two files that reside in a Macintosh client's System Folder. The actual printer driver is a file called *LaserWriter* and another file, called *LaserPrep,* is the PostScript dictionary. Both files must be present in the System Folder for LaserWriter printing to work properly. All Macintosh clients on the network should use the same versions of these files. Figure 3-4 shows how the Get Info command in the Macintosh Finders file menu will show you the version numbers of LaserWriter and LaserPrep.

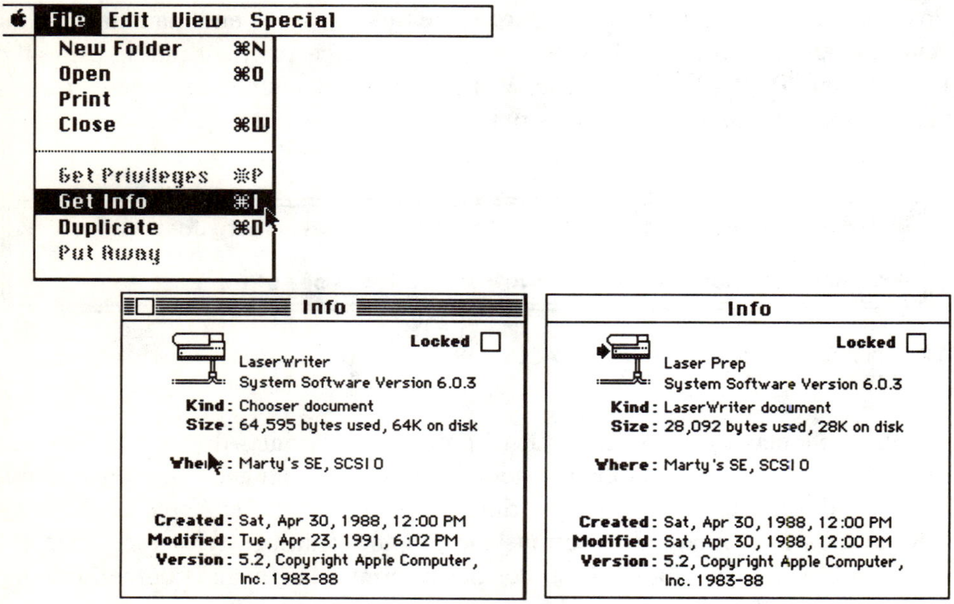

3-4 In System 6.X, Get Info will show you what versions of LaserWriter and LaserPrep you have.

In Macintosh System 7.X, PostScript support is provided by only one file, called *LaserWriter,* which needs to be in a subfolder within the System Folder called *Extentions*. Although both system 6.X and System 7.X use a file called LaserWriter as their printer driver, you can see in Figure 3-5 that the icon is different.

The interface to AppleTalk network services

Access to devices on a Macintosh network is provided through a user interface called the *Chooser*. Though not exclusively used for network access, the

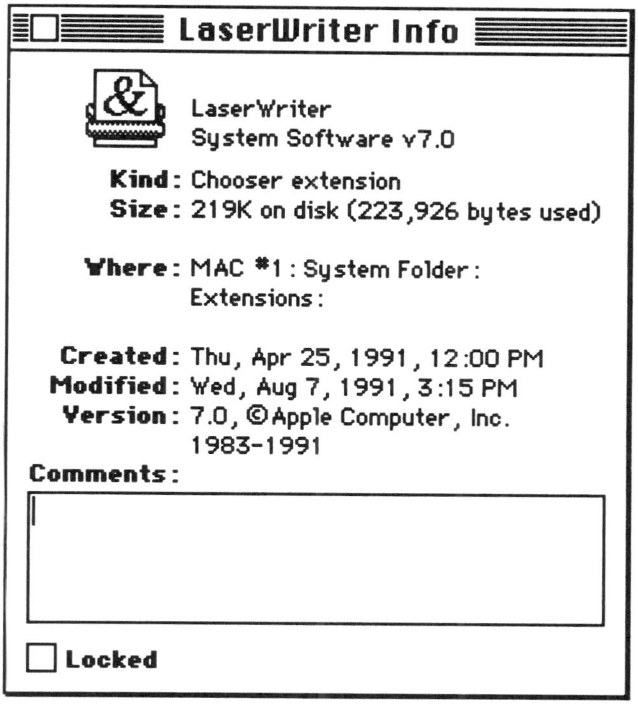

3-5 The LaserWriter file in System 7.X.

Chooser provides an intuitive method for selecting network resources. The Chooser is a menu selection found under the Macintosh's Apple menu. This Chooser works the same in both Macintosh System 6.X and 7.X.

The Chooser window you see in Figure 3-6 shows a number of different devices. The three icons represent an AFP file server, a networked Apple LaserWriter printer, and an Apple Imagewriter printer. The ImageWriter can be attached to the network if it is equipped with a LocalTalk connection. Select the device to be used by clicking its icon. An AppleTalk ImageWriter is distinguished from a nonnetworked ImageWriter by the addition of networking cables to its icon.

Many organizations have more than one AppleTalk ImageWriter or LaserWriter on the network. AppleTalk protocols therefore require that printers be identified on the network by names. Even if only one AppleTalk printer is attached on your network, it still must have a name. After a networked printer icon is selected in the Chooser, you will see lists of available printers by their names, which appear in the window, also shown in Figure 3-6.

Once the printer of choice is selected, Macintosh application programs will send the documents to that printer automatically, when you give the command to

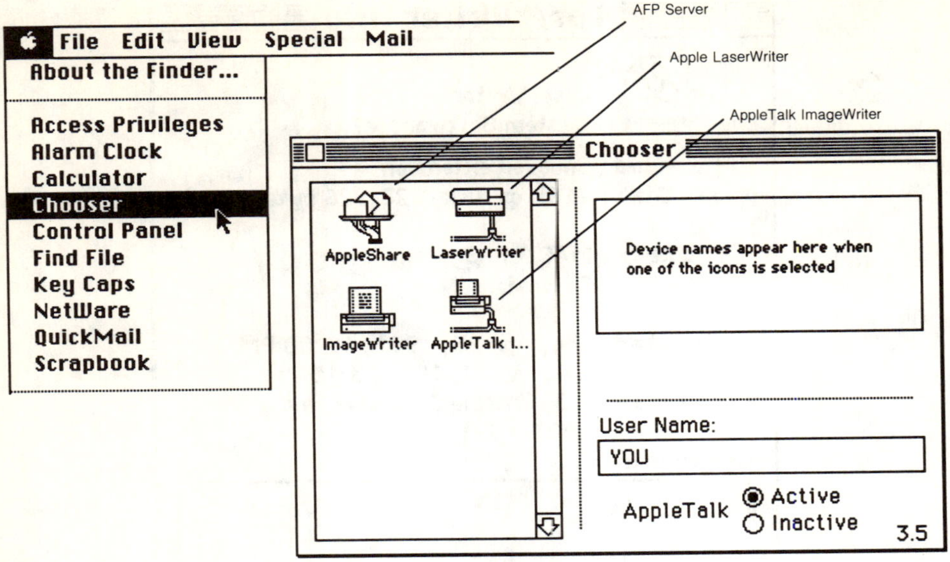

3-6 The Macintosh Chooser interface provides network access.

print from within the application. The printer that you select in the Chooser will stay selected until you go into the Chooser again and select a new one, or select some other device that you use to print.

AppleTalk network file servers

In the Macintosh networking environment, all servers that are compliant with AFP will appear to the Macintosh user as if they are AppleShare servers, even though the server actually might be a Novell NetWare server.

Like AppleTalk printers, servers on an AppleTalk network are identified by names. Figure 3-7 shows how clicking the AppleShare icon in the Chooser will yield a list of the networks AFP server names in the window on the right-hand side. If the network has only one file server, that is the only name you will see. To access a server, double click its name, or click on it to select it, and then click the OK button.

When you select an AppleShare or other AFP servers from the server list, you will be required to log-in to the server in order to access its files or printers. In an AppleTalk network environment, every user of the network's services is required to have a name by which they are referenced when on the network, just like printers and servers. This facilitates communication, when one user wants to send a message to another user, and also assists you and the manager of the network in maintaining its security.

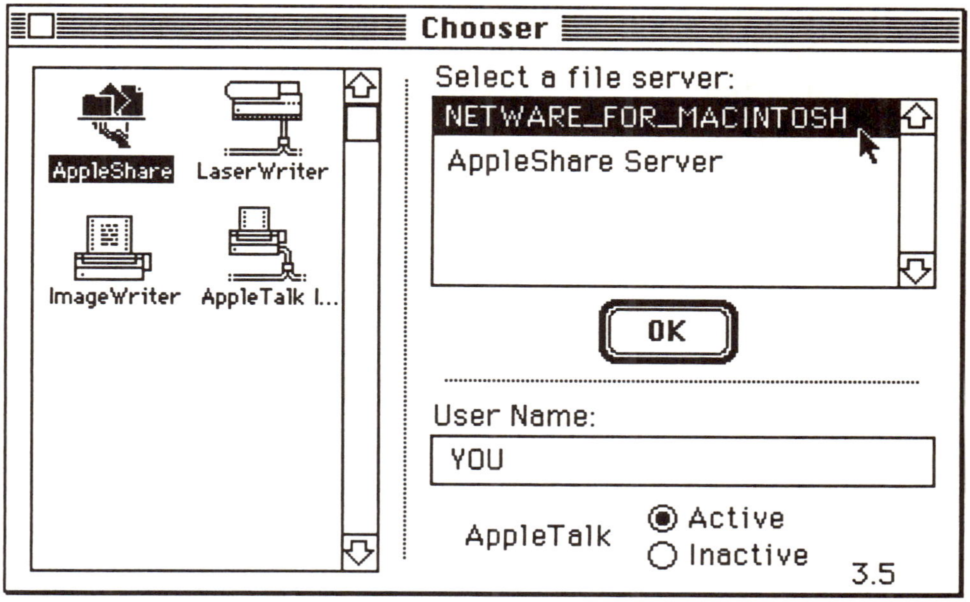

3-7 AppleShare servers are identified by name.

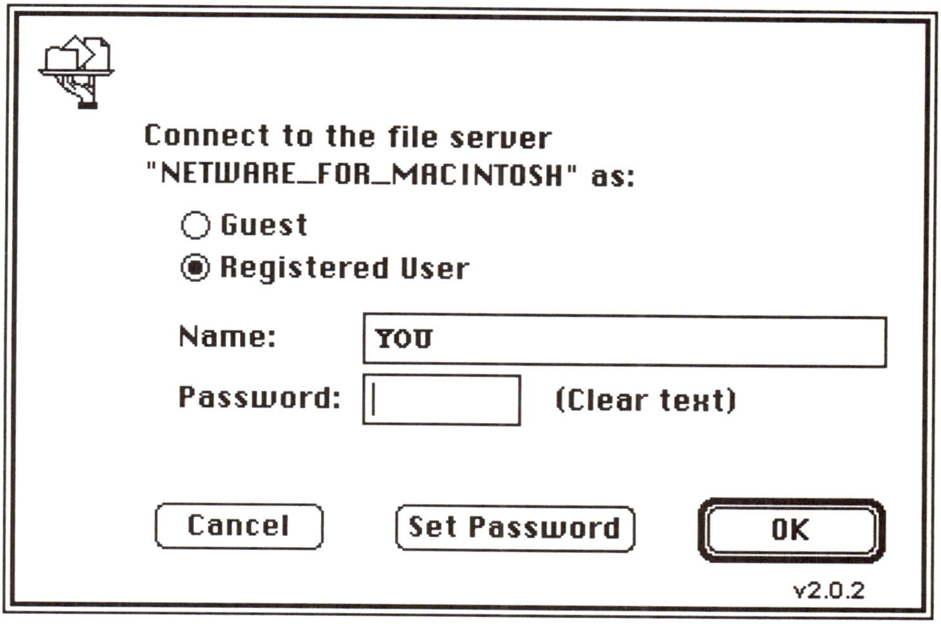

3-8 The AppleShare Login Window.

Servers have a list of valid account names that are created on the server by the person who installs and administers the server (usually the same person). To log in means to sign on to the server by your user name, and often a password that adds access security to that account. Each account has the option to have a password assigned to it. The screen for the account identification, which appears after you select the server you desire, is shown in Figure 3-8. After you type the information in, click the OK button to perform the login.

Password protection on your user account is an important safeguard for your data. If you don't have a password, you should create one. It will prevent others who know your account name from accessing your data unless they also know your password. To create or change a password, click the Set Password button at the bottom of the Login window (Figure 3-8). This button will be gray if you use a NetWare feature called Encrypted User Authentication. The Set Password choice will give you a screen like the one in Figure 3-9, where you can make your password changes. If you use the standard Apple method, you are limited to 8 characters. Naturally, you should keep your password confidential, and avoid choosing obvious ones.

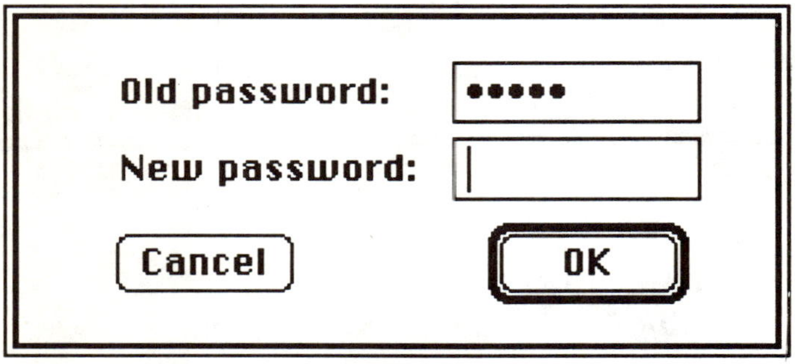

3-9 The window for changing passwords.

After logging in by your account name, you will see a screen that instructs you to select a server volume. This screen is displayed in Figure 3-10. A volume for file services refers to an entity analogous to an actual disk on the server, although one volume could technically be several disks. Any file server can be set up to control multiple volumes or one volume attached to a file server. Whatever the case, choose the name of the volume you want to use from the screen.

In this window you also can specify that you want a volume to be automatically mounted at start-up time. To make a volume mount automatically, click on the check box next to the name of the volume. Click on the box again to unselect the volume. Auto-mounting is disabled if you use encrypted authentication; how-

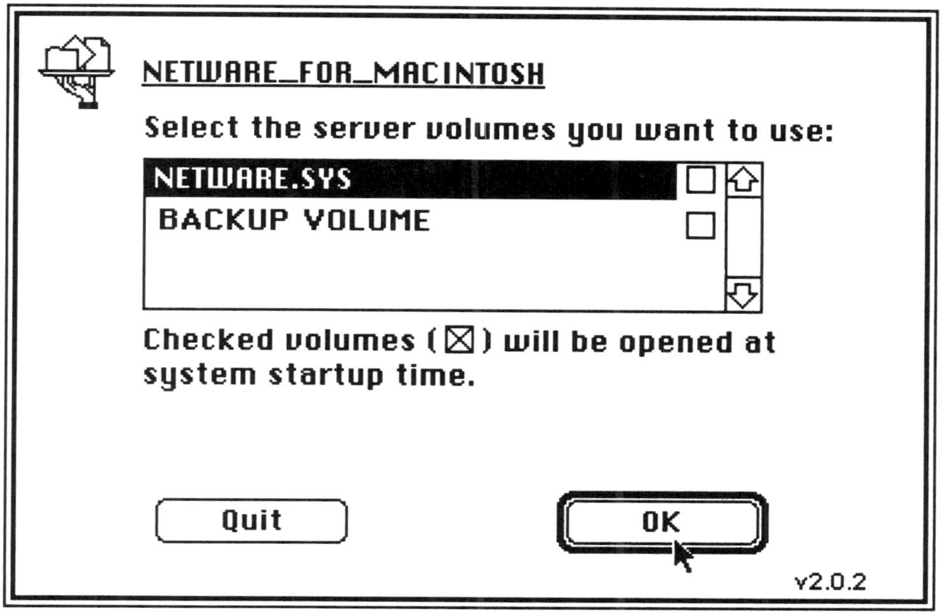

3-10 Selecting a volume.

ever, you can regain a great deal of its convenience through a Macintosh System 7.x feature, called aliasing, which is discussed in chapter 6.

After completing the log-in process, your Macintosh will display the network file services that you have logged into as an icon on your desktop, shown if Figure 3-11.

You can see how the icons differ, but on the desktop, the files and folders of the network volume can be treated and manipulated exactly like the files and folders on the floppy or hard disks. To use the server, click on the icon like you would click the icon of any other disk. Files can be dragged on and off of a server like on anything else, as shown in Figure 3-12.

One way the server is different from other disks is that the server is a shared resource. To protect against data compromise, it has a security system that permits users to set restrictions on some of the information. Sometimes you will see folders on an AFP server that are grayed out. These are folders that you have been restricted from accessing.

AppleTalk zones

A final interface consideration when using the Chooser to access AppleTalk network resources is an AppleTalk networking feature called a zone. A zone is a subdivision of devices and users on a network. Zones are most often used to

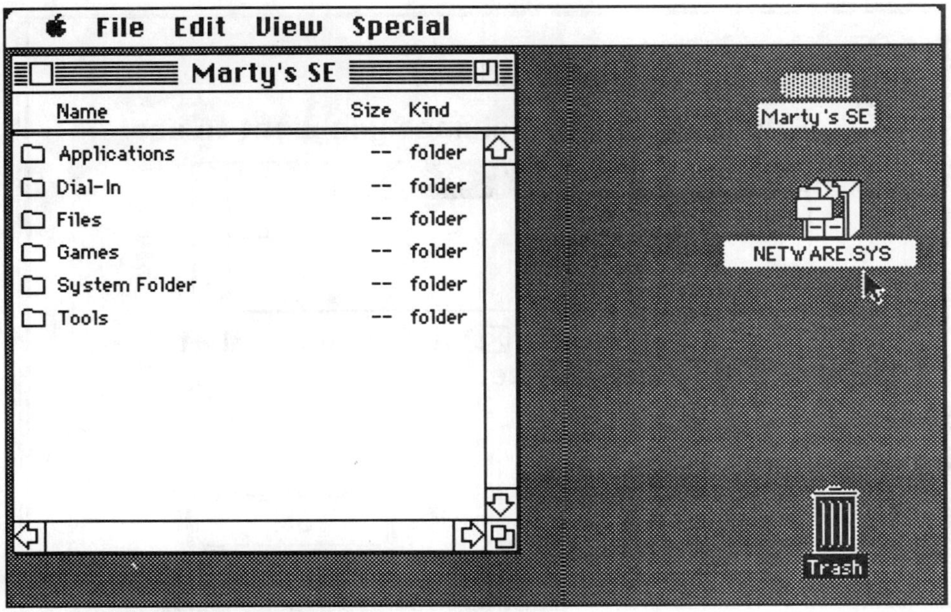

3-11 An icon for a mounted server volume.

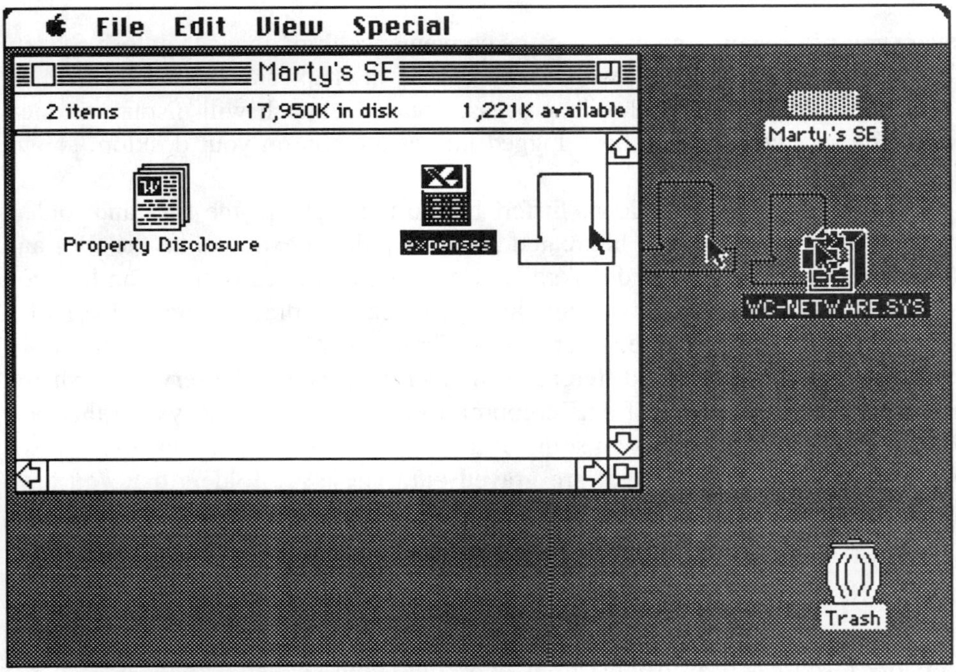

3-12 Files can be dragged onto a server volume as easily as to any other disk.

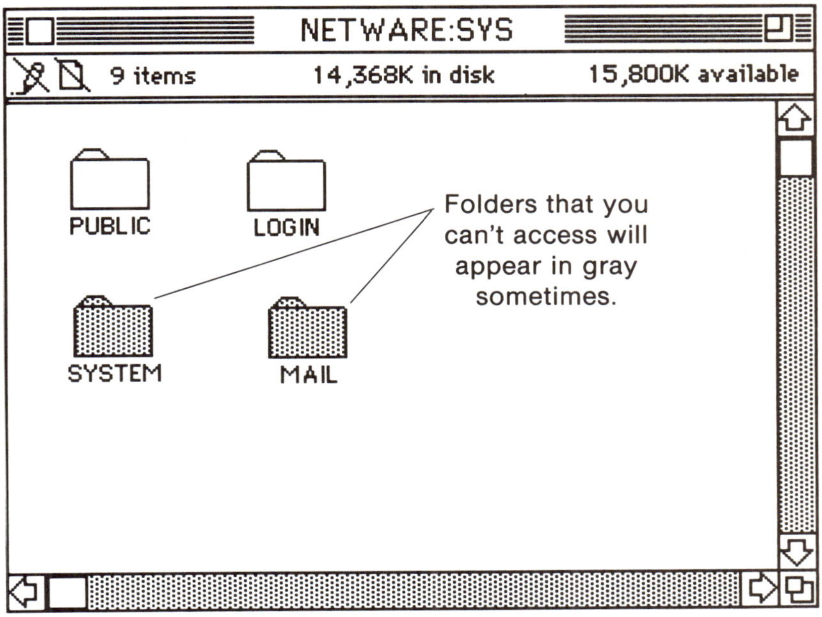

3-13 A look at the contents of a server volume.

reduce the number of servers or devices that are visible in the chooser for a particular section of a network, or for a particular group of users. By reducing the number of devices in the Chooser, zones use the Chooser interface more efficiently.

For example, suppose a company of 50 computer users sets up an AppleTalk network. The network might have two dedicated AFP network servers, one for the accounting group, and one for the sales and administration. The network also might have five or six users at any time who are using Apple system 7.0 and have advertised themselves as Personal AppleShare servers, so they could make some of their computers' local hard disk files accessible by others. Without zones, the network servers would be all mixed together in the Chooser, and in a sense, everyone would be in everyone else's way.

Creating zones organizes the network better, so the users in the accounting group only see servers in their department, and the users in sales and administration would see the servers in their group. With zones, users are not barred from accessing the devices in the other zones of the network, just freed of the inconvenience of working around the other devices when they don't need them. In the Chooser diagram in Figure 3-14, you can see the box in the lower left hand corner of the Chooser interface for changing from one zone to another. Each time you click a different zone, the right-hand window of the Chooser shows you a list of servers in that zone only.

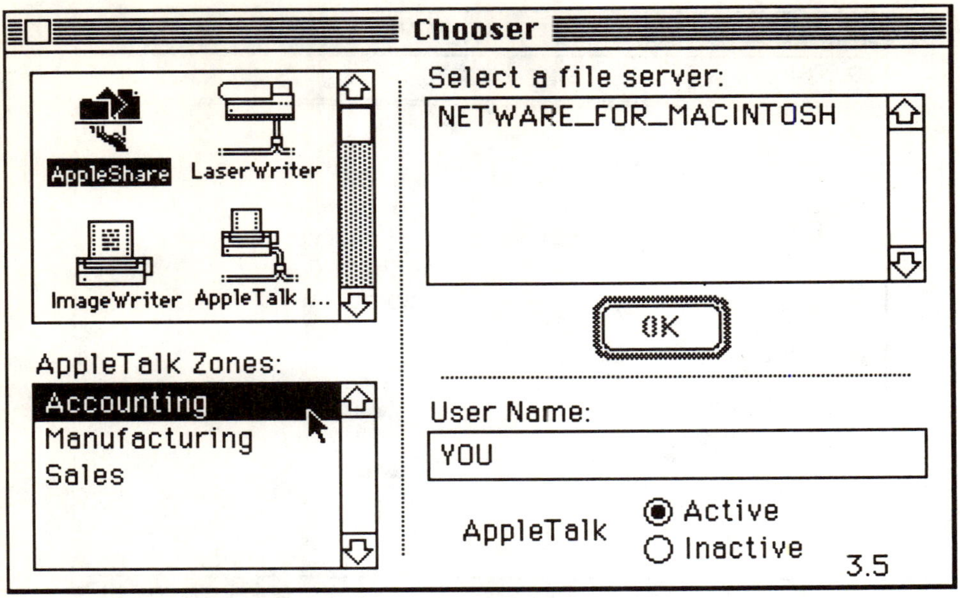

3-14 Zone access is easily accomplished through the Chooser.

NetWare and NetWare for Macintosh

Novell NetWare supports all of the Macintosh networking interface guidelines just described. NetWare supports all AppleTalk protocols, including AppleTalk Filing Protocol (AFP), and Printer Access Protocol (PAP), so that Macintosh networking clients use AppleShare workstation client software to access NetWare resources. NetWare network resources appear in the Macintosh Chooser like the other resources of AppleTalk networks.

Novell's product that supports Macintosh clients was named NetWare for Macintosh. NetWare for Macintosh is client and server software that provides NetWare file and print services to Macintosh computers. NetWare for Macintosh v2.X runs in a NetWare v2.X server environment as something called a Value Added Process (VAP). In the NetWare v3.X environment, NetWare for Macintosh v3.X runs as something called a NetWare Loadable Module (NLM).

NetWare for Macintosh v3.X is the high end of the NetWare for Macintosh product line. It offers some important features not available through NetWare for Macintosh v2.2, but on a basic level of operation, both versions of NetWare for Macintosh work the same way. Both versions of NetWare for Macintosh's AFP support let Macintosh clients store files on NetWare servers, and NetWare for Macintosh's implementation of AppleTalk's PAP allows NetWare print queues to work with Apple LaserWriters.

In addition to supporting Macintosh networking standards through NetWare for Macintosh, Novell NetWare also supports networking standards that connect DOS, Windows, and other personal computers. NetWare, along with NetWare for Macintosh, will integrate multiclient environments of Macintosh, DOS, Windows, OS/2, and even UNIX computers. An organization will benefit from this integration in serveral ways. Macintosh computers benefit because they gain access to NetWare file servers and all the performance advantages, security, reliability, and data safeguards that come with NetWare. The other users also gain, because they have access to the same information as Macintosh users and access to PostScript printers in the Macintosh environment. See Figure 3- 15.

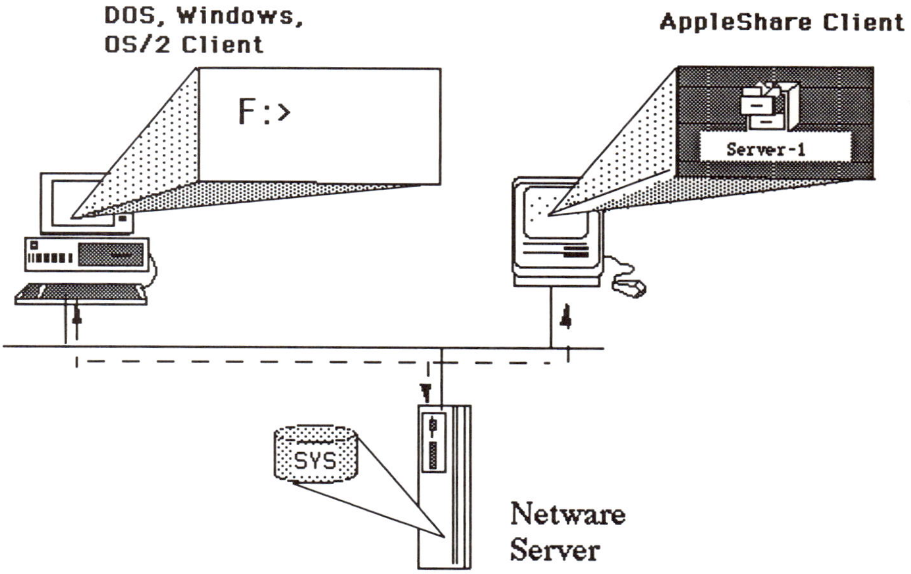

3-15 NetWare preserves the interfaces of all of its users.

You can access NetWare for Macintosh the same way you access printers and AFP servers. Assuming the AppleShare workstation software is installed on your Macintosh, when you pull down the Chooser, you will see an icon that designates an AppleShare file server, which is also what you use to select a NetWare for Macintosh file server, as shown back in Figure 3-14.

Netware for Macintosh

file services

NetWare presents all of its users with a single file system. Through NetWare for Macintosh, Macintosh users have access to the same files that DOS and other users have access to, although each user has a slighty different view of the file (see Figure 3-16). Both Macintosh and the Windows users would see the file as an icon, but DOS users would see the file only by its name.

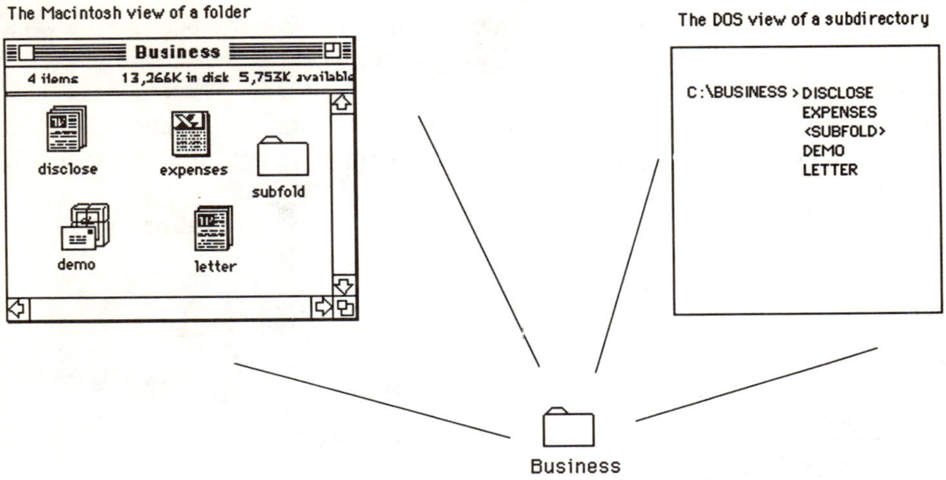

3-16 Different users see the same information in the manner their interface provides.

The AFP support provided through NetWare for Macintosh ensures NetWare compatibility with Macintosh application programs, because Macintosh applications conform to AFP. While conforming to the requirements of AppleShare workstation client software, NetWare offers previously discussed features that extend far beyond the offerings of most other AppleShare-like servers. To distinguish Netware servers that are mounted on the desktop of a Macintosh, Novell has crafted different icons for the different versions of NetWare. Figure 3-17 shows the AppleShare icon, as opposed to NetWare v2.X, and Netware v3.X.

3-17: The icons of AppleShare and NetWare servers.

The process of logging-in to a NetWare for Macintosh server is similar to the process of logging-in to an AppleShare server with two exceptions. If you are using Netware for Macintosh v3.X, a window might proceed the window where you designate your account name and password. That window will be the one shown in Figure 3-18, which let's you select whether you want NetWare's encrypted password protection. The alternative is to use the Macintosh's Apple Standard User Authentication Method (UAM).

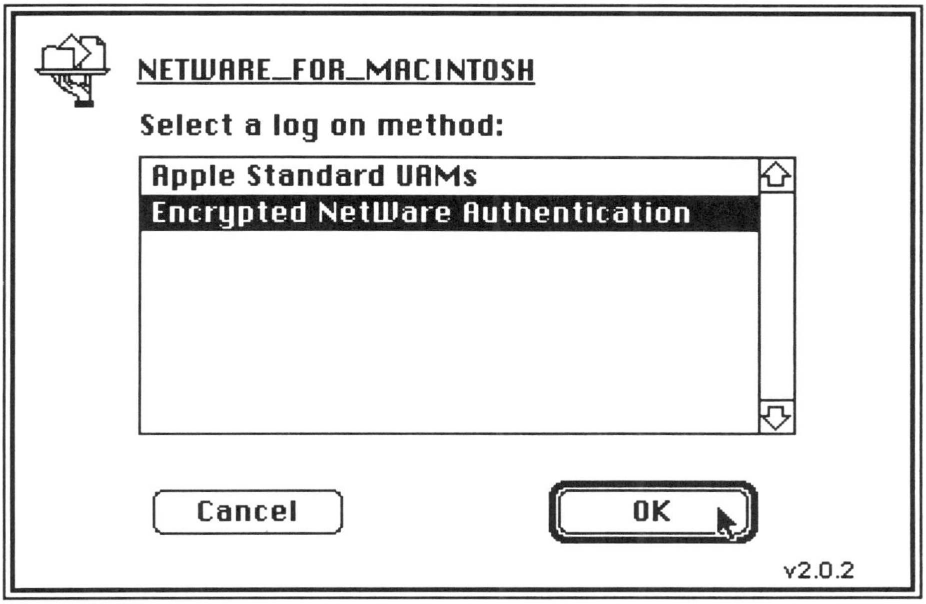

3-18 NetWare for Macintosh v3.0 will encrypt passwords.

The difference between NetWare's Encrypted User Authentication Method and the standard AppleShare User Authentication Method is the way that the Macintosh networking client sends their account name and password over the network wire. In the standard AppleShare method, the acount name and password are sent as normal text inside a data packet. A potential problem with this method of login is that the passwords are discoverable by anyone that uses a network protocol analyzing tool to evesdrop on the network. While this sophistication might be beyond the average computer user, it is not beyond the ability of the average computer professional. Protocol analyzers often are used in organizations with large networks as a standard part of their network management practices. Those who hook up such an analyzer see the information almost as clearly as if it were written on paper.

The NetWare encrypted user authentication method, on the other hand, encrypts the account name and password, so they cannot be read by an analyzer. It thereby provides an additional level of security for the user. NetWare also stores the user account names and passwords on the server in encrypted format.

Another difference between the NetWare UAM and the standard AppleShare UAM is that the NetWare encypted user authentication method allows you to choose a password that is up to 64 characters in length, while the Apple UAM limts its client passwords to 8 characters.

If you use the NetWare for Macintosh User Authentication Method, you cannot change your password from the AppleShare login window, again shown in Figure 3-19. The Set Password button in that window will be grayed out. When you are using the NetWare User Authentication Method you must use an application program, called the NetWare Control Center to change your password.

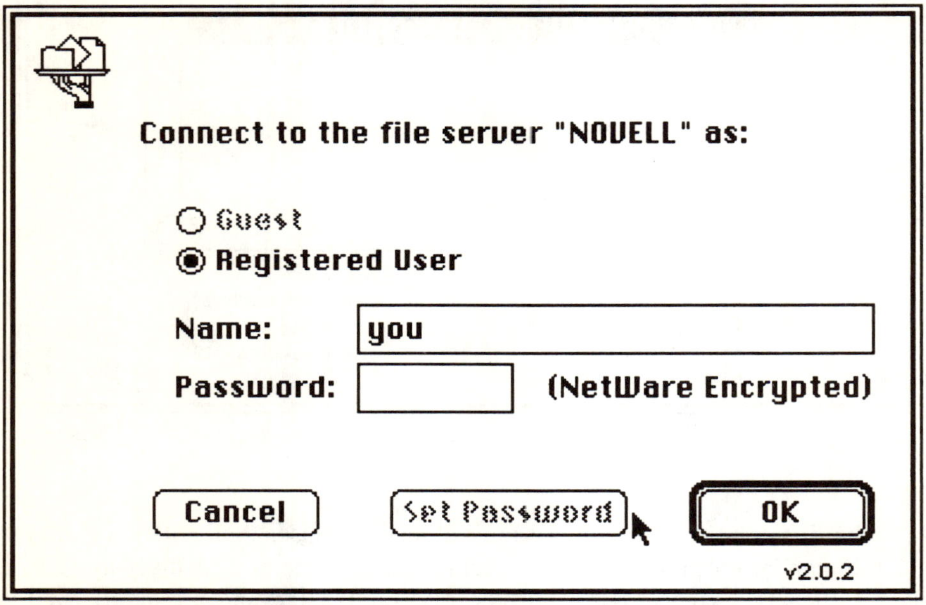

3-19 Your password can not be changed from this screen when you use Encrypted NetWare Authentication.

NetWare for Macintosh

print services

In NetWare and NetWare for Macintosh environments, Macintosh computers can print directly to network printers, such as the Apple LaserWriter, or use NetWare for Macintosh print queues that are configured for Apple LaserWriters.

Printing directly to the LaserWriter is possible because AppleTalk protocols and AppleTalk are built into the LaserWriter. Direct printing is independent of NetWare. PostScript laser printers other than Apple LaserWriters also can be directly accessed from a Macintosh, as long as they support AppleTalk.

NetWare for Macintosh print queues enhance the Macintosh printing process by spooling and queuing PostScript print jobs from Macintosh users before sending them on to Apple LaserWriters. This is possible because NetWare for Macintosh supports AppleTalk and its Printer Access Protocol (PAP). Although the centralized queue is unusual for the typical small or medium sized Macintosh network, the queue sometimes becomes a neccessity in environments with heavy printing demands or in large Macintosh networks. In these environments, the first come, first served policy of the LaserWriter is too chaotic. A NetWare for the Macintosh print queue provides these environments with the ability to manage Macintosh printing. NetWare and NetWare for Macintosh allow both DOS PostScript print jobs, and Macintosh PostScript print jobs to be set up so that they are stored in the same queues, which simplifies overall printing management.

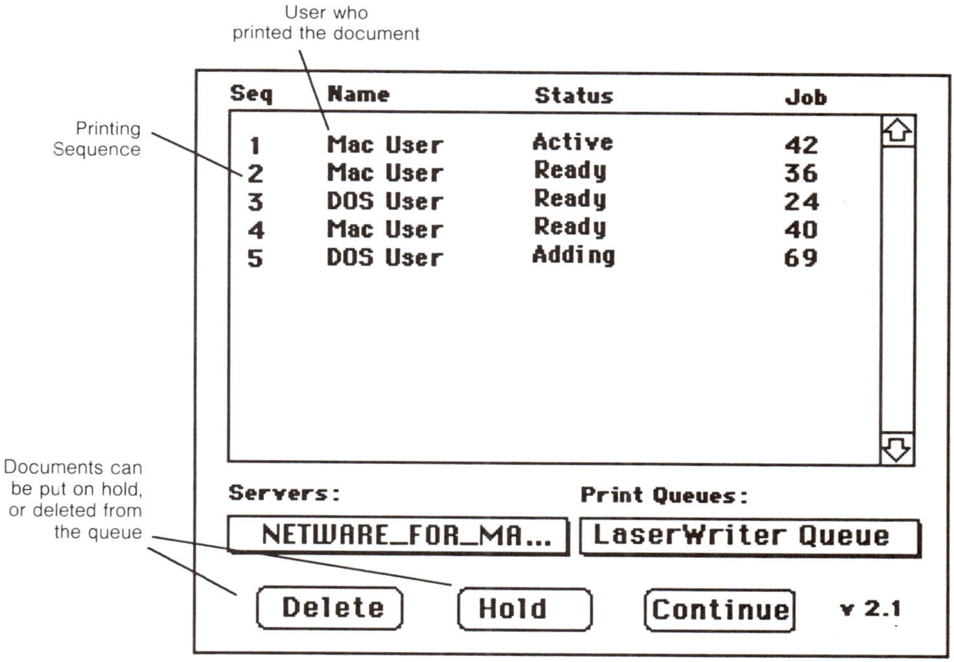

3-20 NetWare for Macintosh print queues consolidate the work of Macintosh users with other users, and allow printing to be easily managed.

You also can benefit by printing to queues because the queues eliminate the need for background printing to run on your Macintosh. Background printing requires local processing of a queue on your Macintosh. Letting NetWare for Macintosh queues handle the printing takes this burden off of your machine and puts it on the server.

Macintosh users access NetWare for Macintosh print queues through the Macintosh Chooser, just as they do when directly accessing a LaserWriter. A program in both NetWare for Macintosh v2.2 and NetWare for Macintosh v3.0 is able to emulate an Apple LaserWriter, so to Macintosh users the queue appears as another LaserWriter on the network. The Macintosh user prints to the emulating program, which accepts the job and puts it into a NetWare queue. When you select a NetWare for Macintosh print queue in the Macintosh Chooser, you go through the same process that you do when selecting an Apple LaserWriter. When you give the Macintosh command to print, the print command sends the print job to the queue exactly the same way it would sent it to an actual LaserWriter.

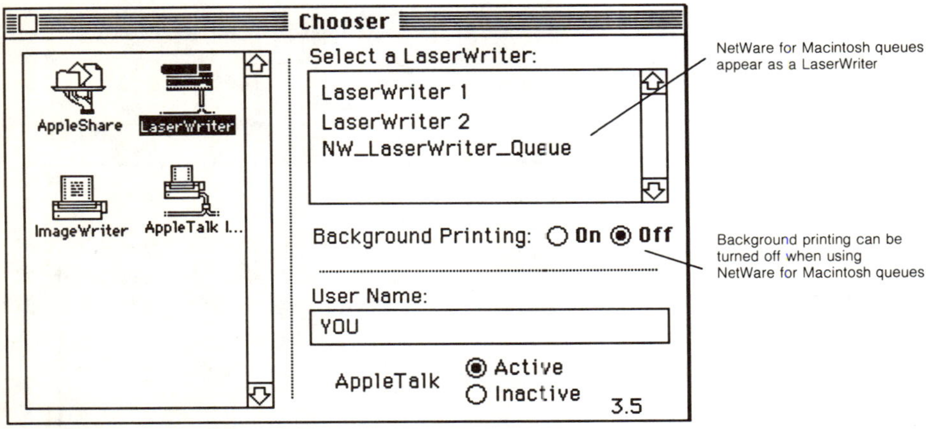

3-21 Accessing NetWare for Macintosh print queues.

NetWare for Macintosh allows Macs to share their LaserWriters with other PCs, shown in Figure 3-22. The common denominator for this printer sharing is PostScript. Print queues that are set up to unspool PostScript print jobs to LaserWriters will accept jobs from DOS, Windows, OS/2, and UNIX computers in addition to Macintosh computers. DOS PostScript support must come from the applications, and today most major DOS applications, such as WordPerfect, Microsoft Word, and many others, come with LaserWriter drivers. Microsoft Windows applications will support the Apple LaserWriter and PostScript, because Microsoft Windows has a postscript driver built-in just like the Macintosh does. OS/2 and UNIX can be set up in a similar way.

NetWare client software

NetWare for Macintosh lets you use the AppleShare client software that is part of the Macintosh operating system to log directly into a NetWare server. NetWare

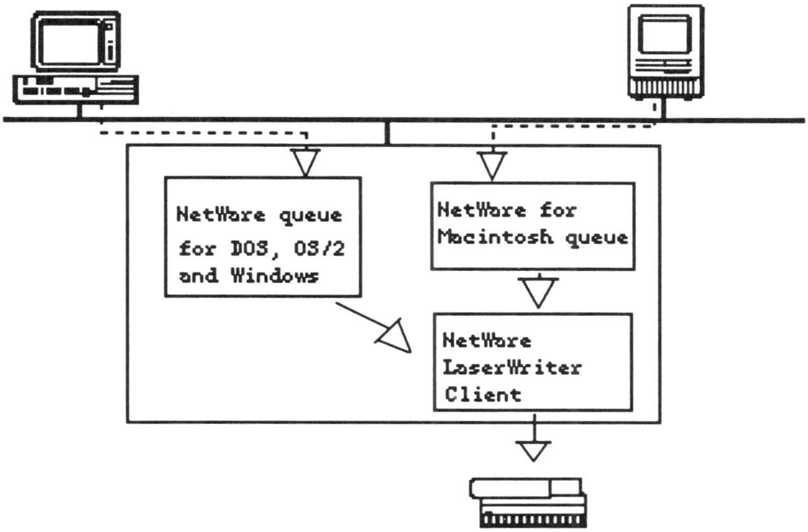

3-22 The flow of NetWare printing to LaserWriters.

for Macintosh also lets the built-in PostScript printer driver of your Macintosh print to NetWare for Macintosh print queues. That's almost all the software you need to do 90% of your filing and printing tasks on the network. Network users also need to organize and secure files, monitor print status, change passwords, and etc. If you are a network supervisor, you also need to create new users and manage existing ones, manage print queues, and the like. NetWare for Macintosh provides some software utilities that can be used from a Macintosh computer for these needs.

Two utilities make up the client software of NetWare for Macintosh. These utilities are a user's window into NetWare. One utility, mentioned earlier, is called the NetWare Control Center. The NetWare Control Center is a comprehensive utility for both users and network supervisors that manages anything that relates to user accounts (at least the ones they can access) and the server's file system. The NetWare Control Center is a Macintosh application program that is pictured in Figure 3-23.

The other utility is a Macintosh desk accessory that can be used to perform a subset of the filesystem tasks of the NetWare Control Center. Like any desk accessory, it can be accessed under the Macintosh Apple Menu, as shown in Figure 3-24. It has significantly less functionality than the NetWare Control Center, but its advantage is accessibility from within another application program because it is a Macintosh menu item. It also can view and manage NetWare print queues and send NetWare messages; two things that the NetWare control center does not do. The desk accessory has three basic modules: a rights module, a print

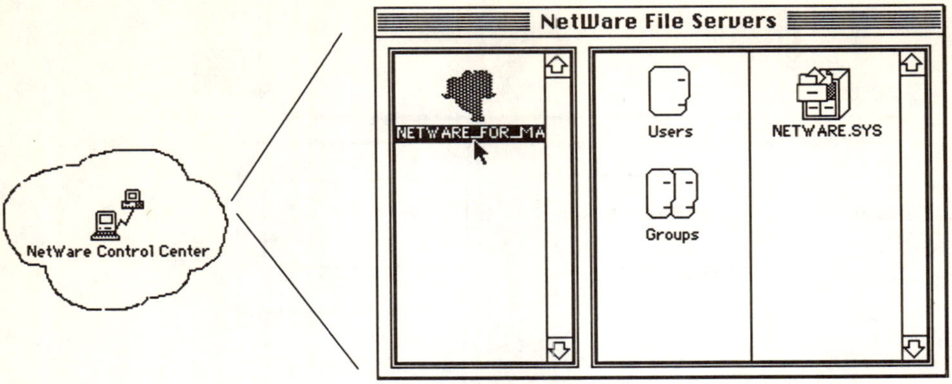

3-23 The NetWare Control Center interface.

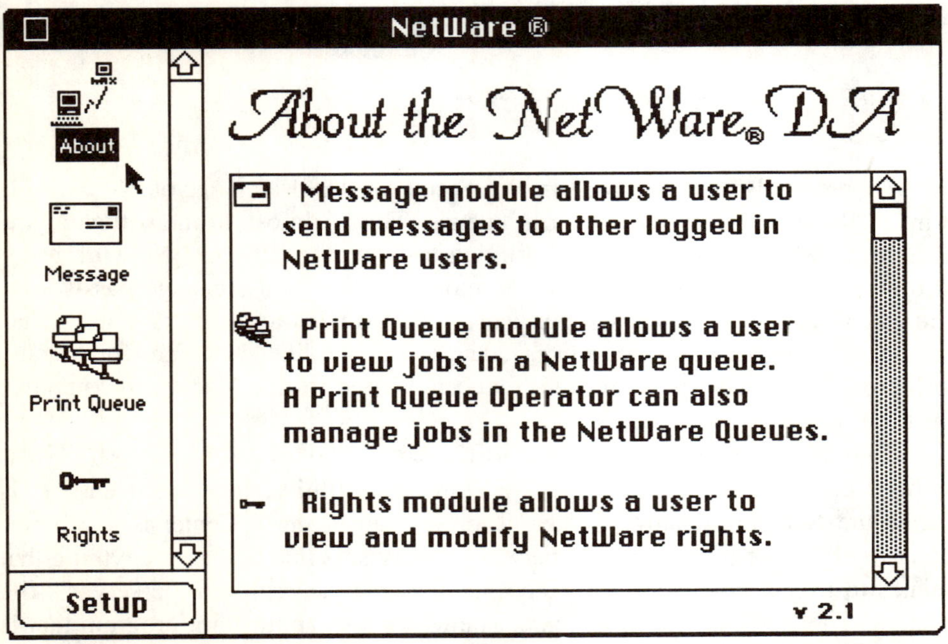

3-24 The interface for the NetWare for Macintosh desk accessory (menu item).

module, and a message module. Their use will be discussed in depth in chapters 6 and 7.

The combination of the NetWare Control Center and the NetWare Desk Accessory allows users and network supervisors to accomplish most forms of day-to-day NetWare for Macintosh environmental network administration from their Macintosh computer.

4
Chapter

Configuring NetWare for Macintosh networks

Chapters 1, 2 and 3 explained some important networking fundamentals and issues, such as the capabilities of the NetWare server operating system, network cabling, and the cost versus performance for computers and interface cards used as file servers or client computers. If your network is still in the planning stage, you probably need to weigh the various alternatives against each other to make decisions on those issues. If your network is already in place, those earlier chapters might help you plan changes to improve your current network configuration. In either case, a grasp of those fundamentals can add greatly to your understanding of the networking environment you work in.

It's time to look at how the network's component choices can be configured in a NetWare network of Macintosh computers. Earlier chapters introduced AppleTalk networks. An AppleTalk network uses protocols from the AppleTalk protocol suite. All of AppleTalk's protocols are supported in Novell networking products for the Macintosh. Therefore, the design of a NetWare for Macintosh network is not materially different from the design of any other AppleTalk network.

NetWare for Macintosh networks usually are not stand-alone networks of Macintosh computers; rather, they are frequently a part of networks that include other kinds of computers that use DOS, Windows, OS/2 and UNIX operating systems. The network designers in organizations who have these mixed environments need to first understand how to set up an AppleTalk network, and then how to combine that network with NetWare's other client environments.

This chapter will explain the design of a Macintosh network, first as if it was a Macintosh-only network, and then as if that network was integrated into a network containing some of these other computers.

The basics of AppleTalk

AppleTalk makes it possible for a Macintosh computer to transmit data on a network by supplying an addressing scheme that identifies the sender and destination of the transmission using node and network numbers. On a single wire network, all of the nodes have the same network number, the number zero, which identifies the local network. This is shown in figure 4-1.

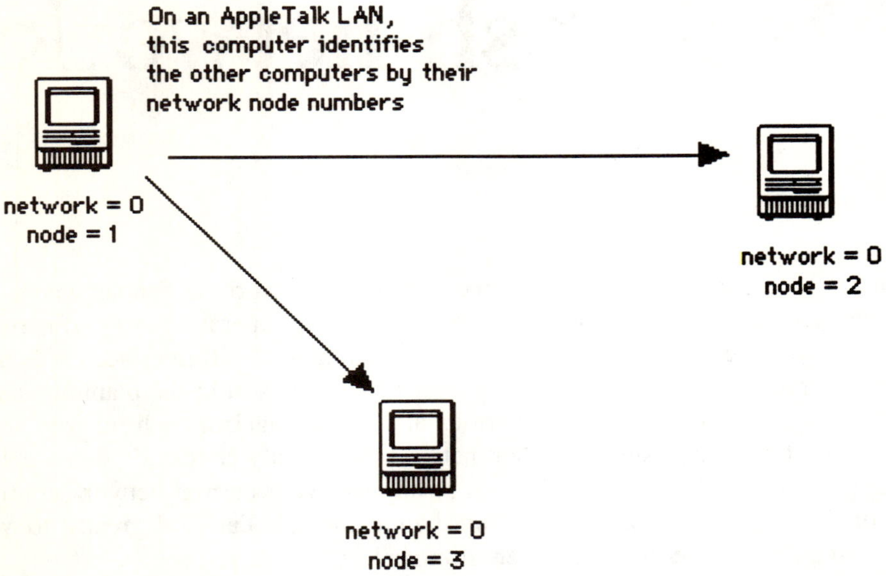

4-1 Node numbers identify the send and recipient of data in the AppleTalk protocol.

In an AppleTalk network, data tranmission are formulated and received on a Macintosh by the AppleTalk Protocol Stack, which is part of the Macintosh operating system. When a Macintosh computer puts data on a network wire, its destination is identified by the node address of the device to which the data will be directed. Part of the AppleTalk stack called the AppleTalk driver takes care of packaging the data into the right format for transmission. For another device to receive the packet, it also must have the AppleTalk protocol stack.

A unique virtue of the AppleTalk networking protocol suite is its ability to permit network devices to self select their node addresses. This technique allows AppleTalk networks to be easily configured by simply plugging in or pulling out devices. This *plug-and-play* capability works because when each device first starts up as a network member, it generates a random node address for itself, and then checks the network to see if another node is using that address already. If the address is not in use, the device keeps it. If the address is in use, the device repeats the process until it finds one that is unused.

In AppleTalk, network devices also are identified on the network by names, in addition to node numbers. This naming capability enhances the protocol's ease of use by enabling Macintosh clients to access these devices by names, through the Macintosh Chooser interface.

The AppleTalk protocol frequently uses a network communications method, called a *broadcast*. In the context of AppleTalk, a broadcast is a message or request sent out to a group of devices, or sometimes to all of the devices, on the network. AppleTalk's broadcast method of communication is another feature that makes the AppleTalk networking system easy to use. For example, when device names appear in a list of available services in the Macintosh Chooser interface, they are responding to a broadcast; however, broadcasts are used in other ways as well. Figure 4-2 shows the results of a broadcast for LaserWriter services.

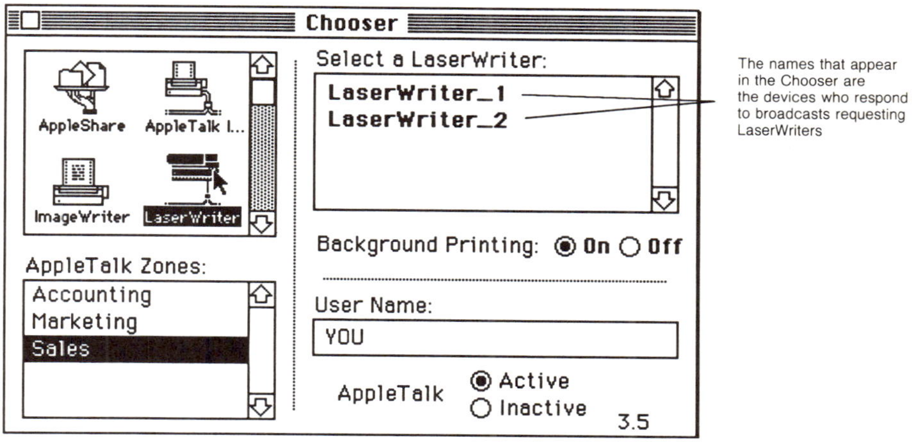

4-2 The Chooser shows network resources by names.

There are two types of AppleTalk protocols: AppleTalk Phase 1 and AppleTalk Phase 2. Both Phase 1 and Phase 2 allow network devices to self select available network addresses, allow devices and services to be displayed through the Macintosh Chooser interface, and allow devices to send broadcasts over the network.

AppleTalk Phase 1 is the orignal AppleTalk. AppleTalk Phase 2 is an expanded version of the original AppleTalk protocol that was enhanced to allow AppleTalk networks to support more than 254 nodes, to be more flexible in the configuration of zones, and to be more efficienct in large networks. Many existing AppleTalk networks have migrated from AppleTalk Phase 1 to AppleTalk Phase 2. If you are implementing an AppleTalk network for the first time, you probably should implement AppleTalk Phase 2 protocols. However, because some existing networks have not implemented Phase 2 and are still using AppleTalk Phase 1, both Phase 1 and Phase 2 will be covered.

AppleTalk cabling

The AppleTalk protocols of Apple's Macintosh environment run over three types of physical cabling: Token Ring, Ethernet, and LocalTalk (a twisted pair standard whose interface is built-in), shown in Figure 4-3. AppleTalk over the built-in LocalTalk interface is called LocalTalk. AppleTalk over Ethernet is referred to as EtherTalk. AppleTalk over Token Ring media is referred to as TokenTalk. TokenTalk is supported in AppleTalk Phase 2 only. In a NetWare for Macintosh environment, AppleTalk also can work over Arcnet cabling systems.

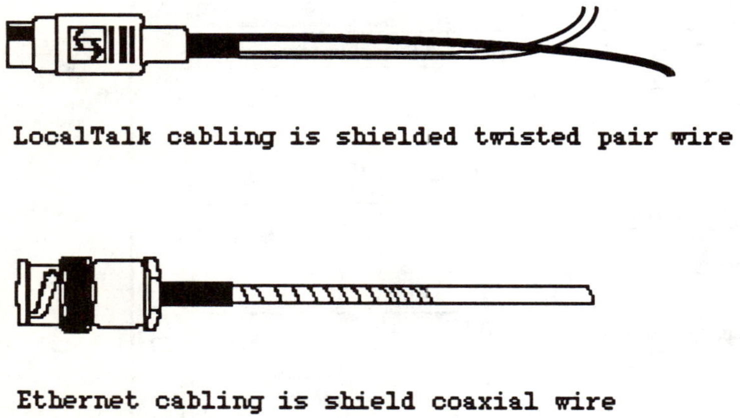

4-3 LocalTalk and Ethernet cabling systems.

To configure a NetWare for Macintosh server for these cabling systems, a network interface card for the cabling system(s) of choice must be installed in the server. Then, in the NetWare for Macintosh installation process, the installer must specify that either AppleTalk Phase 1 or AppleTalk Phase 2 be used on that interface. Table 4-1 lists the network interface cards certified by Novell for use with NetWare for Macintosh at the time of this writing; however, certification is a continous process and Novell frequently updates its lists. Contact your Novell reseller for a more current list.

Table 4-1 List of Novell certified PC LAN cards for AppleTalk:

List of Novell certified PC LAN cards for AppleTalk:

Topology	Network card	File server type	LAN Drivers
Ethernet	Novell NE2000	AT-compatible	With AppleTalk (1 or 2)
	Novell NE/2	Micro Channel	With AppleTalk (1 or 2)
	3COM 3C505	AT-compatible	With AppleTalk (1 or 2)
	3COM 3C523	Micro Channel	With AppleTalk (1 or 2)
Token Ring	IBM Token Ring 16/4 Adapter	AT-compatible	With AppleTalk 2
	IBM Token Ring 16/4 Adapter/A	Micro Channel	With AppleTalk 2
	IBM token ring network II	AT-compatible (4MB)	With AppleTalk 2
	IBM token ring network II/A	Micro Channel (4MB)	With AppleTalk 2
LocalTalk	Dayna DL2000	AT-compatible	With AppleTalk 1
	Dayna DL/2	Micro Channel	With AppleTalk 1
Arcnet	Thomas Conrad	AT-compatible	With AppleTalk 1
	Standard Microsystems	AT-Compatible	With AppleTalk 1

For the Macintosh networking client, Ethernet and Token Ring cabling provide a significant performance advantage over LocalTalk. The bandwidth of LocalTalk cabling is only .23 Megabits/second. Ethernet is 10 Mbits/second, and Token Ring bandwidth can be up to 16 Megabits/second. On high-performance media like Ethernet, transmission speeds are the same for both Phase 1 and Phase 2 AppleTalk, although Phase 1 does not work on Token Ring. AppleTalk Phase 2 has some significant advantages over AppleTalk Phase 1 in areas beyond transmission speed, which this chapter soon explains.

The disadvantage of Ethernet and Token Ring, as compared to LocalTalk, is cost. Unlike the interface for LocalTalk cabling, Token Ring and Ethernet cabling require a separate network adapter to be installed in the Macintosh.

NetWare will support any Macintosh client LAN cards for Ethernet or Token Ring cabling systems. You can use any card that supports AppleTalk Phase 1 or Phase 2. The NetWare for Macintosh AppleTalk environment also supports AppleTalk protocols over ARCnet cabling systems. ARCnet cards for Macintosh clients, and NetWare for Macintosh servers that work with AppleTalk are available from two third-party card vendors; Thomas Conrad Corporation and Standard Microsystems Corporation.

Basic LocalTalk network design

The simplest of AppleTalk networks uses the Macintosh's LocalTalk networking interface to attach one or several Macintosh computers to an Apple LaserWriter. Because the LaserWriter also has a LocalTalk interface and supports AppleTalk, the LaserWriter can be directly attached to the network by the same method as Macintosh computers. Figure 4-4 shows how this network could be layed out.

In a LocalTalk network, the two ends of the network always must be kept separate. They can never be joined to each other so that a LocalTalk network forms a ring, or bus topology. The order of the devices does not matter in a LocalTalk bus.

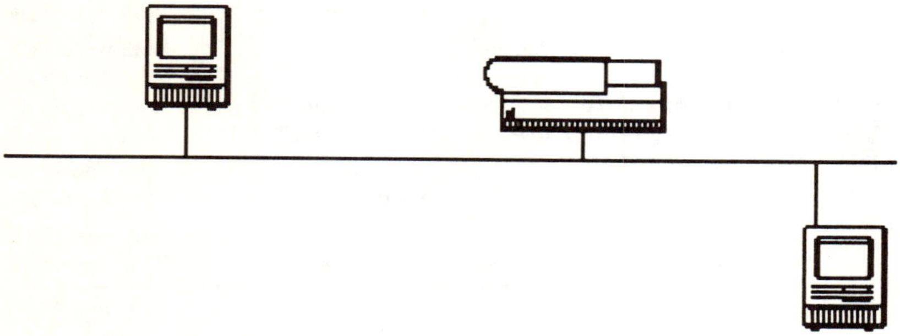

4-4 AppleTalk networks can consist of just a few Macs and a LaserWriter.

LocalTalk networks can be extended by simply plugging in new machines, up to a maximum on one network bus of 32 nodes. An AFP file server such as NetWare for Macintosh, could be added to such a LocalTalk bus, assuming that it had a LocalTalk connection by attaching it to the bus, just like all the other devices. A LocalTalk connection can be added to a NetWare for Macintosh server by installing a card manufactured by Dayna Communications, Inc. For servers based on the IBM AT bus, or the Compaq ISA bus, the card is called the DL2000. For computers based on the IBM MicroChannel bus (MCA), the card is called the DL/2. An expanded network is shown in Figure 4-5.

The wiring in a LocalTalk network is twisted-pair wiring. LocalTalk is actually an Apple trademark name for Apple's cabling system; however, the term LocalTalk has become a generic term for other types of twisted-pair cabling systems, such as Farallon Computing's PhoneNet system, which is a LocalTalk compatible twisted-pair system. LocalTalk and other LocalTalk compatible cabling systems attach to the Macintosh itself by means of a connecting box. The box facilitates the continuation of a LocalTalk bus, because it has two connecting sockets, as shown in Figure 4-6. Networking signals pass through the connectors

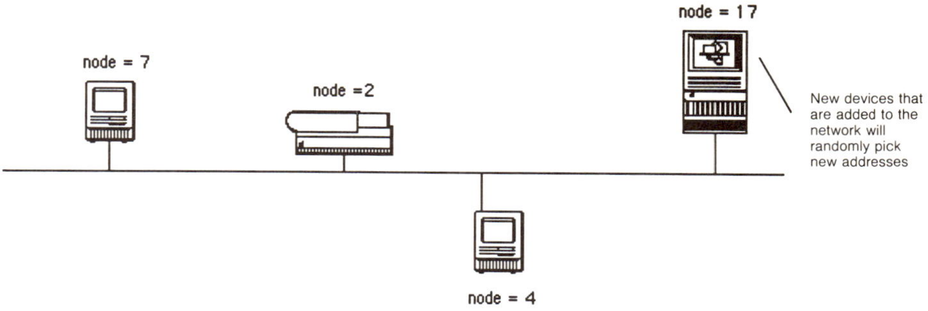

4-5 LocalTalk networks are expanded by plugging in new devices.

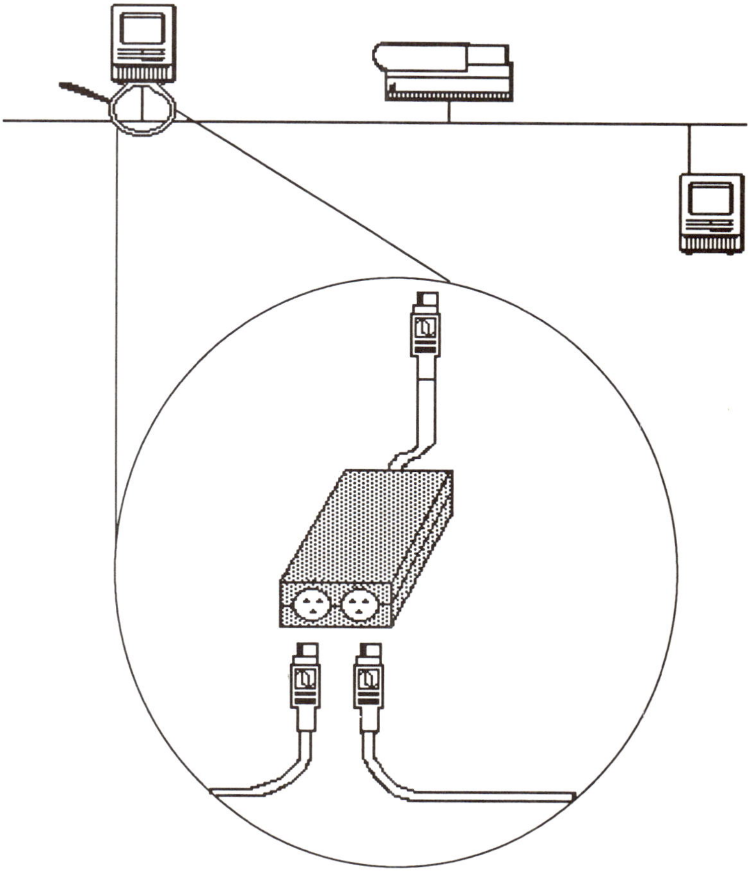

4-6 LocalTalk connectors set up a bus network topology

bidirectionally, so that what comes into one socket goes into the computer or gets passed out the other side to another computer, in both directions.

Macintosh computers on a LocalTalk network bus communicate with other network devices via AppleTalk protocols. The actual sending of data over the network wire is managed by a LocalTalk software driver that is built into the Macintosh operating system. When LocalTalk cables are connected, all a user has to do to activate his or her ability to use the network is to turn AppleTalk on in the Macintosh Chooser. Figure 4-7 shows how this is done with the Chooser.

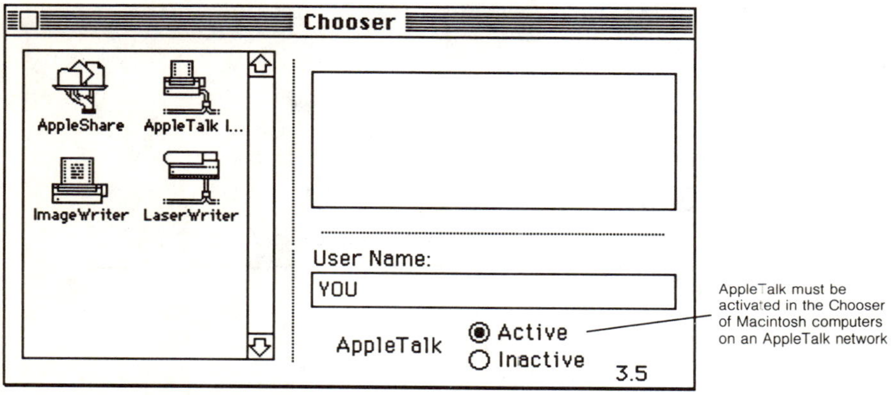

4-7 AppleTalk is turned on in the Chooser.

The maximum physical dimensions of an AppleTalk network are determined by the electrical properties of the cabling media. LocalTalk's twisted-pair wiring has the advantage of being inexpensive as compared to other wiring systems, but its signal is more prone to electrical interference and signal attenuation. Consequently, the recommended maximums for a LocalTalk cabling bus are 1000 ft. of cable and 32 network nodes (computers, printers, etc.). Farallon apparently gets somewhat better performance from its Phonenet cabling system, for which they list maximums of 3000 ft. and 48 network nodes.

However, LocalTalk networks can support more than their recommended maximum number of nodes through the use of *bridges*. Two such devices are the Interbridge from Hayes Communications, Inc., and the NetBridge from Shiva Corporation. Bridges act as an endpoint of one electrical bus, and the starting point of another. Figure 4-8 shows how a bridge can be used to extend the number of nodes supportable on a LocalTalk network. The placement of a bridge in a network cable creates a new electrical bus that also can support 32 nodes. Therefore, the network in Figure 4-8 actually consists of two separate 32-node LocalTalk buses.

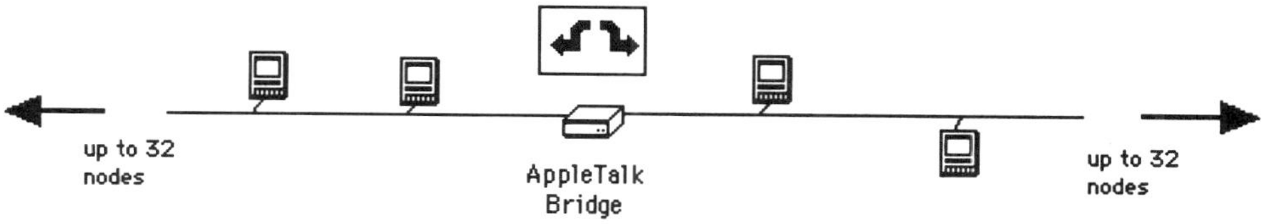

4-8 Bridging a separate network into individual LocalTalk buses.

LocalTalk networks theoretically can continue to be expanded through the use of bridges until they reach a LocalTalk maximum of 254 nodes. On LocalTalk these limits apply to both Phase 1 and Phase 2 AppleTalk. In addition to joining two buses, some bridges also act as signal boosters that send data that comes in one side and out the other side at a magnified strength. These bridges also allow the length of the network to exceed its recommended maximum for distance because the magnified signal will travel further. See Figure 4-9.

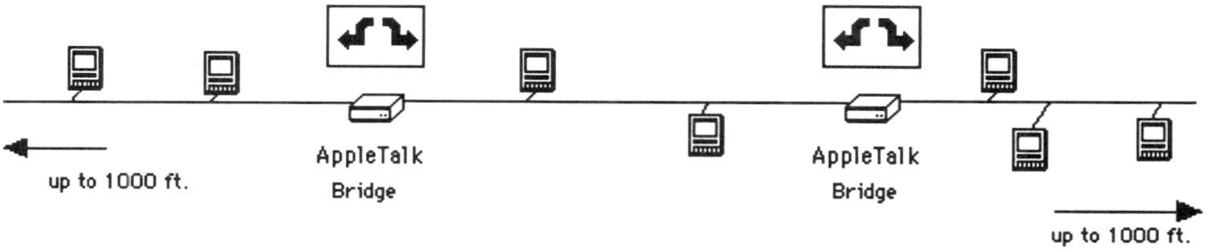

4-9 Bridges can extend the length of LocalTalk networks.

For configuration and performance reasons, a different type of device, called a *router,* is often used in place of a bridge to extend LocalTalk networks. Routers are software programs that run on some kind of computing device that, like bridges, join two electrical buses together. A router, however, has the ability to divide a network of electrical buses into two separate networks. This ability to segragate networks is not a defined characteristic of a bridge, although some bridges provide it. This is shown in Figure 4-9.

By creating two separate networks, the router's software can separate the network traffic in the bus on one of its sides from the traffic on the other side. The router easily will pass data from one side to the other when it needs to, but it doesn't do it all the time like a bridge would.

Along with the ability to separate LocalTalk buses into two separate networks, routers have the ability to map these separate networks into *zones*. Zones are groupings of network devices established for the benefit of the Macintosh Chooser interface. Two buses joined only by a bridge might have as many as 64 nodes all mixed together in a large network, but the same two buses, joined by a router, could act as two separate networks of 32 nodes, each in a different

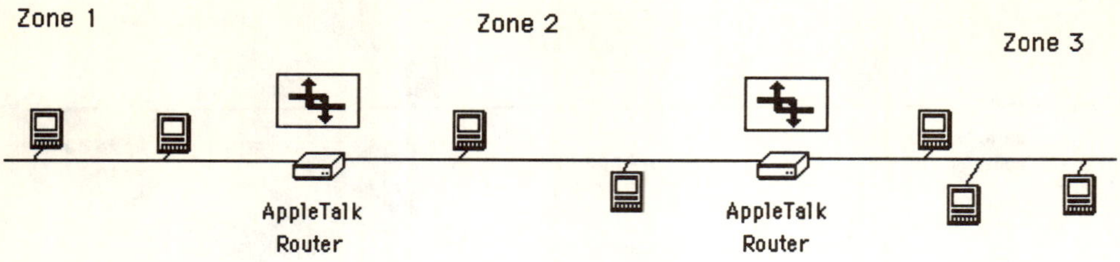

4-10 AppleTalk routers configure the network into AppleTalk zones.

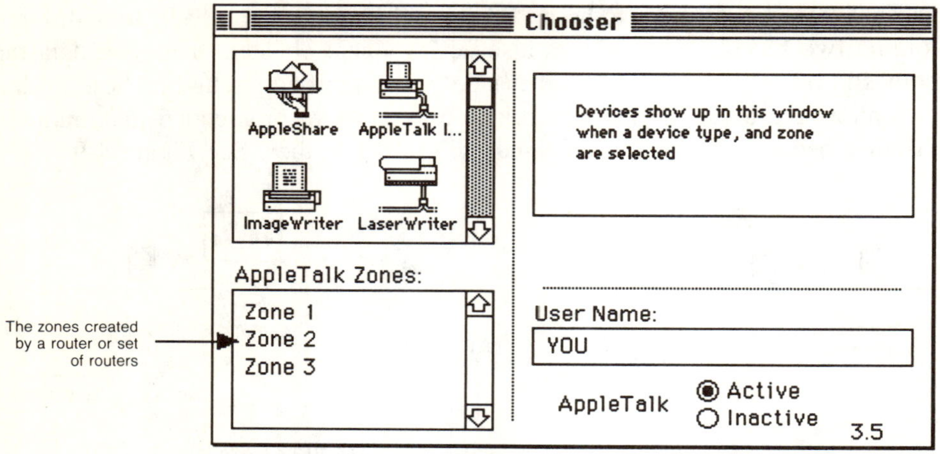

4-11 The zones created by a network's routers appear in the Chooser.

AppleTalk zone. Figure 4-11 shows how zones would appear in your Chooser if they were used in the network, shown back in Figure 4-10.

Sometimes the hardware in which a router program is installed is a Macintosh computer. Apple's AppleTalk internet router, for example, is installed on a Macintosh computer, so the computer becomes a router. Sometimes the router is a specialized box that contains its own microprocessor, such as the Shiva Fastpath or the Cayman Gatorbox, and sometimes the router is a NetWare for Macintosh server, because NetWare for Macintosh v3.X includes an AppleTalk router. NetWare for Macintosh v2.X does not include a router.

In order to configure the router in NetWare for Macintosh v3.X to be an AppleTalk Phase 1 LocalTalk to LocalTalk network router, the server on which NetWare for Macintosh v3.X is installed must have two LocalTalk network interface cards. With the cards installed, the NetWare for Macintosh v3.X router can be setup to use AppleTalk Phase 1 on each of the LocalTalk network interfaces, with routing between them. On a NetWare for Macintosh v2.X server,

AppleTalk routing cannot be done. A third-party router is often used in a NetWare for Macintosh v2.X network when routing is required.

In LocalTalk networks, routers are sometimes used as alternatives to bridges, but at other times they complement bridges. Bridges are typically much less expensive, and are more economical in spots where zone partitions are not required. Routers can be used along with bridges to permit the network to conveniently support large numbers of devices. In Figure 4-12, the router is used to partition for zones, and the bridges are used to extend the length of the network bus.

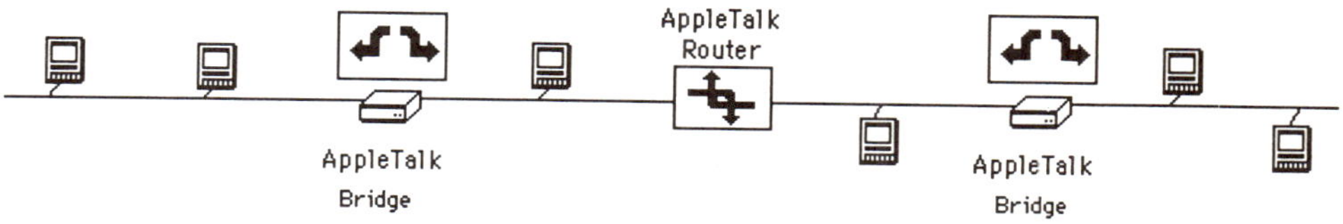

4-12 Routers can be combined with bridges to partition as well as extend the network.

A LocalTalk network with zones should be set up so that users in a zone are grouped in a zone with the users they need to work with most often. Many businesses, for example, might want the accounting people in one zone and the sales people in another zone. Users who occasionally need access to some device in the other zone can still get it, but they don't get it when they don't want it. Through the Macintosh Chooser, users can switch the zone they are viewing.

In a LocalTalk network, the router configures zones by having its software set up so that each of its sides is a different network. LocalTalk network zones must be physically separated from each other by the router. Figure 4-13 shows an example of how the software of a popular router is configured in an AppleTalk Phase 1 LocalTalk network with two zones.

Configuring large LocalTalk networks

When a LocalTalk network needs to support a large number of users, the network eventually might contain multiple routers, and therefore consist of multiple networks. These kinds of networks are referred to as *internetworks*. An internetwork is a grouping of two or more networks interconnectd by one or more routers. In a LocalTalk internetwork, each separate network can contain up to 254 nodes. As you might imagine, internetworks can grow to be very large and might span large distances.

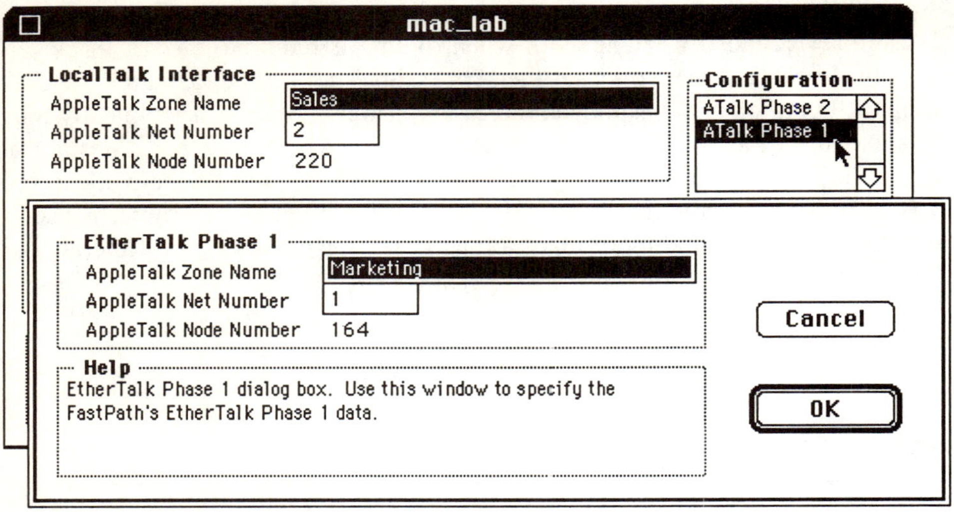

4-13 Routers are configured by software.

As a LocalTalk network grows and begins to run on multiple floors of a building, or through multiple buildings, it becomes more and more difficult to manage from a physical point of view. Running wire in a bus topology all through a building would be a difficult job, not to mention how difficult it would be to try to find and fix a break in the wire if one ever happened. A solution that many organizations turn to as their LocalTalk networks expand is the wiring of LocalTalk cabling through a central wiring closet, much like their telephone cabling (Fig. 4-14). These cabling systems often share the same connection blocks that the telephone system does.

This wiring method makes it easier to add new branches to the bus or to replace a bad section. With a centralized wiring closet, an organization can place nearly all of the routers and bridges in the wiring closet so that they too are in one easy to access place.

The centralized wiring closet also permits the use of more sopisticated multiport bridges in place of several independent bridges. Many companies, including Farallon Computing and NuvoTech, Inc., have brand-name multiport bridges that combine the functionality of many bridges into one box, and make cental-ized wiring hubs relatively easy to manage. These multiport bridges unify individual LocalTalk buses into a star of joined LocalTalk branches (Fig. 4-15).

These hubs make sure that network signals remain strong over all the branches of the network, and even have diagnostic software that works with

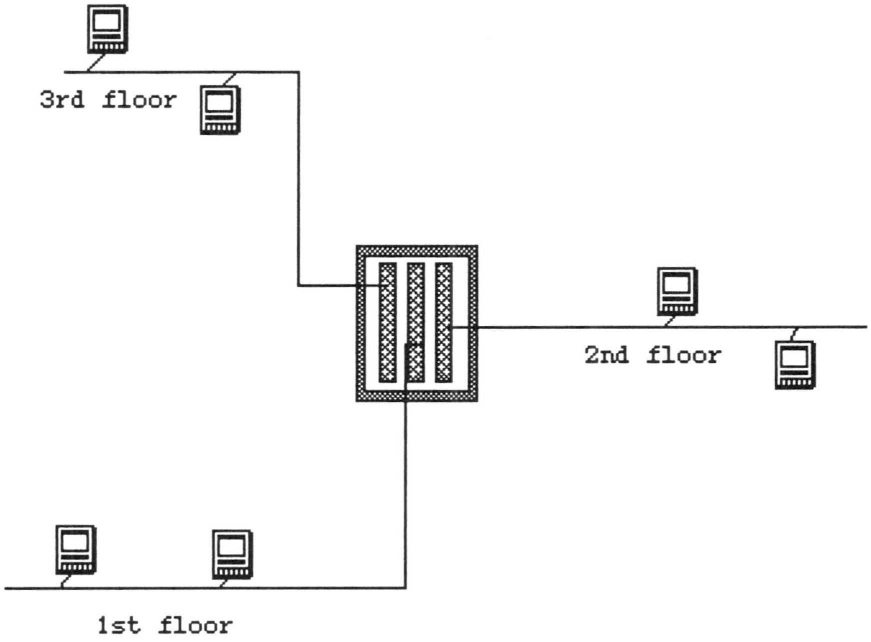

4-14 Large LocalTalk networks can be managed better by laying out a star configuration through a central wiring closet.

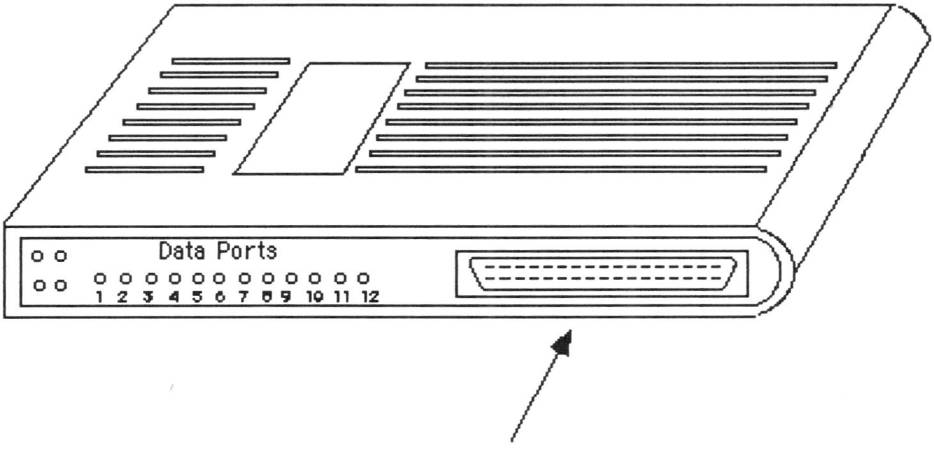

4-15 Multiport bridges faciliate centralized connections them. Their diagnostic programs can report on network noise problems and remove malfunctioning nodes from the network. Even with multiport bridges, LocalTalk networks are limited to 254 network nodes. The only way to overcome that limitation is to configure internet routers into the network. Routers work with these bridges the same way that they do with any other bridge.

Combining LocalTalk cabling systems with other cabling

Routers also can be used to join two separate network cabling systems together. For example, a router can join a LocalTalk cabling network to an Ethernet cabling network so that an internetwork is created between the different cabling systems. This is demonstrated in Figure 4-16. To internetwork two networks together, the router software is configured so that each interface of the router is configured for the type of cabling to which its connected.

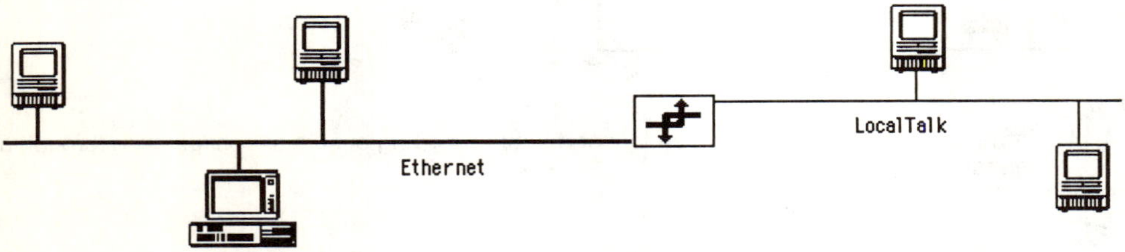

4-16 A router can join LocalTalk to Ethernet cabling systems.

Although the data packets on an Ethernet cabling system would be slightly different than those on a LocalTalk cabling system, in essense they are just AppleTalk packets, and the router can take care of reformatting the packets and passing them from one cabling interface to the other. A router configured in this way changes the AppleTalk format of the network data from what is acceptable in LocalTalk to what is acceptable to Ethernet, and vice versa, without modifying the actual data itself.

Organizations frequently use internetworked cabling systems to optimize networking performance when interconnecting workgroups. Figure 4-17 displays an example where several LocalTalk work groups are joined through an Ethernet cabling system. Because the section of cable in between the workgroups is shared by all the workgroups, it is at times likely to have the heaviest use, in much the same way a city freeway gets heavy use at rush hour. In this example, the Ethernet section is called a backbone, and the LocalTalk sections are called subnets. The backbone serves as a main artery that connects the subnets together. A high bandwidth media, such as Ethernet, is a good choice for backbones because it won't bog down.

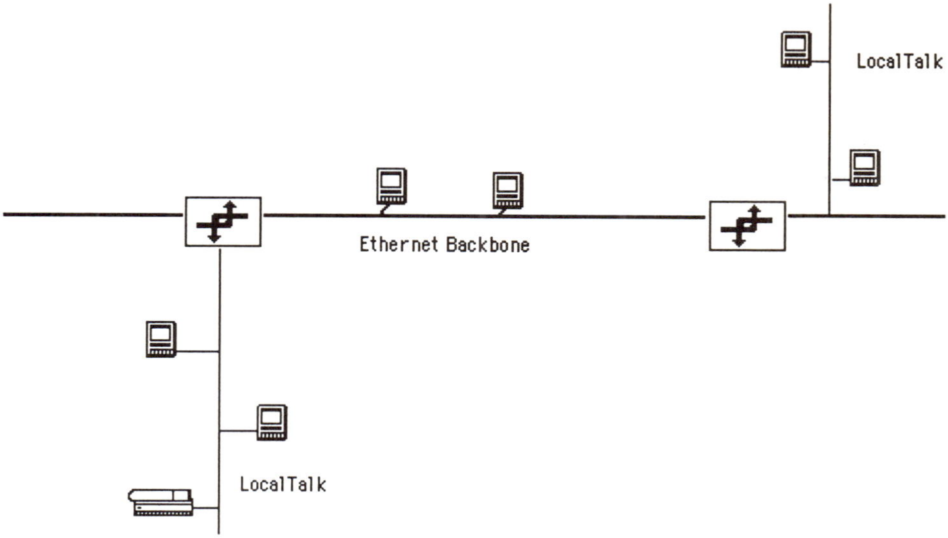

4-17 LocalTalk subnets connected to an Ethernet backbone.

Each LocalTalk subnet attaches to the Ethernet backbone through a router, and each router packages and repackages data to the right format of the cabling segment that the data is going to enter. This can be understood by tracing the movements of an imaginary data packet. As a data packet leaves the LocalTalk subnet of its origin, the router that joins the LocalTalk subnet to the Ethernet backbone repackages it for Ethernet, and sends it out on the Ethernet wire toward its destination. As the same packet arrives at the destination subnet, another router repackages the packet back to a LocalTalk format, and sends it on to its final target.

The router in NetWare for Macintosh v3.X can be configured in this way by putting both a LocalTalk card and an Ethernet card that support AppleTalk in an Intel based computer. The same computer, if running the NetWare for Macintosh v3.X file and print services, can act as both a server and a router, shown in Figure 4-18. The built-in router of NetWare for Macintosh v3.0 allows users to consolidate file services, print services, and router services all into one server.

AppleTalk routing capabilities are a major point of distinction between NetWare for Macintosh v3.X and NetWare for Macintosh v2.X. Even though NetWare for Macintosh v2.X will support AppleTalk and Ethernet interfaces simultaneously for concurrent access to file and print services, it will not act as a router to other services. In NetWare for Macitosh v2.X networks, third-party AppleTalk routers, such as the Shiva FastPath or the Apple Internet Router, must be used to provide routing services.

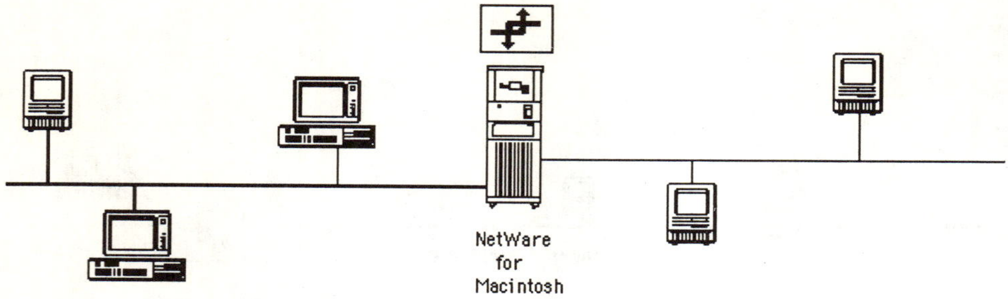

4-18 NetWare for Macintosh v3.X can be configured as an AppleTalk router.

AppleTalk networks with Ethernet cabling

Ethernet backbones help improve the internetworking performance of LocalTalk subnets, but for higher overall networking performance, a Macintosh network could be completely laid out with an Ethernet bus. Again, *bandwidth* is a term that describes the capacity of a network to pass data. LocalTalk bandwidth is 0.23 MBits/sec. Ethernet bandwidth is 10 MBits/sec., which is clearly a significant improvement.

There is, however, a cost for this performace improvement. With Ethernet cabling systems, each Macintosh needs an Ethernet network interface card installed, which is not necessary when using LocalTalk cabling systems. Although significantly less expensive than they were a few years ago, these still will cost several hundred dollars each.

The cabling for an Ethernet bus is also more expensive than LocalTalk cabling. LocalTalk uses twisted-pair wiring, while most Ethernet uses a special coaxial cabling. The most common form of Ethernet cabling is usually referred to as *Thin Ethernet,* and is connected to the interface card with BNC connectors, like in Figure 4-19. A more heavily shielded form of Ethernet is Thick Ethernet, which uses heavier DB pin connectors. Another version of Ethernet that runs over twisted-pair wiring is called 10 Base-T, and is becoming increasingly more popular. 10 Base-T connections look just like the snap-in connections most telephones use to plug into the wall. 10 Base-T Ethernet cabling systems require a device called a concentrator box for every network bus. These concentrators are similar to the multiport bridges that are available for LocalTalk networks.

Connecting Apple LaserWriters to Ethernet networks also requires a network interface change. Because LaserWriters have no built-in Ethernet connections (the built-in network connection is LocalTalk), an external adapter to connect the LaserWriter to the network is required. This kind of adapter, a product called EtherPrint, is available from Dayna Communications, Inc.

Another option for connecting the LaserWriter to a primarily Ethernet network or internetwork is to install a LocalTalk card in a NetWare for Macintosh v3.X server, and set up NetWare for Macintosh v3.X's router to route data

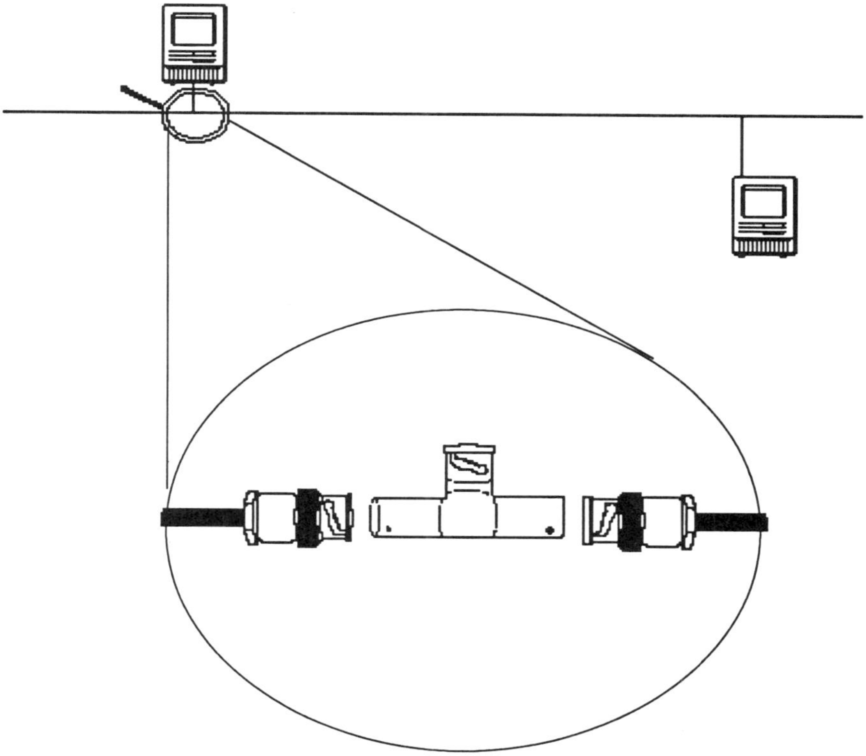

4-19 Thin Ethernet cabling systems also are configured as a bus.

between Ethernet and LocalTalk. The LaserWriter then could be attached to a short length of LocalTalk cabling coming from the LocalTalk interface in the server. The router would ensure that the Laserwriter could be seen by the nodes on the Ethernet cables, and makes sure that the data intended for the LaserWriter got there.

The final option available is to connect the LaserWriter to the server via a parallel or serial interface cable. Netware for Macintosh v3.01 will support client access to LaserWriters attached this way through print queues. NetWare for Macintosh v2.2 does not support a parallel or serial LaserWriter connection.

When the AppleTalk protocol is running over Ethernet cabling systems, it is referred to as EtherTalk. An EtherTalk network bus can support up to 100 network nodes, spanning 1640 ft. As with a LocalTalk bus system, an EtherTalk network can be expaned by the placement of a bridge, which creates a new bus that can support 100 new nodes. This way the 254-node limit of AppleTalk Phase 1 could be reached with only 3 buses and 2 bridges, as shown in Figure 4-22. When the entire network is laid out with Ethernet cabling, routers are not needed to adapt data to changing cabling media; they only need to be added to

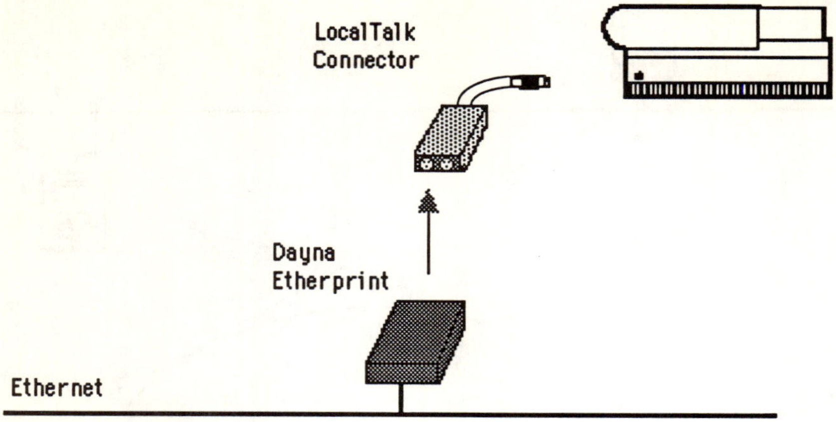

4-20 LaserWriters can be connected through their LocalTalk interface, or adapted to Ethernet through Dayna's Etherprint.

create a new network so that more than 254 nodes can be supported, or if the network requires zones.

EtherTalk works over Ethernet cabling systems in both Phase 1 and Phase 2 varieties, if all of the network devices are installed with one or the other. Both AppleTalk varieties should not be run on the same network at the same time. Phase 2 is usually the best choice for Ethernet cabling. AppleTalk Phase 2 is a much more robust and flexible solution for large networks, but even for small NetWare networks that have a mixture of Macintosh and other PC clients, EtherTalk Phase 2 has advantages over EtherTalk Phase 1 because it is less "chatty."

Extended AppleTalk networks

Routers are often used to internetwork both LocalTalk and EtherTalk networks, because they overcome the 254 node per network AppleTalk Phase 1 limitation by permitting an internetworked configuration of two LocalTalk networks that can have up to 254 nodes each (assuming bridges are used to connect multiple electrical buses together).

The 254 node limitation per physical network of LocalTalk cabling is the result of the 8-bit addressing scheme used by AppleTalk Phase 1 protocols. On Ethernet cabling systems, however, AppleTalk Phase 2 has a feature called extended addressing that can support up to 16 million nodes. Extended addressing within AppleTalk Phase 2 networks overcomes AppleTalk Phase 1's node limitations on a physical network by allowing the addressing scheme that uses the 8-bit node number plus a 16-bit network number (Fig. 4-21).

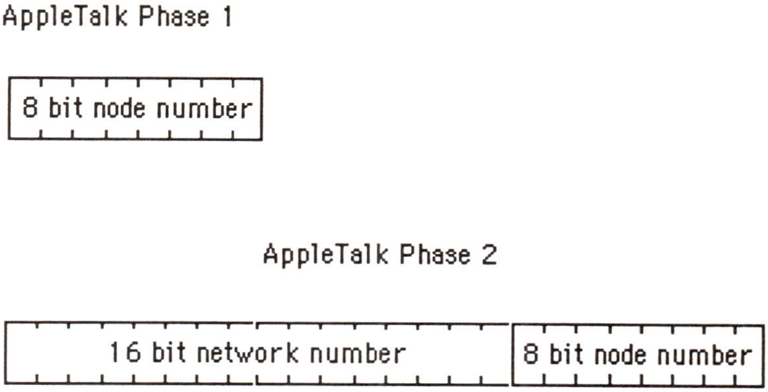

4-21 AppleTalk Phase 1 addressing versus Phase 2 addressing.

With AppleTalk Phase 2 extended addressing, a range of continuous network numbers can be assigned to each physical network. For example, a physical network using AppleTalk Phase 2 can have more than one network number assigned to it, shown in Figure 4-22. Each of the nodes in the physical network can be assigned to any of the network numbers.

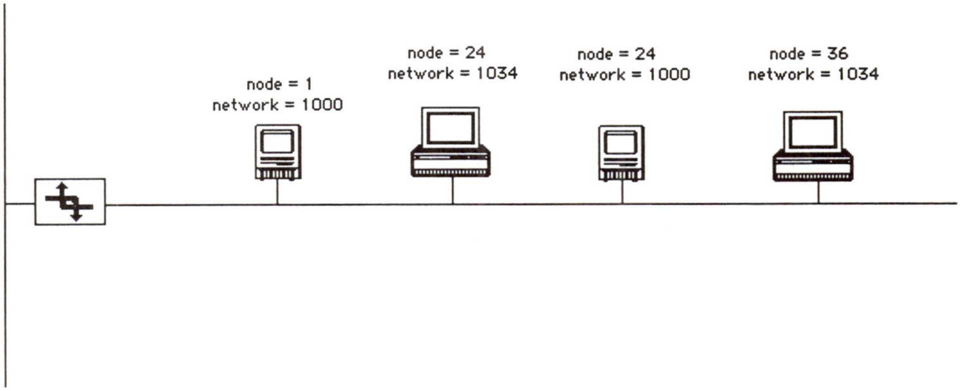

4-22 Extended AppleTalk Phase 2 networks can have more than one network numbers assigned to the same segment of cable.

As long as the routers on an AppleTalk Phase 2 network are properly configured to reflect the proper network numbers, and no other router on the same internetwork uses the same network numbers for a different physical network, the router always can send data packets to the right destination.

Routers on AppleTalk Phase 2 extended networks are not confined to mapping zones to match the physical layout of the network. On an AppleTalk Phase 2 internetwork, physical partitioning is not a requirement for the creation of a zone. There is no strict relationship between zone names and network numbers. Therefore, AppleTalk Phase 2 networks are said to support *logical* and *physical* zone configurations. In an AppleTalk Phase 2 network, devices can be grouped without regard for the physical location of the devices. This is depicted in the internetwork diagram of Figure 4-23.

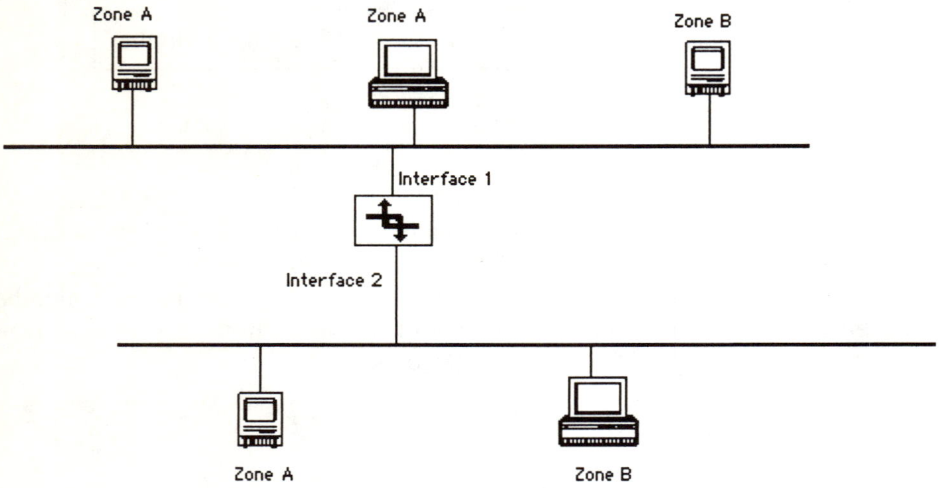

4-23 AppleTalk Phase 2 supports logical zone configurations that are not bound to the physical network.

Two adjacent nodes on the same physical network can belong to two different zones. Similarly, you can see from the diagram that even though some of the Macintosh computers are in a different physical network, they are in the same zone. The diagram in Figure 4-23 is depicting a *default zone* for the Macintosh workstations on this network. A default zone is the zone that a Macintosh computer will appear in when it starts up. The default zone for a Macintosh can be set through the Macintosh Control Panel. The procedure for setting a Macintosh's default zone will be demonstrated in chapter 5.

Mixing AppleTalk with other NetWare protocols

A cabling system, such as Ethernet, is not protocol limiting. The network interface cards and cable for an Ethernet cabling system can transmit data in virtually any protocol as long as the computer that wants to use it has a software driver for it that works (Fig. 4-24).

On a NetWare and NetWare for Macintosh network, AppleTalk can be simultaneously transmitted over the same cabling systems as NetWare's SPX/IPX, which is what NetWare uses to communicate with DOS, Windows, and OS/2 computers. TCP/IP, which is what UNIX computers use for networking, also can work over the same wire. Each of these NetWare client computers can use the networking driver appropriate for their operating system to send data onto the network in the format of one of those protocols, and the NetWare network operating system can understand them.

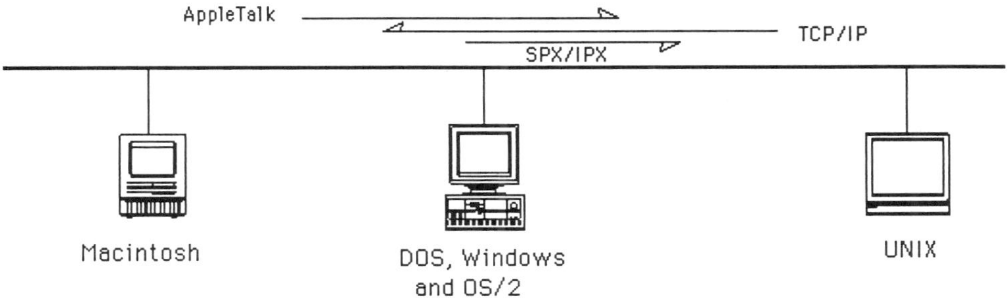

4-24 NetWare supports multiple protocols over the network.

Because NetWare for Macintosh clients can share a cabling system with any one of the other NetWare clients mentioned, another advantage of AppleTalk Phase 2 with NetWare networks is that it is more efficient on Ethernet than AppleTalk Phase 1. Two characteristics in particular enhance this efficiency. These characteristics involve a less chatty routing method and a more directed broadcast method.

AppleTalk Phase 2 benefits for NetWare

The AppleTalk protocol has a certain amount of overhead created by AppleTalk's use of network broadcasts that network devices use to idenfify themselves, and that routers use to communicate with each other. Routers use these broadcasts to tell nodes and other routers what networks they are connected to, so that nodes and other routers can send data packets to the right places. Routers then store the information sent to them in tables so they can keep track of how to get data to other parts of an internetwork (Fig. 4-25).

When AppleTalk Phase 1 was created, routers were required to broadcast the entire contents of their routing tables to all available routers on their networks. This enabled each router to keep its routing tables up to date, and allowed

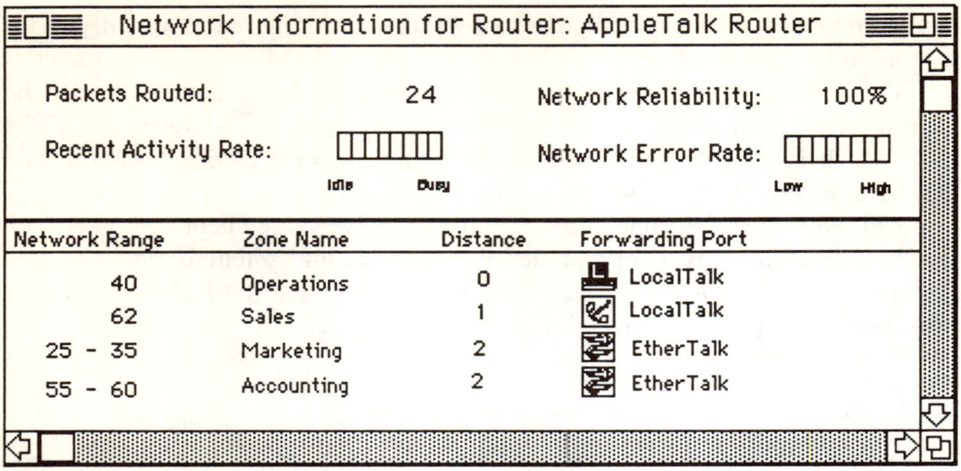

4-25 A look at the routing tables of the Apple Internet Router.

routers to record the shortest path across the internetwork. Unfortunately, this also generated a lot of overhead in large networks and backbone networks with many routers. AppleTalk Phase 2 has adresssed this problem by significantly reducing the amount of router information that is broadcast onto the network.

AppleTalk Phase 2 requires that routers send routing information out a network interface to only those networks it can reach through that interface. That way, AppleTalk Phase 2 routers send only relevant information onto the network, and reduce uncessesary broadcast traffic. Figure 4-26 might help you understand how AppleTalk Phase 2 can reduce routing traffic. In AppleTalk Phase 1 all of the network's routers would have broadcast information about the network subnets, however, in AppleTalk Phase 2, router B does not have to transmit its entry for Network 1 to router A, because router A is on Network 1 and already knows about it. Likewise, router B need not transmit this information to routers C and D, because they will be told about Network 1 by router A.

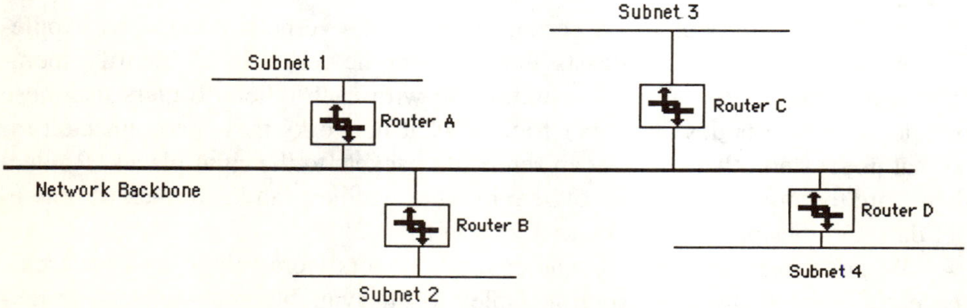

4-26 AppleTalk Phase 2 routers reduce router traffic.

Even networks with relatively few routers will be more efficient on AppleTalk Phase 2 than on AppleTalk Phase 1 because of reduced broadcasting; however, the larger the network, the greater the reduction in traffic. Reducing the routing traffic on NetWare and NetWare for Macintosh networks benefits all of NetWare's clients, not just Macintosh clients, because less routing traffic makes more of the network's bandwidth available for other uses.

Another benefit that AppleTalk Phase 2 brings NetWare networks is the ability to use an enhanced feature of the EtherTalk Phase 2 protocol to direct AppleTalk broadcasts only at EtherTalk nodes, shown in Figure 4-27. This directed broadcasting makes the overall network more efficient by cutting down on the broadcast interruptions to NetWare clients that are inherent in EtherTalk Phase 1 networks.

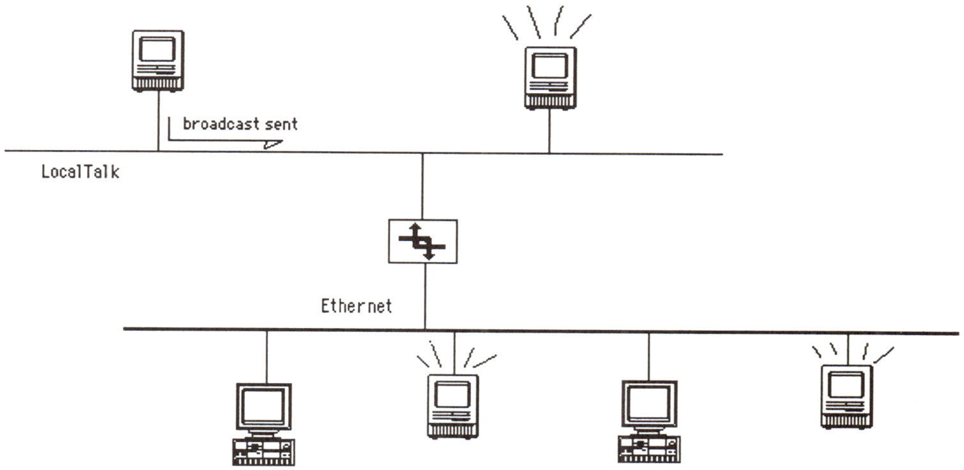

4-27 AppleTalk Phase 2 sends broadcasts only to AppleTalk nodes.

In AppleTalk Phase 1, broadcasts were directed at all nodes attached to a network cable, whether they were AppleTalk nodes or not. Even non-AppleTalk nodes had to receive these broadcast nodes, if only to process them and immediately discard them. AppleTalk Phase 2 on NetWare and NetWare for Macintosh networks can direct broadcasts through a feature called *Multicasting* at only the AppleTalk nodes on the network, so these broadcasts do not interrupt the NetWare nodes using one of NetWare's other protocols. AppleTalk Phase 2 defines a specific *multicast address* to all AppleTalk nodes on an EtherTalk network. EtherTalk nodes register to receive the packets when they start up. Nodes that do not use AppleTalk and therefore, do not register on that address, will not receive or be interrupted by EtherTalk broadcasts.

Wide area networks with AppleTalk

With the right routing or bridging equipment, an AppleTalk network can be extended across great distances. Networking sites can be joined together with other networks in remote locations by wide area AppleTalk bridging equipment, or by wide area AppleTalk routers.

The difference between joining remote AppleTalk networks with bridges and joining remote AppleTalk networks with routers are the same as the differences between joining networks with bridges or routers on a LAN. An AppleTalk bridge joins two electrical buses, but maintains a single network. An AppleTalk router joins two different networks into an internetwork. The only visible difference between the two methods that users will notice is whether the devices on the remote network will appear in the same zone that they work in locally, or whether the remote devices are in a different zone.

WAN bridging solutions tend to be the most economical, so they probably make the most sense for LocalTalk networks (Fig. 4-28). Most products that link remote sites on LocalTalk media use public telephone lines and computer modems to establish connections over those lines. Both of the two AppleTalk LAN bridges mentioned earlier, the Shiva NetBridge and the Hayes Interbridge, can be used as WAN bridges when combined with modems. On a local area network these devices acted as a full bridge, but over a wide area network they act only as half bridges.

A *half bridge* is a bridge that allows a network to communicate in only one direction. It works like a one-way window that allows you to see people on the other side, but they can't see you. Users in Network 1 can look into Network 2, but users in Network 2 can't look into NetWork 1. It takes one unit and one modem at each location to establish a full bridge with these products. This requirement is demonstrated in Figure 4-28. Shiva Corp. also makes a very popular product called the NetModem, which is a single unit that contains both a modem and an AppleTalk half bridge. This is shown in Figure 4-29.

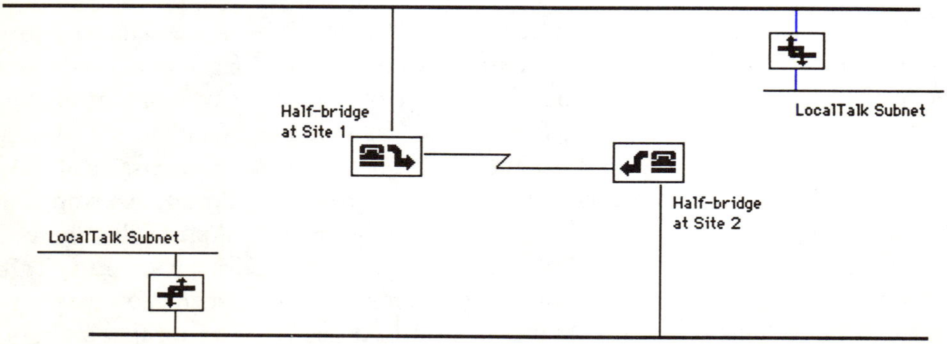

4-28 Some AppleTalk bridges will link remote LANS together into a WAN.

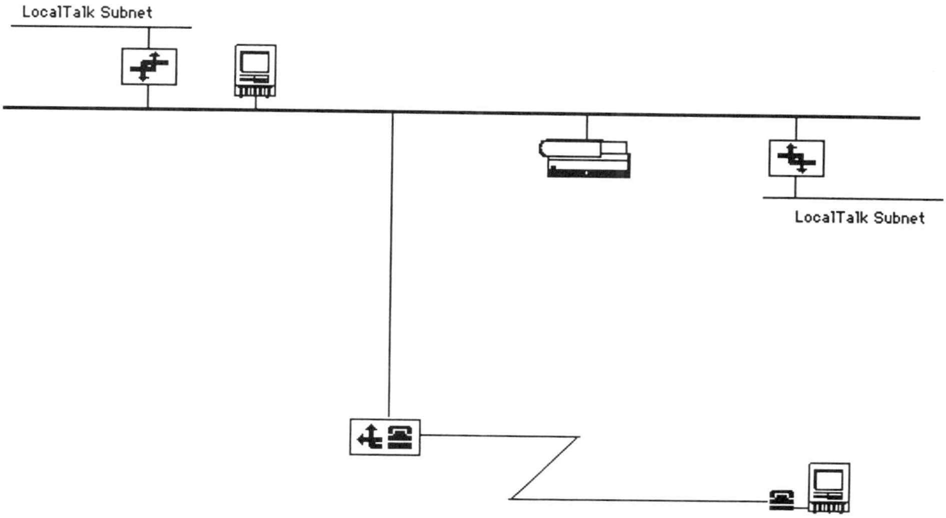

4-29 Shiva NetModems allow remote user access from standard modems.

The Shiva NetModem allows users in remote locations to dial in and make half-bridge connections, even if they only have a regular computer modem instead of another Shiva NetModem. NetModems often are used as a means to allow users, such as salespeople in the field, to make a temporary connection to the headquarters network to read their E-mail, or to perform some other administrative task. They allow a single user to dial up the bridge and modem in the remote network, access services on the remote network, and then terminate the connection.

Because the NetModem at the headquarters network is only a half bridge, the remote user can see the Network but the network cannot see the user. Figure 4-30 shows how you would use the Shiva Netmodem to dial in and bridge to a remote network.

Modems allow the digitized data of network transmissions to be converted to electrical impulses that can travel over telephone lines in an *asynchronous* format. An asynchronous format means that the sending and receiving modems do not precisely time the sending and receiving of data; they just tell each other when the data is starting and stopping, and let the elements of the phone system control the flow. The icon being selected in Figure 4-30 represents an asynchronous driver that allows you to send AppleTalk data packets through the modem attached to your computer, and over the telephone lines.

For NetWare networks, Shiva makes an especially useful version of the NetModem, called the NetModem E, that supports both AppleTalk and SPX/IPX protocols and works on various types of Ethernet networks, shown in Figure 4-31. The NetModem E can bridge NetWare networks and allow Macintosh, as

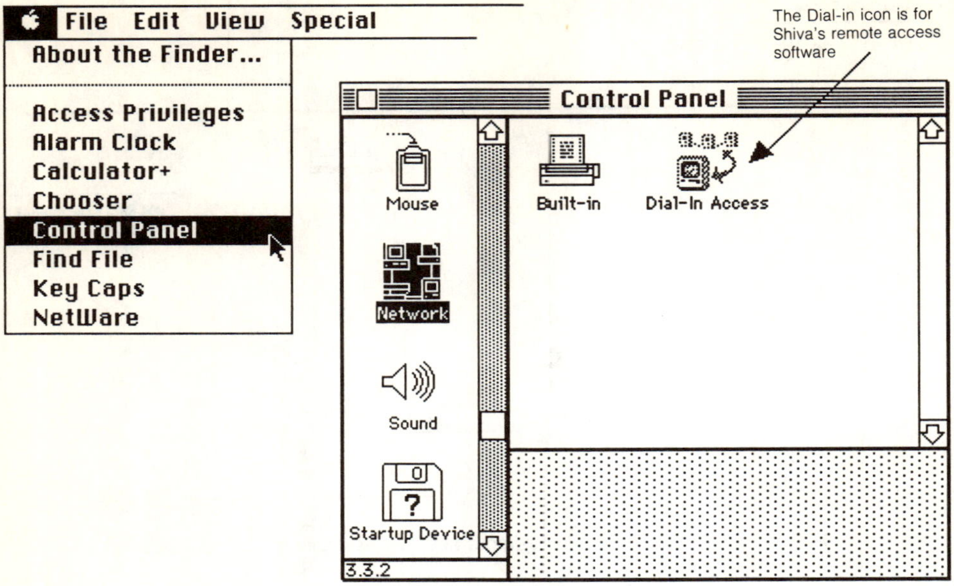

4-30 Shiva Dial-in software uses an asynchronous network driver.

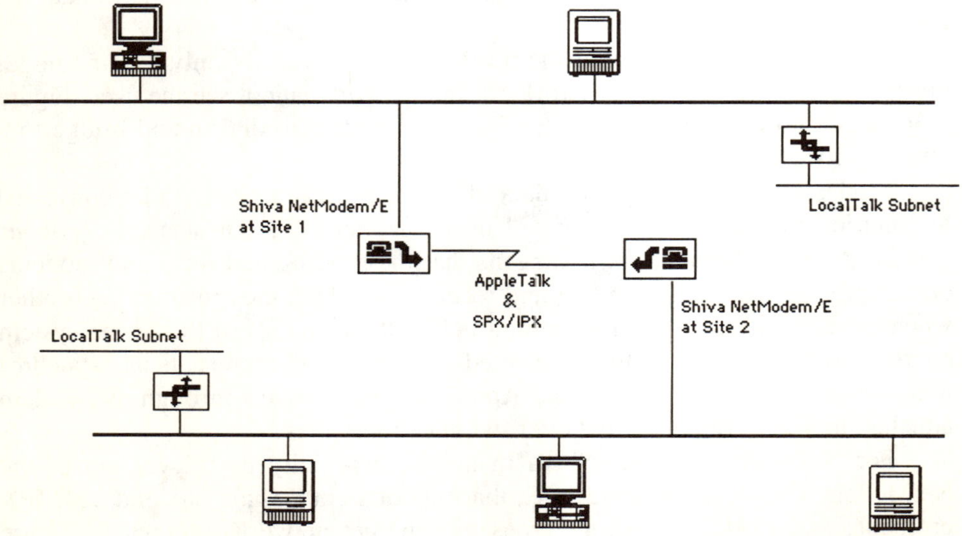

4-31 The Shiva NetModem E will bridge SPX/IPX networks in addition to AppleTalk.

well as DOS, Windows and OS/2 users, to access NetWare services through NetModem E half bridges.

The Advantages of AppleTalk Phase 2 are magnified on Ethernet wide-area NetWare networks of multiple clients, because the overhead of broadcast and unnecessary data traffic over wide-area links are especially hard on WAN network performance. The ability of EtherTalk Phase 2 to determine the most efficient route to internet subnets, and the reduced router traffic required over bridges allow Phase 2 networks to minimize the data passing through the WAN bridges, and to keep them running much more effectively than they can with AppleTalk Phase 1.

Wide Area Network routers

The alternative to WAN bridging is WAN routing. WAN routers differ from WAN bridges in their internetworking abilities. WAN bridges link remote sites into a continuous network, whereas WAN routers link remote sites into an internetwork of separate networks. The internetwork configuration can improve per-

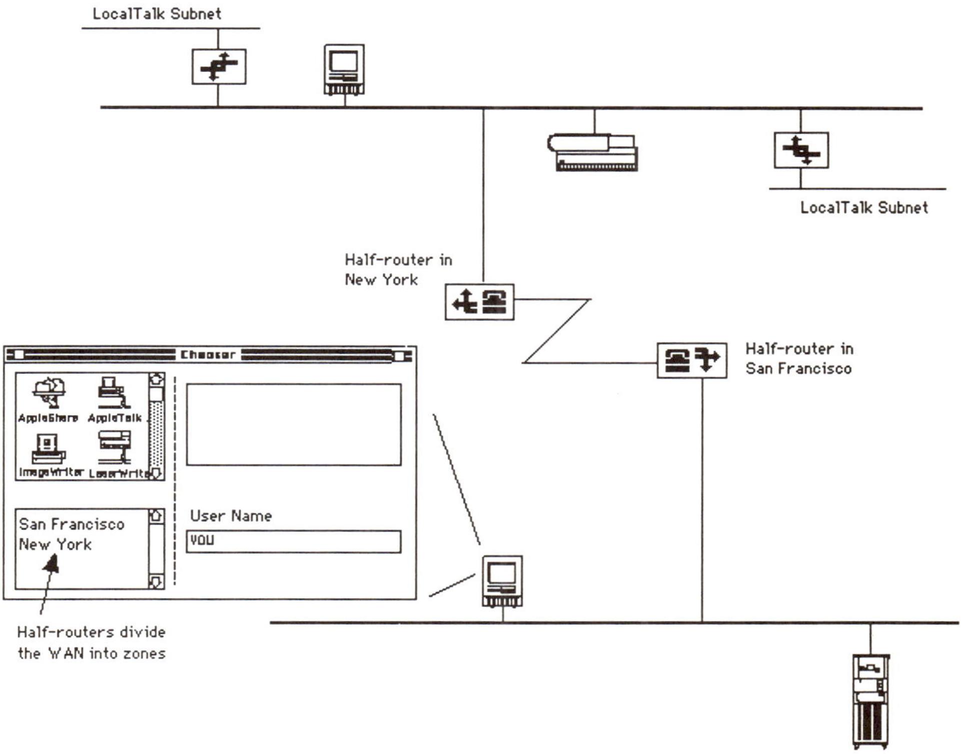

4-32 Farallons PhoneNet Liaison router connects remote zones into a WAN.

formance because broadcast traffic passes over the WAN router only when destined for the remote network. WAN bridges are not able to be so selective. WAN routers also have the benefit of convenience for users, who do not need to see the remote devices unless they change zones.

WAN routing for LocalTalk networks is available with a WAN router, called the PhoneNet Liaison software router, from Farallon Computing, Inc. The PhoneNet Liaison router runs on a Macintosh computer and works as a half router when run over asynchronous connections via some kind of modem (Fig. 4-32). To establish complete routing between two sites, each site must be equipped with a Macintosh running a Liaison half router and modem.

More sophisticated WAN routers are available from companies such as Cisco Systems, Inc. and Wellfleet Inc. that support AppleTalk, as well as SPX/IPX and TCP/IP. These routers are specially designed hardware/software combination solutions. Their features and design make them appropriate for highly integrated, high-performance WANs.

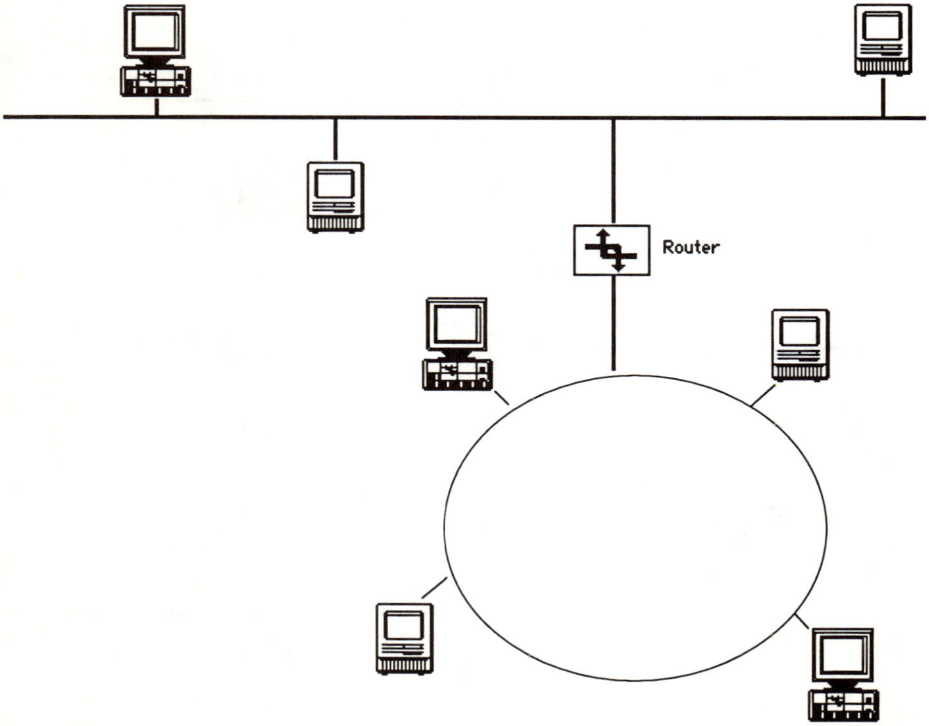

4-33 Macintosh computers can connect to Token Ring systems via routers, or by connecting directly.

These kinds of WAN routers will route data from all of the above protocols simultaneously over high bandwidth T1 lines, leased lines, and various other sophisticated communications transport methods.

AppleTalk Networks with Token Ring cabling

Macintosh networks that are being integrated into IBM environments often need to integrate with a cabling system called Token Ring. Token Ring is an IBM standard that IBM uses to network PCs to other PCs, and to IBM mainframe or midsized computers. The Macintosh has several ways of connecting to Token Ring. See Fig. 4-33.

AppleTalk running over Token Ring cabling systems is referred to as TokenTalk. TokenTalk is not supported by AppleTalk Phase 1, so Macintosh net-

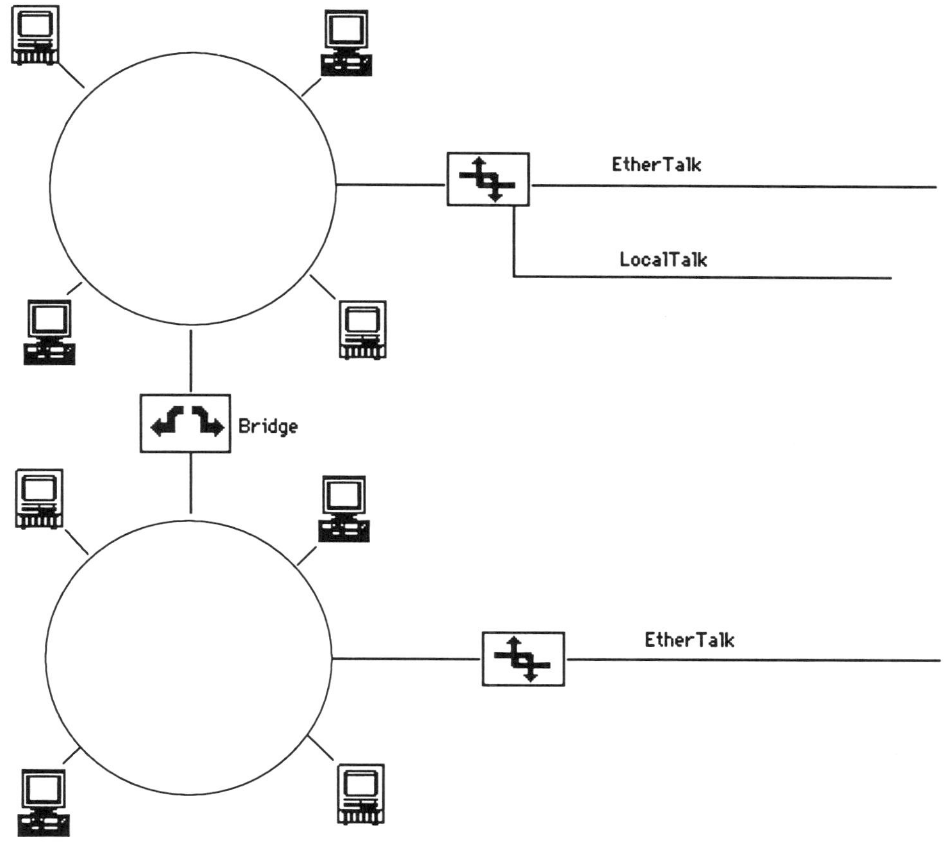

4-34 TokenTalk supports IBM source routing.

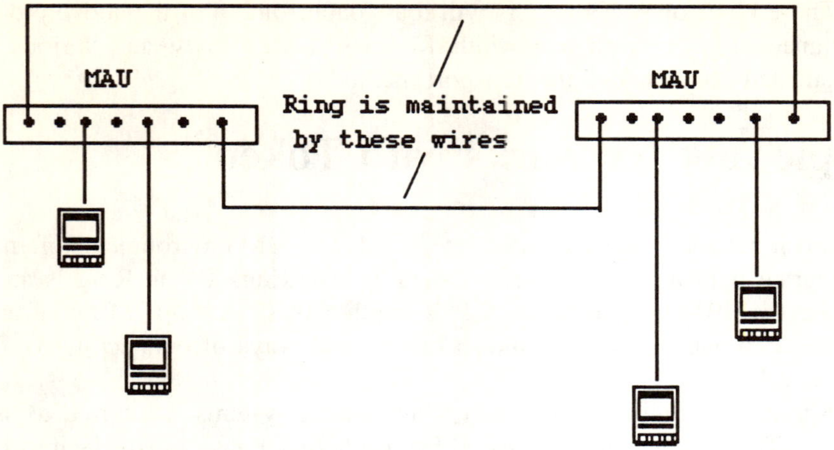

4-35 Token ring clients are linked within a ring by a multiple access unit.

works on Token Ring cabling systems always will use AppleTalk Phase 2. Macintosh clients on Token Ring networks are supported by both NetWare for Macintosh v3.X and NeWare for Macintosh v2.0 or later. NetWare v2.15, which supported NetWare for Macintosh v1.1 will not support Macintosh Token Ring clients.

As with Ethernet, Macintosh workstations can be connected to Token Ring networks in two ways. They can be connected to a LocalTalk network that is attached to a NetWare for Macintosh v3.X server that routes data onto Token Ring, or they can be attached directly to Token Ring by placing Token Ring interface cards in the Macintosh.

Token Ring networks can be linked together through a Token Ring source routing bridge. The source routing bridge is not an AppleTalk bridge, but it accomplishes the same ends for Token Ring networks. TokenTalk will work with the source routing bridge so that AppleTalk protocols can pass between internetworked Token Rings (Fig. 4-34).

Within the rings themselves, Token Ring clients originate from a controlling device called a Multiple Access Unit (MAU). The MAU simulates network connections as if they were a physical ring. This is shown in Figure 4-35.

5

Chapter

Installing a Macintosh client

Assuming that the planning and implementation of your AppleTalk network infrastructure has been completed, at some point you will need to connect Macintosh client computers into it. This chapter covers the basics of hooking a Macintosh into the Novell network, and discusses both hardware and software configuration. Software configuration is covered for both System 6.X and System 7.X clients

Macintosh client requirements

The computers that are supported by NetWare for Macintosh are Macintosh Plus, Macitosh Classic, Macintosh LC, Macintosh SE, and Macintosh II models. In order for these models to work, they must use the Macintosh System version 6.0 or above, and Macintosh Finder version 6.1 or above. NetWare for Macintosh works with any version of Macintosh 7.X software. To see the version numbers for both the Macintosh System and Finder software on your computer, pull down *About the Finder* from the Apple menu within the Finder of your computer (called *About this Macintosh* in System 7.X). Figure 5-1 shows this process on a System 6.X version of the Macintosh operating system.

You also must check your Macintosh Chooser to make sure it is a version 3.3 or above. To check the version of Macintosh Chooser that you are using, pull down the Chooser and check the version number in the lower right-hand corner.

If your Macintosh is not running one of the above mentioned compatible versions of system software, you should update your Macintosh to one of those

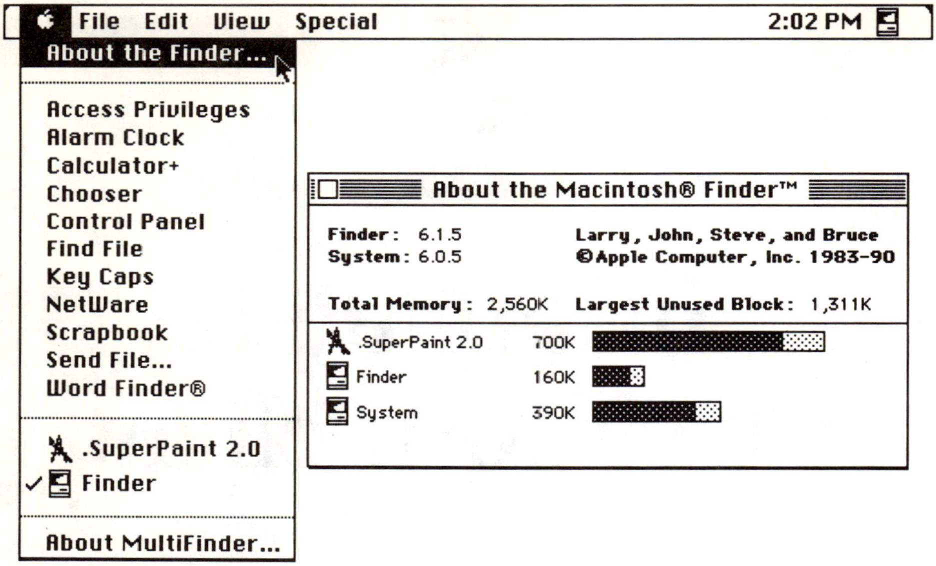

5-1 About the Finder will tell you what version of the Macintosh operating system you have.

versions. You always can acquire the latest version of system software from your Apple dealer if you do not have it at your site. Later in this section, you will be shown how to install or update Macintosh system software.

Connecting a Macintosh into a NetWare network

The process of networking a Macintosh client into a NetWare for Macintosh network can be broken down into two steps. The first step involves making the physical connection. That means installing a network interface card, if required, and making the proper link with the network cabling. The second step is installing the required components of networking software on the Macintosh.

LocalTalk connections for a Macintosh client are plug-and-play. For LocalTalk, or LocalTalk compatible cabling systems, the networking interface is built-in. All that is required is a network attachment plugged into the LocalTalk port at the rear of the Macintosh computer. The position of the Macintosh LocalTalk port and a drawing of a LocalTalk connector are shown in Figure 5-2. The connector has two sockets: one for in-going and one for out-going cabling.

The LocalTalk port on a Macintosh computer is identified by the printer icon above it. Next to the LocalTalk port is a modem port, identified by an icon of a telephone receiver above it. Both of these ports are serial ports controlled by a chip on the motherboard of the computer. All Macintosh computers have a

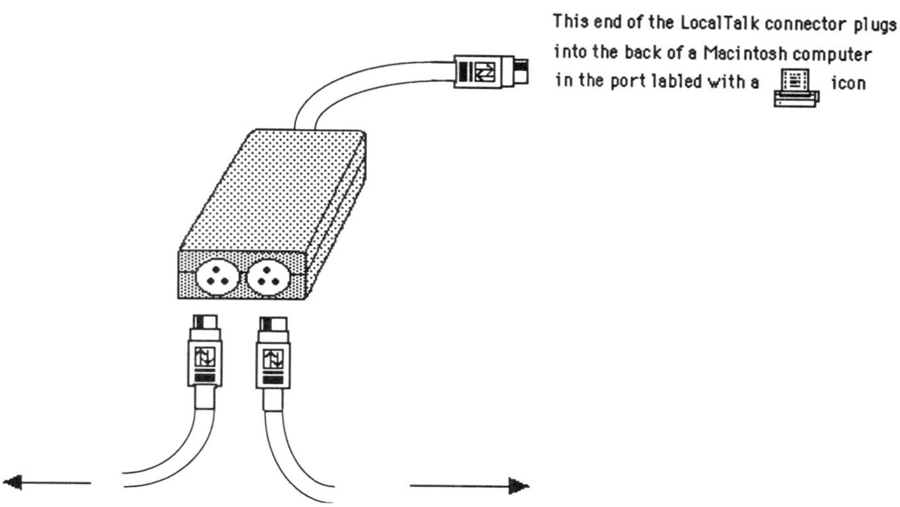

5-2 LocalTalk connectors are made for bus topologies.

LocalTalk port, and all versions of the Macintosh operating systems come with an AppleTalk driver for LocalTalk. To activate the driver, you need to select it in the Macitosh Control Panel, shown in Figure 5-3.

You also need to make sure that the *AppleTalk on* button in the Chooser is selected. Figure 5-4 shows how this is done for both System 6.X and System 7.X versions of the Macintosh operating system. While you are at it, you might want to change your Chooser's user name to your NetWare account name. That way you will not need to re-enter your account name every time you use the AppleShare login screens to mount a NetWare for Macintosh server. The login screens pull your username from the Chooser as a default.

The drivers for the various AppleTalk network resources that you might need to access are shown on the left hand side of the Chooser in this figure. If you don't see all of these icons, it is because they have not been installed in your system. If you want, you easily can install them. In a moment, you will read about how to install the AppleShare client workstation software, and other AppleTalk resource drivers.

Connections for Ethernet (and other cabling systems)

For Ethernet and Token Ring cabling systems, your Macintosh must have an Ethernet or Token Ring network interface card installed, or it must be equiped with a device to adapt the Macintosh SCSI or LocalTalk interface to those cabling systems. For a Macintosh Classic or Plus computer, Dayna Communications, Inc. makes an external Ethernet adapter that attaches to the LocalTalk port. For Macintosh SE and Macintosh II computers, Ethenet network interface cards

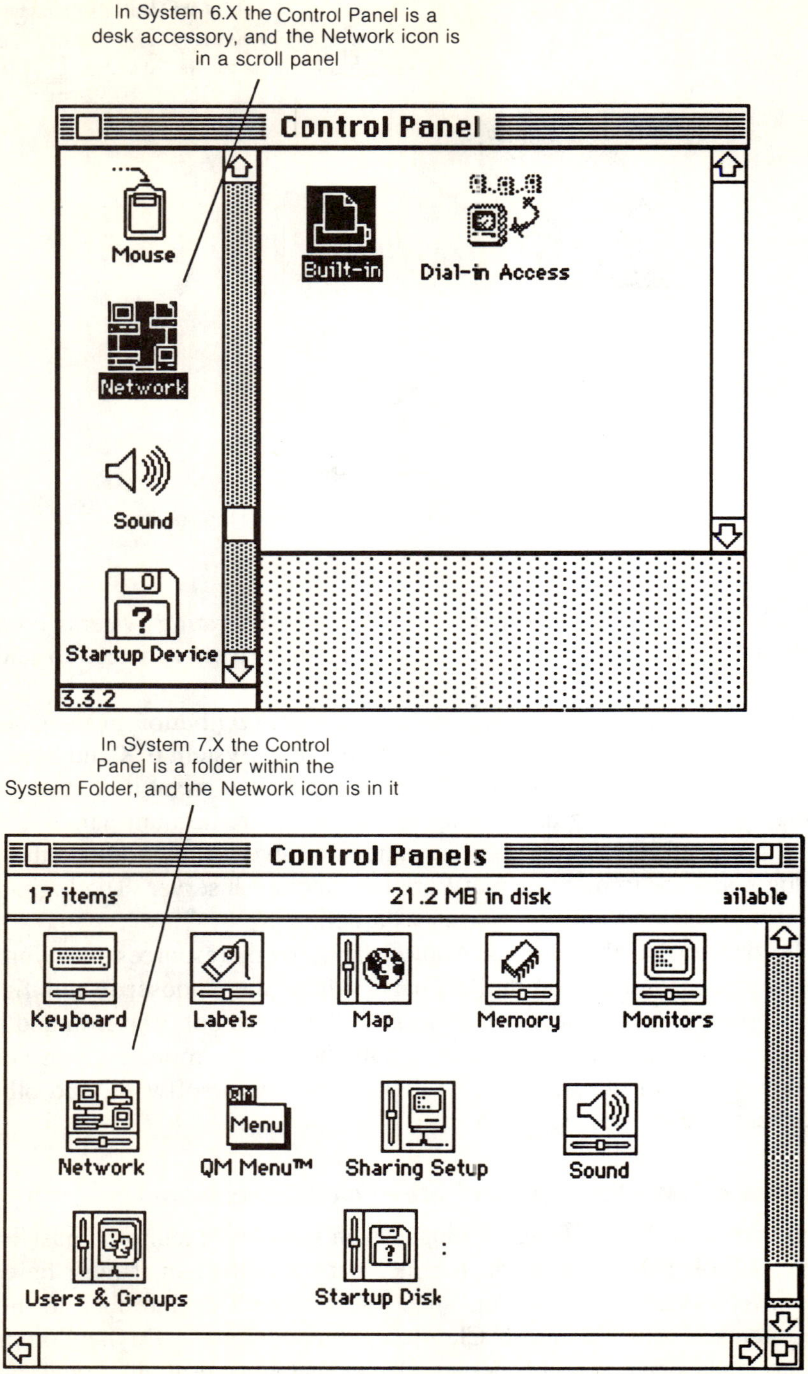

5-3 System 6.X and System 7.X Control Panels.

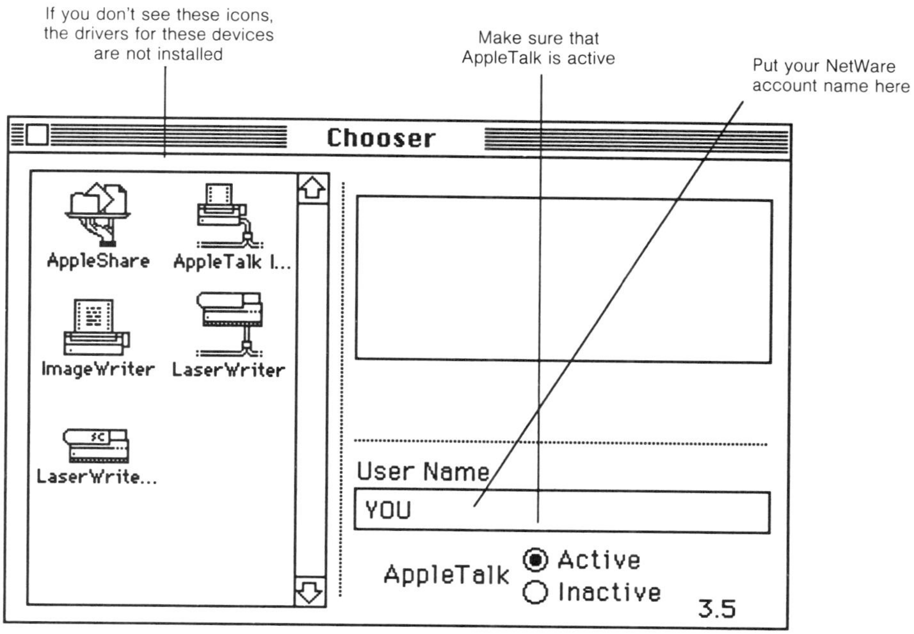

5-4 Setting up your Chooser.

are manufactured by Shiva, Dayna, Farallon, Asante, Dove, and others. Any card that supports AppleTalk Phase 1 or Phase 2 should work with NetWare for Macintosh. NetWare has no special requirements for cards on a Macintosh client.

To install a network interface card on a Macintosh II type computer, the Macintosh's cover must be removed, and the card inserted into a slot in the computer's internal bus. Popping the cover on the Macintosh II computer family can be done with your hands. SE computers require a long screwdriver. Most Macintosh Ethernet cards, when installed, typically have both Thin Ethernet and Thick Ethernet connections exposed in the back of the computer. If your card lets you externally switch between the thick and thin connections, it will probably look something like the diagram in Figure 5-5. The figure also illustrates the connector you will need to attach your Macintosh with its Ethernet card to a Thin Ethernet cabling system.

Once the Ethernet or Token Ring card is installed, you will need to install an EtherTalk driver on your Macintosh, so that the Macintosh's operating system can use the card. EtherTalk is what the AppleTalk protocol is called when it is used on Ethernet cabling. Unlike the Macintosh LocalTalk driver, which was a part of the Macintosh operating system, an EtherTalk driver is not built-in. It must be installed from the floppy disk that most likely came with the card. For example, Figure 5-6 shows the contents of the floppy disk that come with Shi-

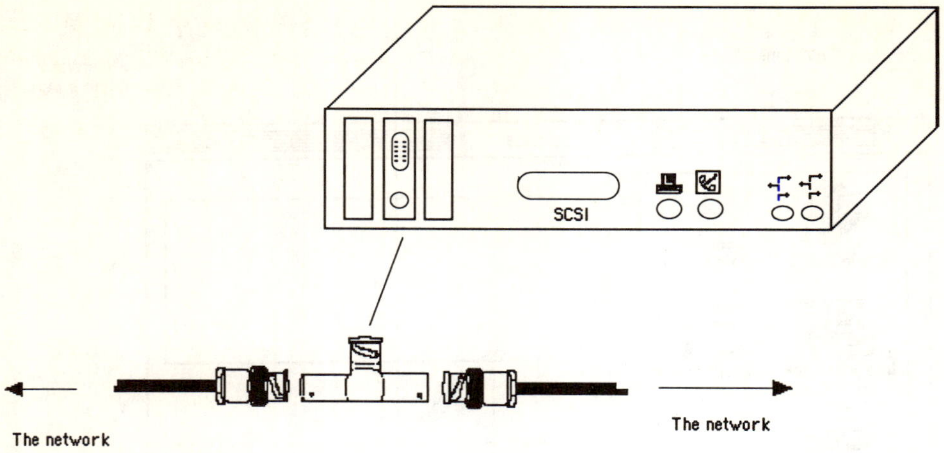

5-5 Thin Ethernet cabling system attach to the connector of an installed Ethernet card.

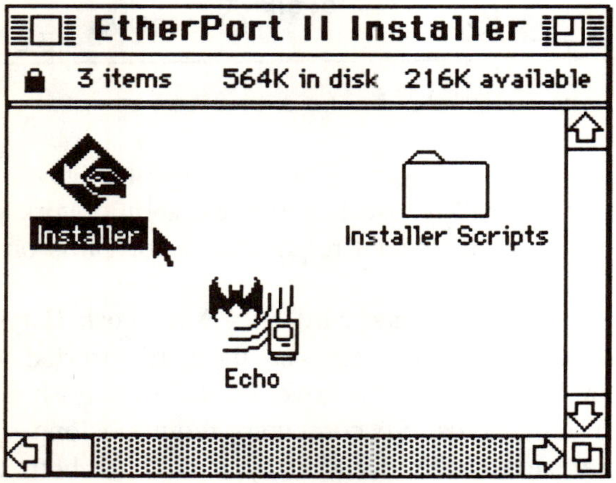

5-6 Ethenet drivers are installed from a floppy disk that comes with the card.

va's Etherport cards for Macintosh computers. To install the driver, double click on the install program.

When you run the installer program, the program copies some files into your Macintosh system folder, and patches some information into the Macintosh System File. After it finishes, you need to activate the driver to make the card work. To activate the driver, use your Macintosh computer's Control Panel. Refer to Figure 5-3 if you are not sure how to get to the Control Panel.

If you are using Macintosh System 6.X, when you select the Control Panel's Network icon you will see the window displayed in Figure 5-7. This figure is displaying an example of how the drivers for all Macintosh Ethernet cards support EtherTalk Phase 1 and EtherTalk Phase 2. The icon with the double arrow should be selected if your network is AppleTalk Phase 2, the single arrow if your network is AppleTalk Phase 1, and the icon that says built-in if your network is LocalTalk.

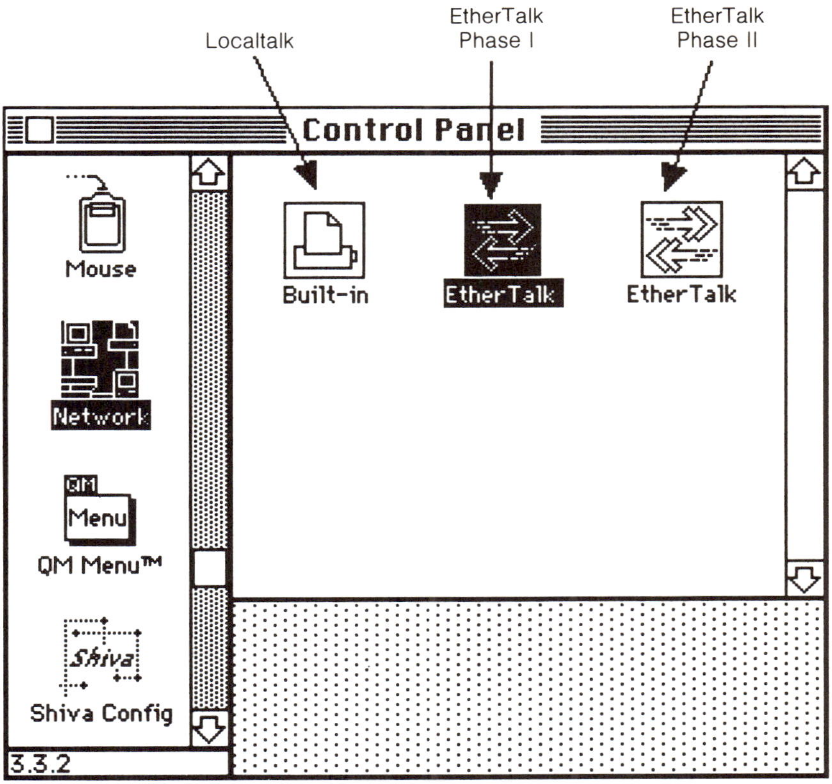

5-7 Selecting the appropriate AppleTalk Connection in the System 6.X Control Panel.

For Macintosh System 7.X, the theory of selecting drivers is the same, but the interface is completely different. Figure 5-8 shows the driver selection process for System 7.X. After making the driver selection, close the Control Panel window and your card and driver should be working. If they are not, restart your Macintosh.

Other cabling connections

If your network cabling scheme is a LocalTalk or Ethernet bus, each computer on the network is a link in a continuous chain. Even the servers on such a

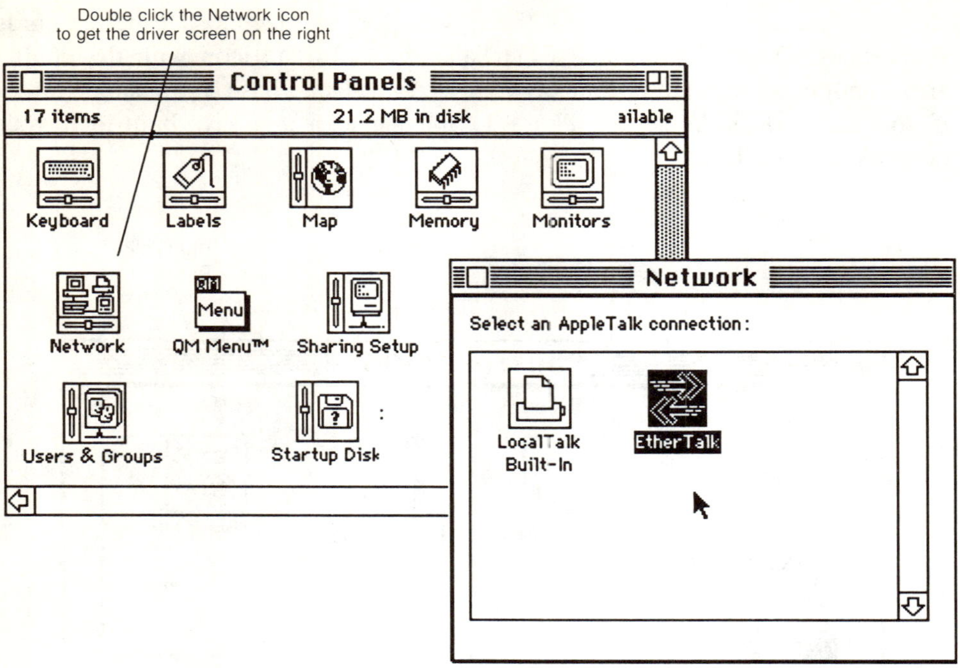

5-8 Selecting the AppleTalk dr ver in System 7.X.

network bus are points in the chain. The connectors that attach to the Macintosh computer facilitate the chain's continuation by having attachments for a wire in, and then out again. Both the LocalTalk connector and a connector for a variety of Ethernet, called Thin Ethernet, are depicted in earlier figures. For Thick Ethernet, 10 Base-T, and Token Ring cabling, the principle of the continuous chain is the same, but the connectors are a little different. These cabling systems use external signal tranceivers and concentrators. Consequently, a single wire usually is all that plugs in to the network interface card for these systems.

For 10 Base-T, a RJ-11 or RJ-22 connector is usually used that resembles the snap-in connectors you see on most modern telephones, as shown in Figure 5-9. For Think Ethernet, the connector is usually a DB-9. A Token Ring cabling system uses still a different arrangement. What actually hooks to the Macintosh is a single cable with an insulated prong connector.

Configuring your AppleTalk Phase 2 driver

When your Macintosh is a client on an AppleTalk Phase 2 network, a number of different zones might be set up on the network cable to which you are attached. If this is the case, you have the opportunity to select which zone you want as your *default zone*. Your default zone is the zone in which you will automatically

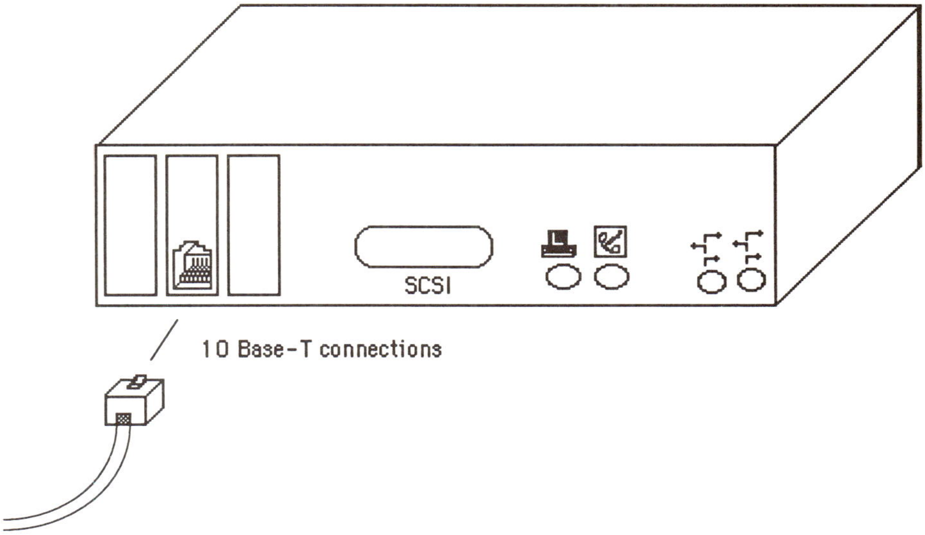

5-9 10 Base-T Ethernet uses RJ connectors.

be registered when you start-up your computer, shown in Figure 5-10. When you pull down the Chooser after your computer starts, it first shows you devices in that zone. To reach devices in other zones, you can use the Chooser to change zones.

Specify the AppleTalk Phase 2 zone that you wish to be your default zone through the Macintosh Control Panel. The Control Panel is accessed as a desk accessory under the Apple menu. To get to the AppleTalk Phase 2 driver, you must find the Network icon in the Control Panel's resource list and click on it. Your AppleTalk drivers will be displayed, as shown in Figure 5-11.

The default zone has no relevance to AppleTalk Phase 1. If your network is running AppleTalk Phase 1, your default zone will be determined by your computer's placement in the physical network topology. If your network uses AppleTalk Phase 2, however, you can determine your default zone by clicking on the EtherTalk Phase 2 driver icon, which is distinguishable by the double arrows (rather than the single arrows that identifies the EtherTalk Phase 1 driver). To make your specification for a default zone, click twice on the EtherTalk Phase 2 driver and select the zone from the window that is shown in the right-hand side Figure 5-11.

Installing Macintosh client software

Two elements of software are required on a Macintosh in order to network to any AFP server, including a NetWare for Macintosh server. The first is AppleShare

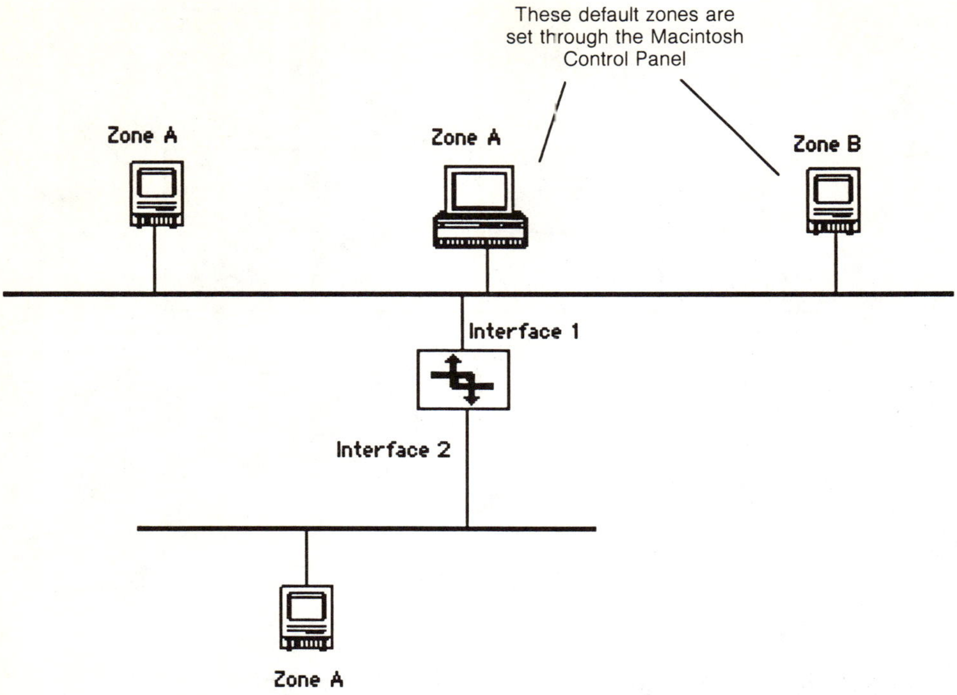

5-10 The default zone is the zone your Macintcsh will consider its normal zone.

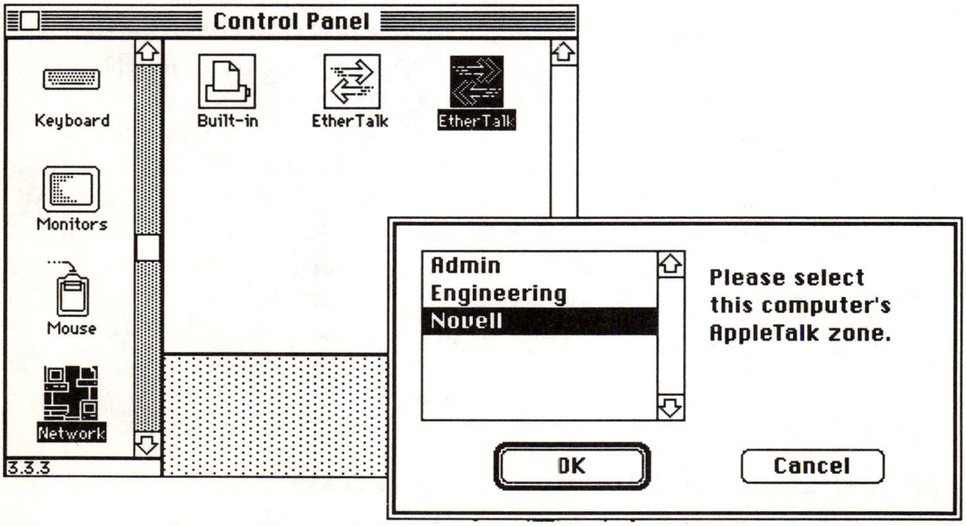

5-11 Double-click on the Phase 2 driver to set the default zone.

client software. This does not come from Novell, it comes from Apple. The second element of client software is a set of software tools that comes on a floppy disk with NetWare for Macintosh.

AppleShare client software can be found on the Macintosh System Software disks that are packaged with every Macintosh, whether a version in the System 6.X family, or System 7.X. AppleShare client software allows a Macintosh to access NetWare for Macintosh servers via AppleTalk and AFP protocols. There is actually another client workstation piece of software on those disks as well, the drivers for Apple LaserWriters, which permits your Macintosh to print to a networked LaserWriter. Figure 5-13 shows the set of disks you need for full NetWare for Macintosh client installation. The set of disks on the left are the system software disks for Macintosh System 6.X. The disk on the right is a NetWare disk, not a Macintosh system software disk which contains tools used by Macintosh clients to manage the file security and print queueing features of NetWare and NetWare for Macintosh. These utilites work with both System 6.X and System 7.X.

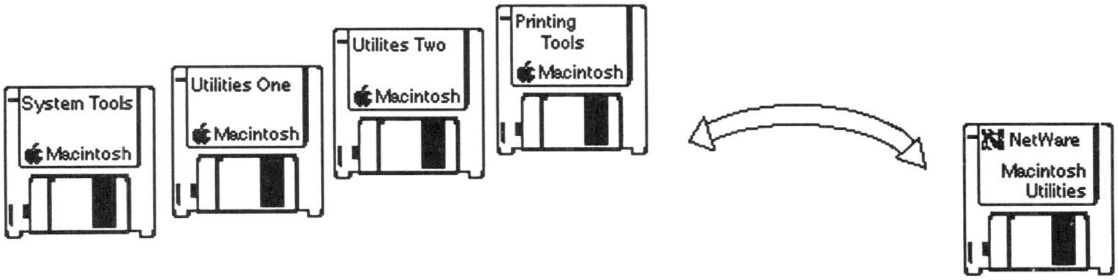

5-12 The disks you need in System 6.X to install everything for a NetWare for Macintosh client (on LocalTalk).

If AppleShare workstation software, LaserWriter printer drivers, and the NetWare for Macintosh client utilties are not installed already on your Macintosh, you must install them. This is a simple process. To begin installing the Macintosh system software and AppleShare workstation client software on a Macintosh running the System 6.X operating system, insert disk number one, titled Startup, and click on the Installer icon, as shown in Figure 5-13.

The System 6.X installer program brings up a menu that allows you to choose the elements of Apple System 6.X on your Macintosh from a menu. Choose the selection for AppleShare workstation software and the version of LaserWriter you will be using, as well as any other network resources, such as an AppleTalk ImageWriter, that you want installed. This is shown in Figure 5-14. When your selections are made, click the Install button and the Installer program will do the rest. When the Installer tells you the installation is complete, click the Quit button and exit the program.

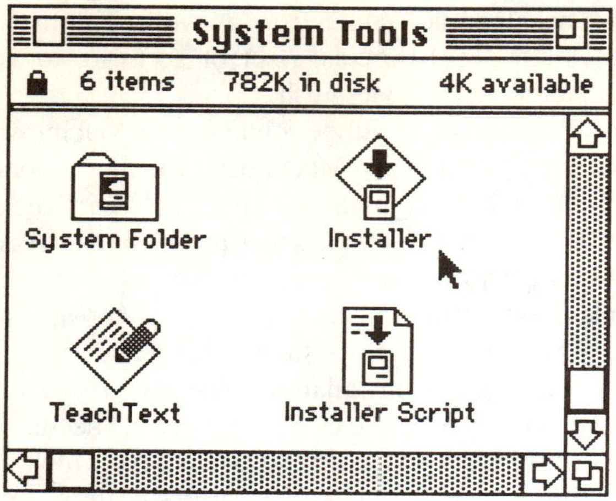

5-13 The Macintosh System installer.

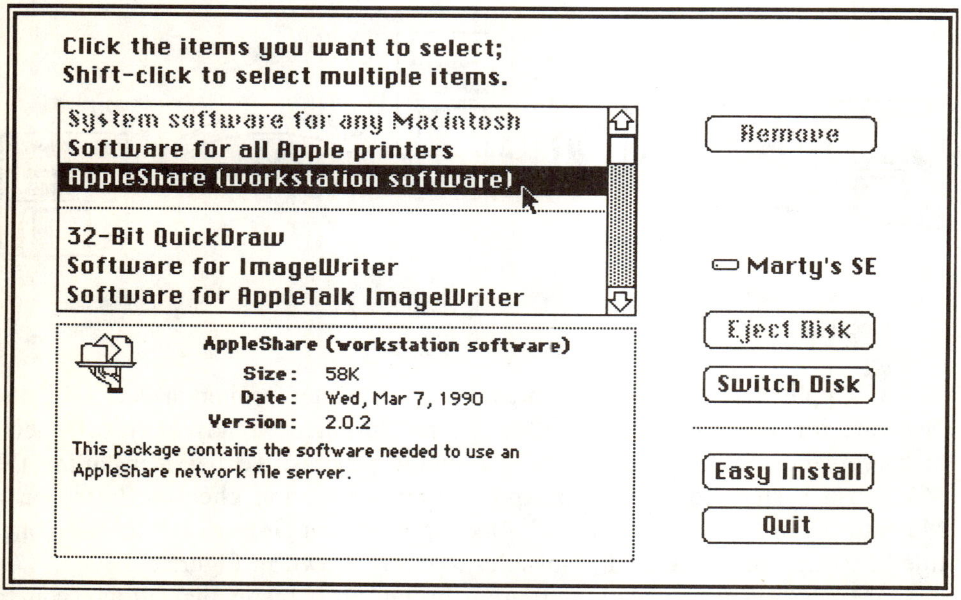

5-14 Select the system components you wish to install.

In an organization that is using System 6.X on Macintosh networking clients, it is imperative that all of a LaserWriter's Macintosh users be installed with the same versions of the LaserWriter drivers. If they are not all using the same version, the LaserWriter constantly will need to be reset between users. If your organization has a mixture of users, some running system 6.X and some running 7.X, you can install system 7.X printing resources on all the computers to achieve compatibility.

Installing NetWare client utilities

The two main tools on the NetWare for Macintosh utilities disk are a NetWare desk accessory, and an application called the NetWare Control Center. When installed, the desk accessory is accessible on a Macintosh under the Apple menu at the top of its screen. It allows you to set limits on the rights of other users to access your data. The NetWare Control Center is an application that contains a superset of the capabilities of the NetWare Desk Accessory, which also lets you set NetWare file attributes and manage NetWare users and groups. Use of these tools is explained in detail in chapter 6.

To install the NetWare desk accessory, you need the disk titled NetWare for Macintosh Utilities. Its contents are displayed in figure 5-15. There are two procedures to installing these utilities. First, run the Apple Font/DA mover to install the NetWare DA under the Apple menu. Second, drag some files into your System Folder.

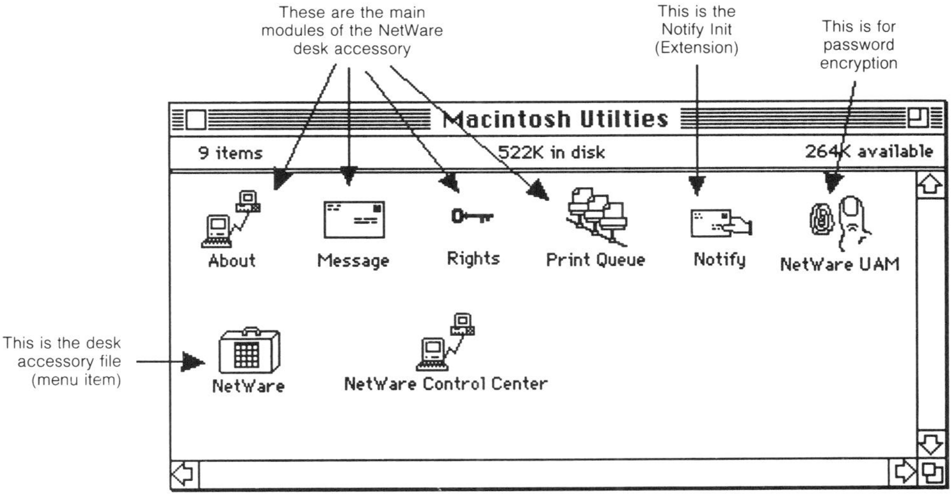

5-15 The contents of the NetWare for Macintosh Utilties disk.

To install the NetWare desk accessory in a Macintosh using System 6.X, use the Macintosh Font/DA mover. The icon for the desk accessory is the one that looks like a suitcase. The easiest way to start its installation process is to double click its icon and, like most Macintosh files, it will launch the application that it belongs to, which in this case is the Macintosh Font/DA mover. In Macintosh System 7.X, you can install the NetWare menu item by opening your System Folder and dragging the icon into the folder called Apple Menu Items. System 7.X has made the installation of menu items very easy. See Figure 5-16.

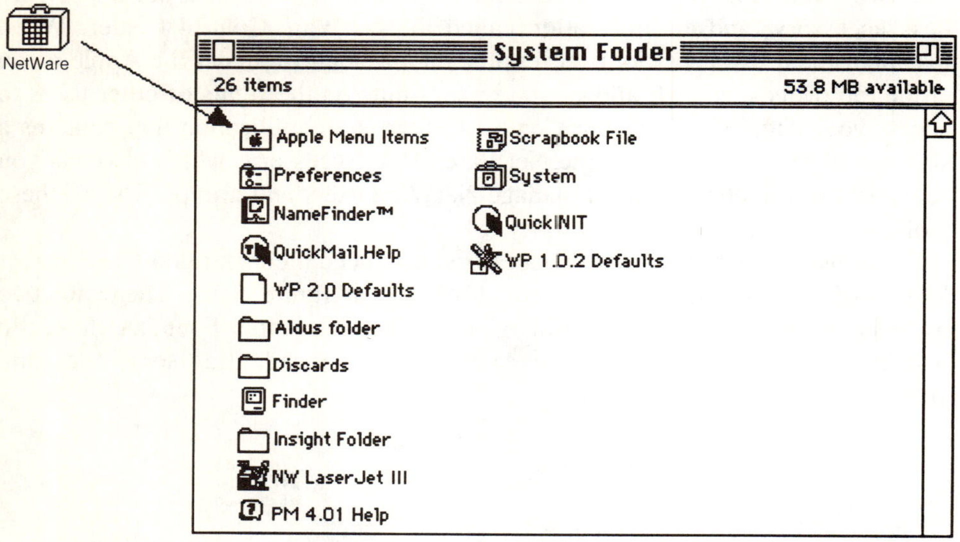

5-16 In System 7.X, drag the NetWare suitcase into the menu items folder.

The Font/DA mover of Macintosh System 6.X copies the NetWare DA resource into the Macintosh's system file. Figure 5-17 shows how this is done in the Font/DA mover. The box on the left is the System File. The box on the right is the desk accessory(ies) that you will be copying. Select the desk accessory resource on the right, click copy, and the process is complete. Click Quit to exit the Font/DA mover, and your DA will be under the Apple Menu. If you are running System 6.X Multifinder, you will need to restart your computer before it will appear. Before you restart, however, you should drag the files that the NetWare desk accessory modules into your System Folder, or another folder of your choice. The icons for these files are shown on the first row in Figure 5-18. Drag them with your mouse. Their names are About, Message, Print Queue, and Rights.

After you restart, the NetWare desk accesssory will be available under the Apple menu. When you pull it down, you will see the window diplayed in Figure 5-18.

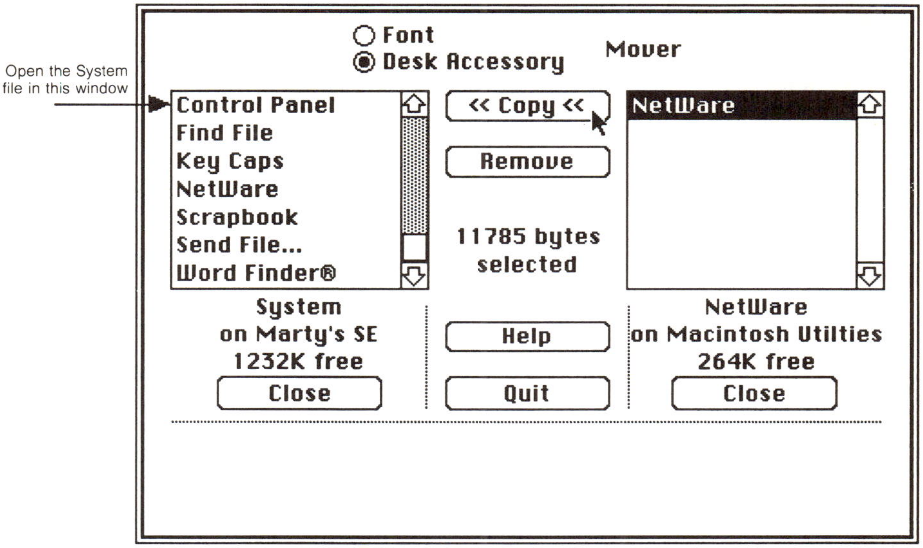

5-17 Use the Font/DA mover to install the NetWare desk accessory in System 6.X.

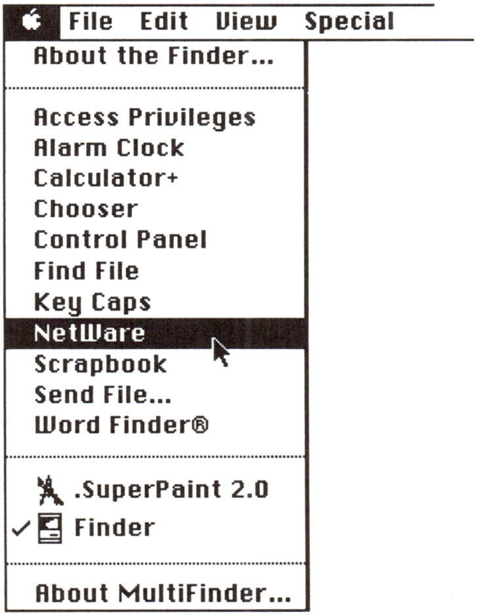

5-18 After installation, the NetWare item will appear under the Macintosh Apple Menu.

Another file you might want to install in your System Folder is named Notify, which is called an *init* in the terms used with Apple System 6.X. In Apple System 7.X, it would more appropriately be called and extention. An init, or extention, file on a Macintosh is a program that is launched when the Macintosh is started. With Macintosh System 6.X, this file can be anywhere in your System Folder. With Macintosh System 7.X, you will find a folder called Extentions, in which you should place the Notify file. You already might have some of the same types of files on your Macintosh, which display themsleves at the bottom of your screen as your Macintosh starts up.

The Notify init (extension) listens for incoming NetWare messages and displays them on your screen. This is discussed in more detail in chapter 6. The other files are resources for the Macintosh desk accessory, which by default are expected to be in the System Folder for the desk accessory to work properly. However, a setup option is available that allows these files to be stored anywhere, including on a NetWare server.

Installing NetWare for Macintosh v3.X's encrypted authentication

The NetWare User Autentication Method (UAM) of NetWare for Macintosh v3.X is software that encrypts the user's password before sending it to a NetWare for Macintosh file server. This is a feature of NetWare for Macintosh v3.x only; it is not available for NetWare for Macintosh v2.X. The NetWare UAM is recommended in security conscious environments as a measure to ensure that passwords are encoded before they are sent over a network wire, so they will not be discovered by some kind of network evesdropping. See Figure 5-19.

To install the NetWare UAM in both Macintosh System 6.X and 7.X, you must create a new folder in your System Folder named Appleshare Folder. Then copy a file called NetWare UAM into the folder. The icon for the NetWare UAM file is displayed in Figure 5-20. When you restart your Macintosh, the NetWare UAM will be in effect when you log into NetWare for Macintosh servers.

The NetWare UAM has several other minor effects on the Appleshare interface, other than the one displayed in Figure 5-20. One effect is that the NetWare UAM allows you to choose a password up to 64 characters in length, as opposed to the 8 character default limit of AppleShare. Another effect is that the NetWare UAM does allow a client to do startup mounting. If you attempt to select the check box next to a volume name, which you see in Figure 5-21, an error message is displayed. Finally, When the NetWare UAM is installed you can not change your password from the AppleShare login screen. The Set Password button will be grayed-out. To change your password, you must use the NetWare Control Center.

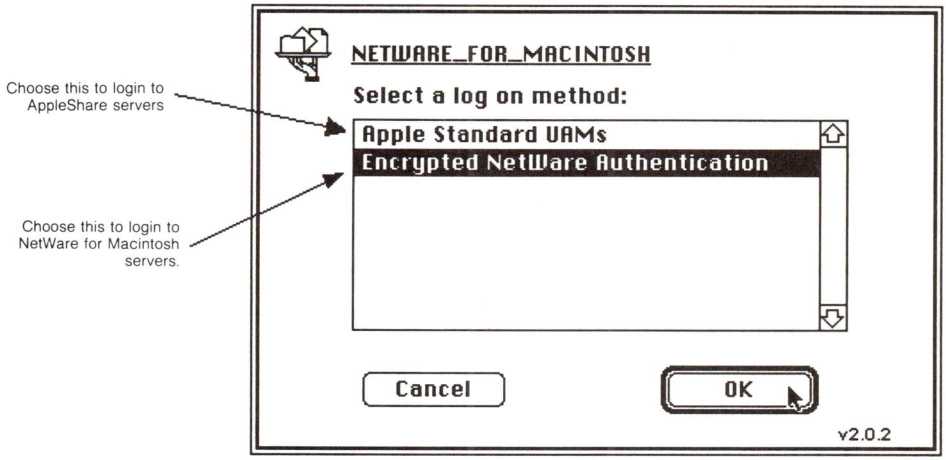

5-19 This screen is added to the AppleShare login process when you install Encrypted NetWare Authentication.

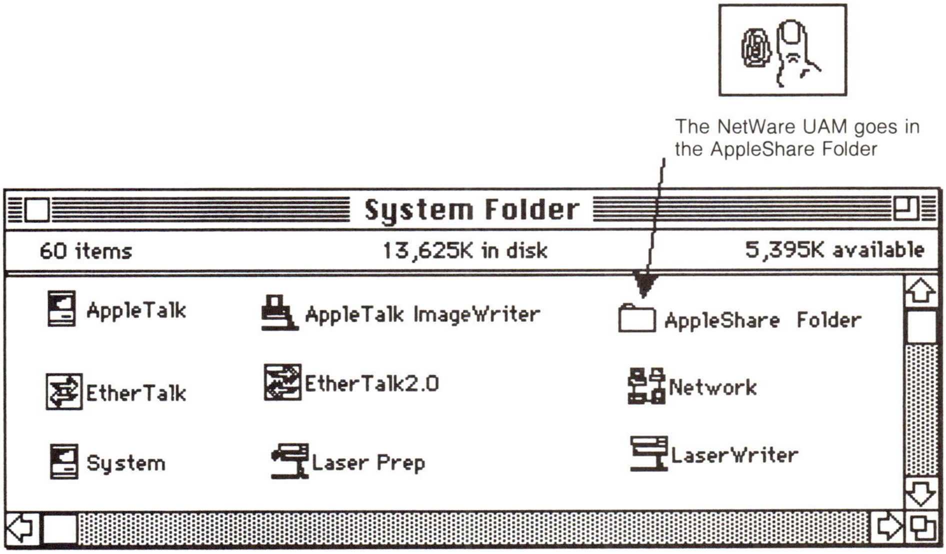

5-20 The Encrypted NetWare UAM is installed in a folder called AppleShare within the Macintosh System Folder.

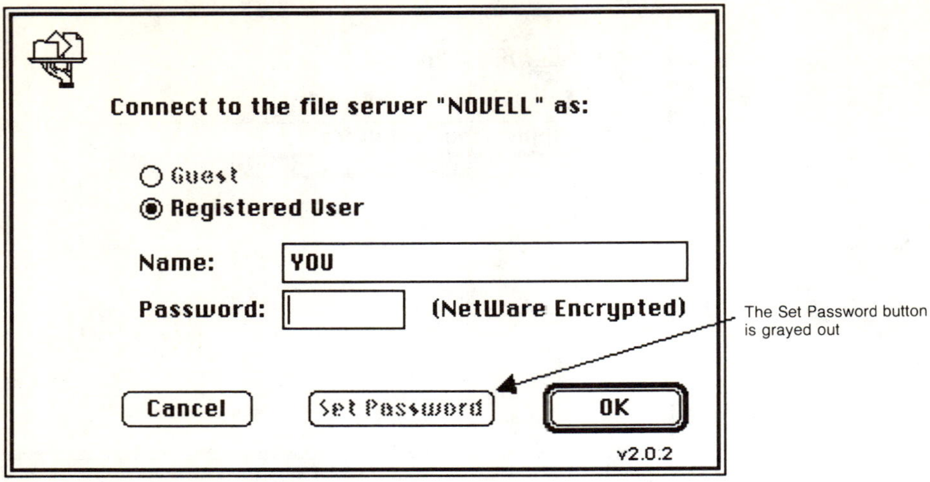

5-21 Encrypted Authentication will disable some normal AppleShare options.

Installing the NetWare Control Center

The NetWare Control Center is also on the Macintosh Utilities disk of NetWare for Macintosh. It is an application program file that is installed on a Macintosh client by simply dragging a copy from the floppy disk onto the hard disk (if the Macintosh is so equipped), or onto the disk of a server. Then, like with any Macintosh application progam, it is launched by double clicking with the mouse, or by selecting it and giving the file open command.

6
Chapter

Basic operations

Considering their capabilities, one might expect NetWare services to be difficult to use; but they are not. For example, chapter 3 explained how easy it is for a Macintosh user to log-in to a NetWare for Macintosh server and copy files onto it, because its icon appeared on the desktop like a local disk icon. However, a NetWare for Macintosh server is a shared resource so there are features and issues unique to networking environments that you should be aware of.

This chapter explains basic issues related to working with other users and using Macintosh application software in a shared server environment. Also discussed is the use of NetWare for Macintosh in environments that integrate you with users of other desktop computers, such as DOS, Windows, UNIX, and IBM mainframe computers.

Using the file services of NetWare for Macintosh

Once you've logged on to a NetWare for Macintosh server volume, you have the ability to access files created by other users, or to store new files. Your Macintosh Finder—the graphical interface that controls the icons on your desktop—treats the NetWare for Macntosh volume much like any local disk.

NetWare for Macintosh v2.X and v3.X both have complete compatibility with the Macintosh Finder and its interface. Users work the same basic way no matter which version of NetWare for Macintosh their organization has installed. Because NetWare for Macintosh is a shared resource, however, each individual user does not create their own workspace or control everything on the server, as they would on their own local disks. NetWare for Macintosh users work within a system that is preinstalled. One user, called the supervisor in NetWare terminology, installs a volume and creates accounts that permit others to log-in.

One of the first and most visable effects of the control that users relinquish on preinstalled NetWare for Macintosh volume is the sizing and positioning of windows. Generally, folders that are shared among multiple users do not allow users to permanently alter the dimensions or placement of the windows when you open them. You can resize and move them on your desktop in any given working session, but when you log out or close those windows, the changes will not be remembered. The next time you open those folders, the windows will have reverted to their old settings. When you resize or move a folder's window on any of your local disks the window stays in the position that you leave it in, even after you close and re-open the window. See Figure 6-1.

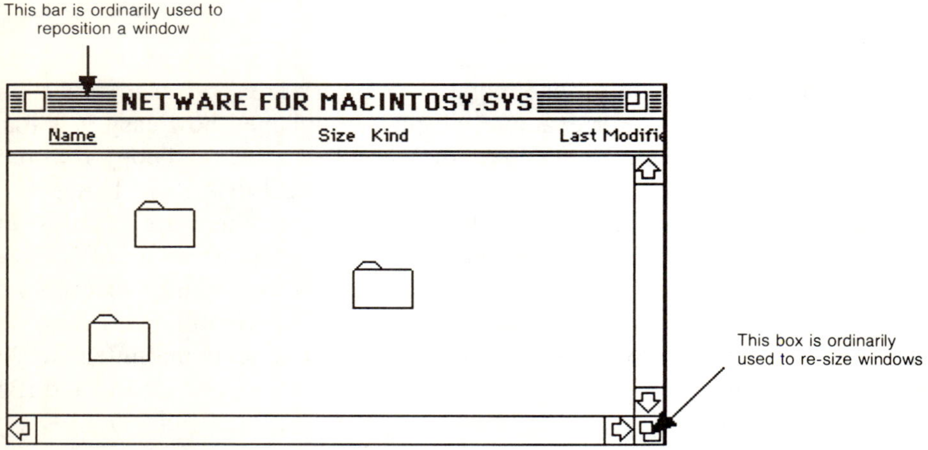

6-1 The windows of shared volumes can not be permanantly resized by the average user.

Local disks remember window size and positions because the Finder saves the window size and positon information on the disk in a file called the desktop file. Each local Macintosh disk has its own desktop file. When you close a window on a local disk after resizing it, the next time you open it, the Finder reads the placement from the desktop file. On a shared NetWare for Macintosh volume, you and other users do not have the ability to save your personal window settings in the desktop file, because you all share the same desktop file. Allowing each individual to make changes would cause pandemonium. On a NetWare for Macintosh volume (or any AFP volume), the supervisor is usually the only one who has the ability to update shared window settings; you inherit those settings when you use the window.

Another difference between working on local disks and working on NetWare for Macintosh volumes stems from the Finder's use of a shared desktop file. Neither you nor any other user can take files from a shared volume, and place them on your personal desktop. The Finder will not permit it because if it did, a user could undermine another users ability to see shared data. You will get the error message shown in Figure 6-2, if you try to take files from a shared volume.

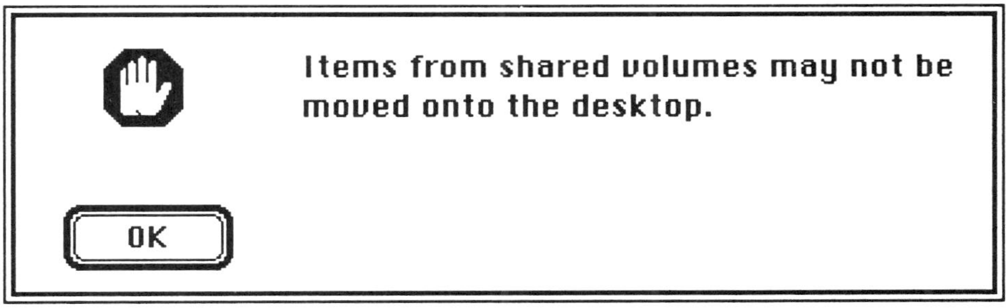

6-2 The error message you get with shared volumes if you try to put one of its files on your desktop.

You also will not be able to drag a server volume icon from your desktop and into the trash if you have files on that volume that are open. If you try, you will find the volume icon stubbornly removes itself from the trash and re-appears. This usually happens if you use MultiFinder in Macintosh System 6.X or Macintosh System 7.X, and you have an application open in the background when you are in the Finder. If this happens to you, you will have to re-enter the application with the open file, and close the file before you can get rid of the volume icon.

Common elements of NetWare for Macintosh volumes

When installed, NetWare requires that the first volume on a server be named by the name of the server, and the extention SYS. Other volumes can be set up on the same server after the SYS volume if the network supervisor creates them. When a server has multiple volumes, they are listed in the AppleShare client Volume window, as shown in Figure 6-3.

If you wish to mount more than one of a server's volumes, you must mount them both at the same time. For security reasons, NetWare will not let you mount one of its server volumes now, and then come back and mount another volume later. If you try to mount a second volume later, you will see all the volumes on the server grayed out in the volume mounting window. If after you mount one volume you decide to mount another one as well, you must unmount

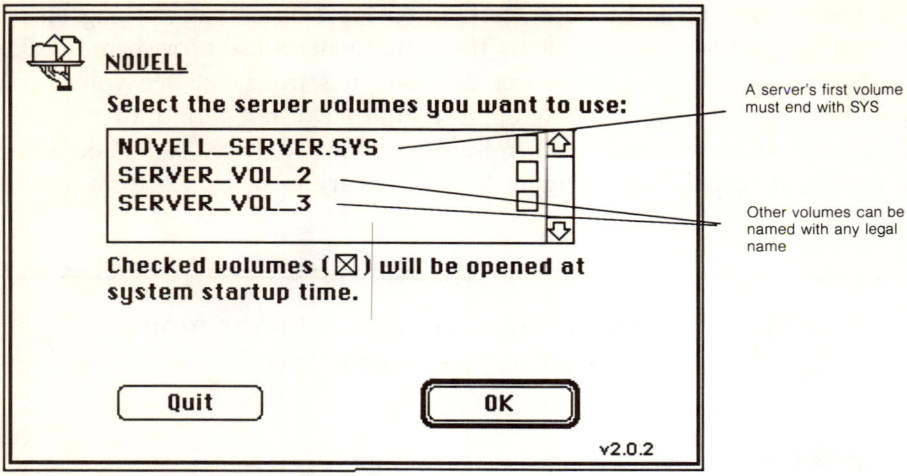

6-3 NetWare for Macintosh supports multiple volumes per server.

the one you already have and then login in to the server again and mount them both.

Each mounted volume of a server acts like a different disk resource. Even if two volumes are on the same server, when you mount them you will get a separate icon. If you choose, you can have more than one volume from the same server or different servers mounted on your desktop at the same time. Figure 6-4 shows two volumes that were mounted from the same server.

The SYS volume on any server always has certain characteristics in common. The SYS volume has at least the four folders shown in Figure 6-5. Sometimes the server's SYS volume is the server's only volume. In this case, the supervisor generally creates a set of folders in which users will do most of their work at the same time as the installation. This is depicted in Figure 6-5 in a folder called User Work. When the server has more than one volume, the other volumes are often set up for the use of clients in any way the supervisor wants, and the SYS volume is rarely accessed.

Figure 6-5 illustrates a NetWare v2.X volume. The folders shown in Figure 6-5 are mandatory on both NetWare v2.X and NetWare v3.X SYS volumes; however, with NetWare v3.X, you might not see some of the folders because they are shielded from your view. The following is a brief description of the SYS volume, and the purpose of the four required NetWare folders on the SYS volume:

Servername_SYS The NetWare file system originates from a volume that is identified by the name of the server, and the suffix SYS. At that level, as you saw in Figure 6-5, sit the NetWare folders Login, Mail, Public, and System.

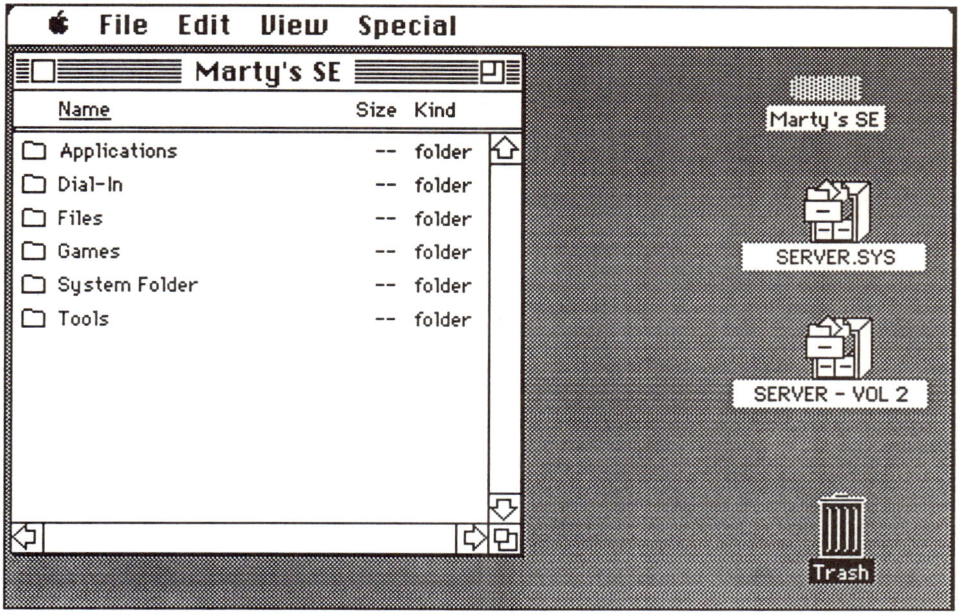

6-4 Volumes mounted from the same server.

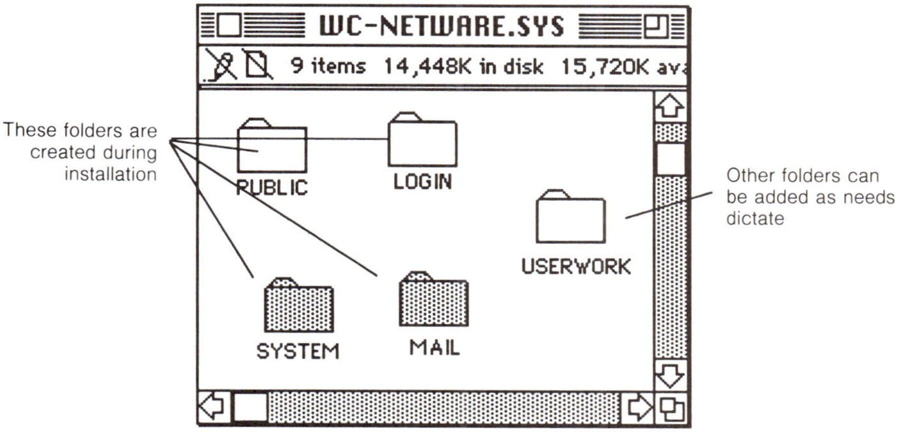

6-5 A hypothetical volume configuration.

LOGIN This folder holds operating system programs that permit DOS and OS/2 computers to log-in to the server. It has no purpose for Macintosh users.

MAIL The Mail folder is provided by NetWare for use by electronic mail programs. A user can open this folder, but nothing can be saved to it.

SYSTEM This folder contains NetWare supervisory and diagnostic programs that are used to manage the server. You will not see this folder on NetWare v3.X unless you are a NetWare supervisor. On a NetWare v2.X server, it will be gray. When a folder is gray, you can't access it.

PUBLIC The Public folder holds menu programs and command utilites that DOS users use to secure their user environment. A user probably can see the items in this folder. The user can run the programs from a DOS machine, but probably will not be able to write or delete files. Macintosh users do not need the utility programs in this directory, although they too can access this folder. Macintosh users have their own set of utilities in the form of the NetWare desk accessory and NetWare Control Center.

Beyond these four required folders, there is no typical example of how the folders on a NetWare for Macintosh volume are organized. The organization of files and folders is often determined by the needs of the network manager who sets the server up. Unless you are the supervisor, however, you generally will have only limited access to any of the four required NetWare folders.

The NetWare system of rights

Because there sometimes might be information on a server that should not be accessible by just anybody, NetWare has a system of *access rights* that can be used to give only certain users access to certain files or folders. If you do not have access rights to files and folders, you cannot open them. In Figure 6-6, you can see the SYS volume of the server that was described in the previous section. Some of the folders in the diagram are gray folders. NetWare v2.X shows the

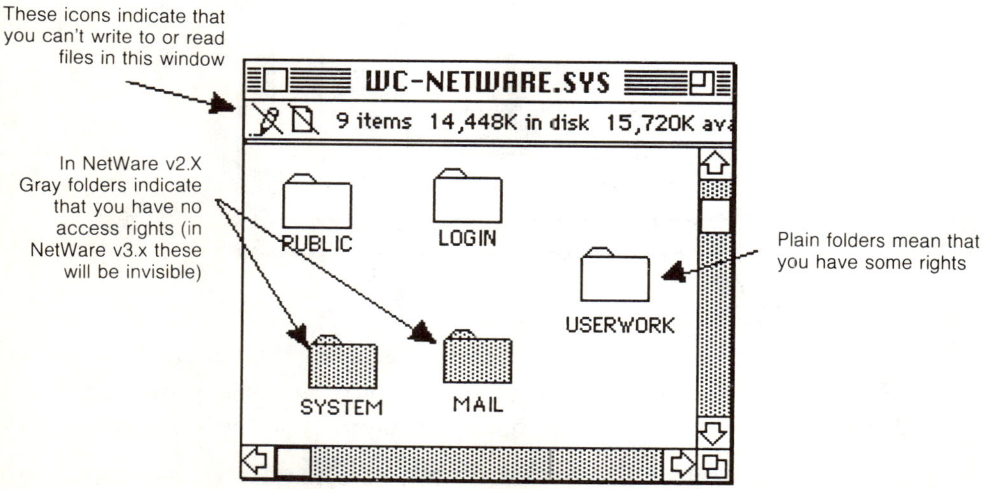

6-6 Icons for access rights in NetWare.

folders that you can't access in gray. The reason the System folder is made inaccessible to all but the supervisor is that it contains some critical files for the server operating system, and most organizations want to protect those files from inadvertant harm.

Only if you are given the right to access the folders that you see in this diagram can you open them, browse through their contents, and use their space to store files. If you try to open a folder or file, or write to a folder in which you did not have a NetWare right, you get a message informing you of your limitation. Figure 6-7 shows you a brief sample of some of the error messages displayed when you try to do something you don't have rights to do.

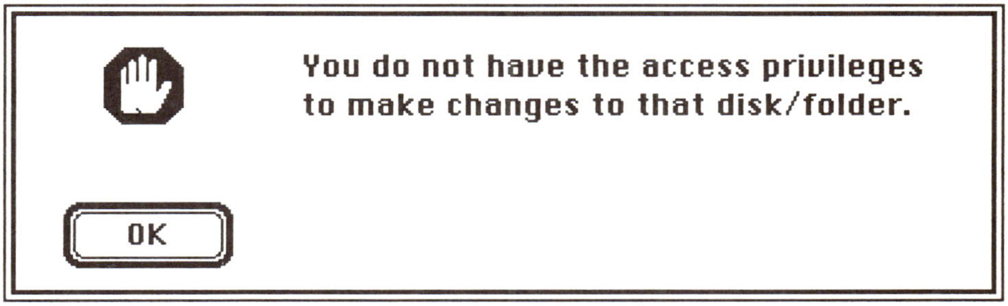

6-7 You recieve an error message when you try to open a gray folder.

NetWare v3.X has a rights system similar to NetWare v2.X, but it is a little more comprehensive. In NetWare v2.X, the folders that you don't have rights to are in gray, but in NetWare v3.X, if you do not have rights to a folder, you do not even see it. For example, unless you are the server's supervisor, you cannot see the folder called System, because you have no rights to that folder. Even though you cannot see it, it is there nonetheless, and if you are given rights to it, then you will be able to see it.

The NetWare rights system works the same for all NetWare users, Macintosh, DOS PC, UNIX, or others, which is an important characteristic. If that was not the case, then some of NetWare's desktop clients would have more or less security than the others. The consistency of NetWare rights is a considerable achievement when you realize that there are some significant file system differences between the various native client operating systems that NetWare serves. Using the NetWare rights system is discussed at length in chapter 7.

The NetWare file system

Network Supervisor's usually add directories to a NetWare SYS volume or some other volume, as the organizations needs dictate. This was shown as an example in Figure 6-5 with a folder called User Work. If you are given the ability to write data to this or some other folder on a volume, you can use it as a storage resource. A NetWare for Macintosh volume basically acts like any other Macintosh disk, to the extent that it shows up within your Macintosh application software's Mini-Finder when you save files to the server. You can see from the arrow in Figure 6-8 how Claris's MacWrite II, and other Macintosh application software, identifies and treats a server volume in its Mini-Finder.

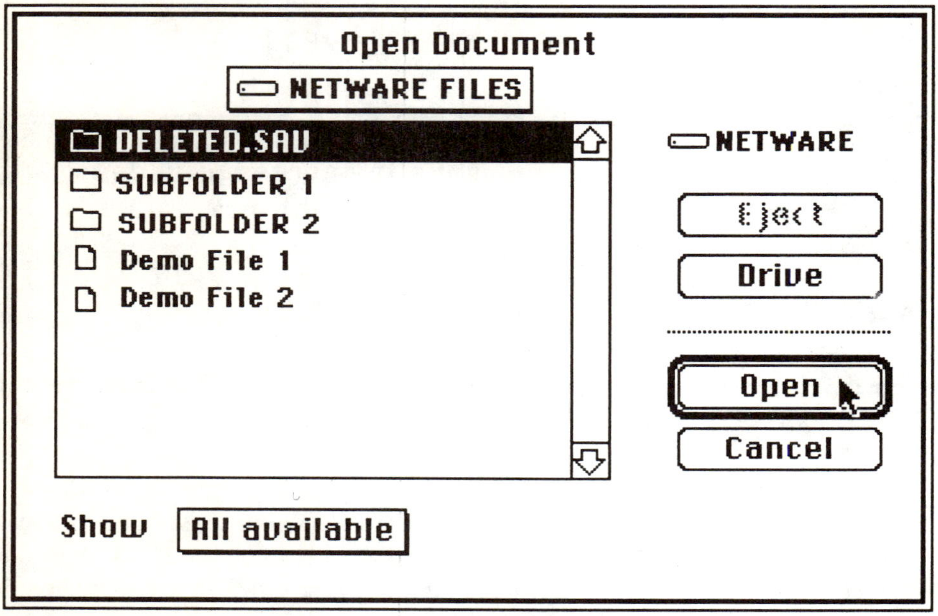

6-8 NetWare for Maicntosh volumes appear like any other disk volumes in an application's Mini-Finder window.

Files on a NetWare file service volume are displayed to a Macintosh as icons, which the Mac user would expect. However, a NetWare volume has the ability to store files from users of DOS, Windows, and other computer systems in addition to Macintoshes. For that reason, icons for files from other computer systems are displayed as different types of icons. The way that data files created with both Macintosh and DOS applications are displayed on a NetWare for Macintosh volume is demonstrated in Figure 6-9.

Although NetWare for Macintosh gives Macintosh users the ability to access files created by other computer users, NetWare for Macintosh does not alter the data within DOS, OS/2, or UNIX data files to make them readable by Macintosh application programs. It merely acts as the platform to make them acces-

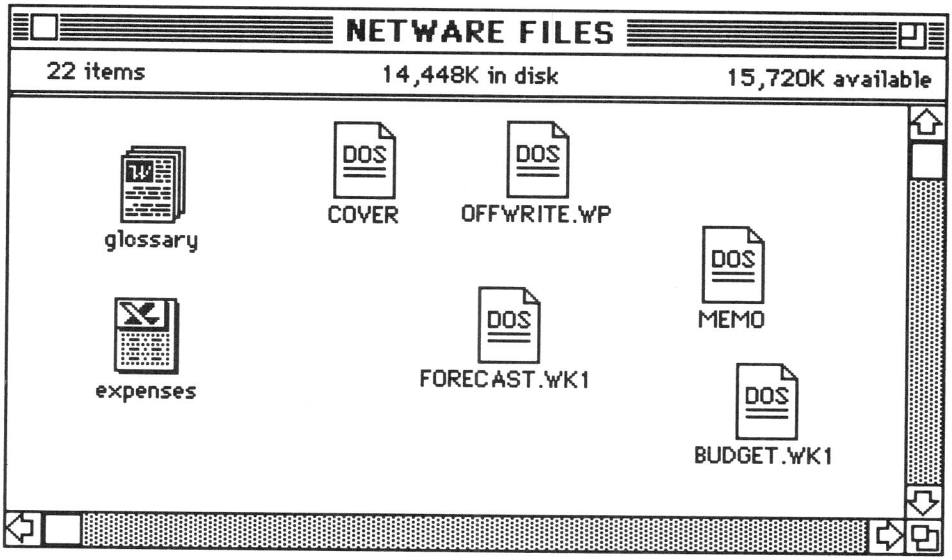

6-9 NetWare for Macintosh displays even DOS files as icons.

sible. To use the DOS files on your Macintosh, you need to treat them as Macintosh files. A Macintosh user can work with DOS files in several ways. One way is to translate the DOS file to a Macintosh file. Another way is to use a Macintosh application that can read the DOS file without translation. These and other methods are discussed at length in chapters 8 and 9.

On a NetWare for Macintosh file server volume, Macintosh files are displayed in their customary manner, which designates the application in which they were created. Macintosh files can be shown in this way because Macintosh files are stored with information that designates the application program with which they were created. The Finder, which is the desktop manager of the Macintosh operating system, reads this information and includes it in the icons that it displays. The non-Macintosh files, which in this case happpen to be from a DOS computer system, are shown generically as DOS icons, because they have no information about their creators. Neither the DOS operating system nor DOS applications programs provide this kind of information, but NetWare provides enough information so the Finder knows that they are not Macintosh files and shows them with a DOS icon.

The structure of Macintosh files is one of the big differences between the Macintosh file environment and the file environments of DOS, Windows, OS/2, and UNIX computers. Macintosh files are unique because they actually consist of two parts. These parts are called *forks;* the user only sees a fork called the *data fork*. The other fork, called the *resource fork,* is invisible. Figure 6-10 shows an illustration of this two-part file structure. NetWare and NetWare for Macintosh

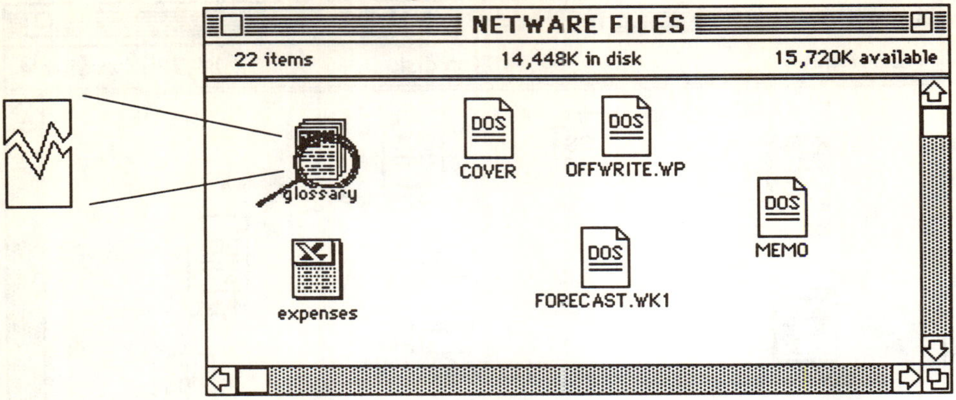

6-10 Macintosh files have two forks.

simulate a resource fork for DOS and other types of files, so that they are compatible with the Finder and will appear on the Macintosh desktop, but the information in those resource forks is as generic as their icons.

The resource fork is one of the features that make it possible for Macintosh documents to be opened by double clicking them on the desktop. Because the resource fork of a document keeps track of the application it was created in, the Finder is able to find out the application that belongs with the file and open that application for the file. If you double click one of the DOS, Windows, OS/2, and UNIX files on a NetWare for Macintosh volume, they will not be launched, partly because they do not have this information in a resource fork. Instead, you will receive an error message that tells you the application program where the file came from is busy or missing, shown in Figure 6-11.

Every Macintosh application program uses the data fork and resource fork in different ways. Some word processing programs keep most of their data in the data fork, and almost nothing in the resource fork, while some graphics programs

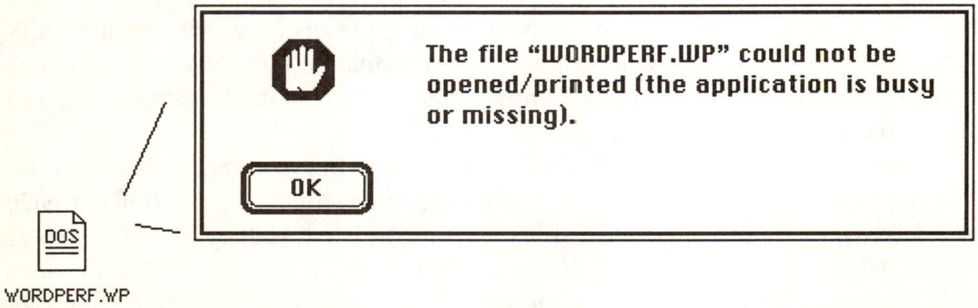

6-11 DOS files will not be launchable by double-clicking.

keep most of their data in the resource fork. Every application works a little differently. Perhaps the only valid generalization about the data fork and resource fork relationship of files is that once a Macintosh file is separated from its resource fork, it usually will not work any longer. Even though the resource fork in invisible, it is a critical part of the file.

Users and network administrators should be aware of the dual fork structure of Macintosh files when a DOS client or some other client is handling the files of Macintosh users. Clients, such as DOS computers, that do not have the dual fork structure of the Macintosh do not have native operating system commands that will manage both of the Macintosh's file forks. The DOS copy command, for example, copies only the data fork of a Macintosh file because it was intended to work with DOS files, which only have one part. See Figure 6-12.

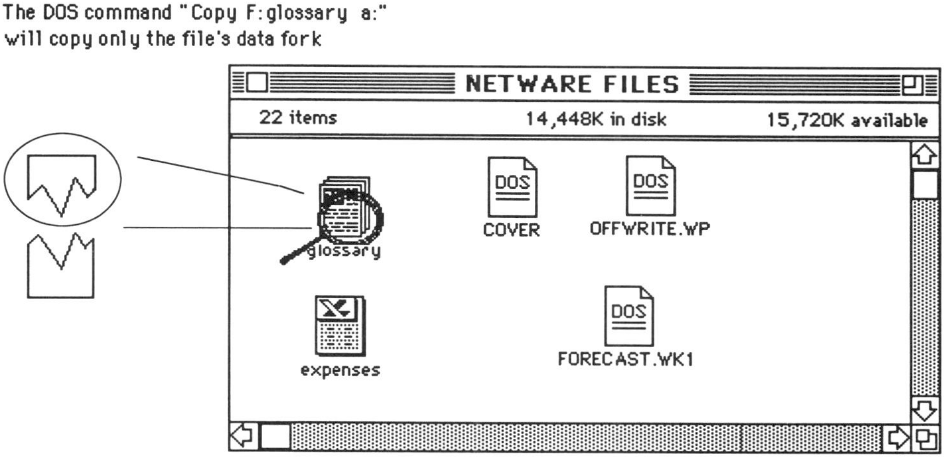

6-12 DOS commands will not recognize both forks of Macintosh files.

To work with Macintosh files, you must use tools that are aware of, and will handle both forks of a Macintosh file. Utilities, such as NetWare's Ncopy, are the most appropriate tools for DOS clients to use to manage Macintosh files, because they handle the resource fork as well as the data fork of a Macintosh file. Instructions on how to use NetWare's N-utilities are beyond the scope of this book. Consult the NetWare utilities manuals for informnation on these commands.

File naming differences between NetWare clients

Another set of file differences between Macintosh and other NetWare client environments are the file naming systems that each environment supports. The

Macintosh computers operating system supports file names that are up to 31 characters long. File names for a Macintosh file can contain spaces and any other keyboard character except the colon. In contrast, the permissible names for DOS files are more restricted. OS/2 is even more generous than DOS in its rules for naming files, but also is more restrictive than the Macintosh. UNIX and the Macintosh are pretty much the same, except UNIX distinguishes between upper and lower case characters. Table 6-1 summarizes the naming rules for all supported NetWare environments.

NetWare has a system that supports the allowable file names of all of its clients. Macintosh users can store a file under any legal Macintosh file name, even if the name violates the naming rules of one of the other client environments. However, the other environment will not see the file with the name the Macintosh user gave it when it is in violation of the other environment's rules. For example, when a Macintosh user gives a file a name that has a space in it,

Table 6-1 File naming rules.

Macintosh Rules

- File names can be up to 31 characters, include blank spaces, and include all other special characters except the colon.

Unix Rules

- File names can be up to 256 characters, include blank spaces, and all other special characters except the colon.
- Upper case and lower case are considered different characters in file names.

DOS Rules

- File names follow the format FILENAME.EXT
- File names can up to 8 characters, no spaces, optionally followed by a period and up to 3 more characters.
- File names allow characters that are numbers 0–9, and the letters A–Z, plus the following special characters:

~ ! @ # $ % & ( ) - _ { } '

- File names can not be one of the following:

AUX	COM1	CON	LPT1	NUL
PRN	COM2	LPT2	LPT3	CLOCK$

- Some extentions have special meaning to DOS, and should not be used for documents. They are:

COM EXE BAT SYS BAS

the DOS user would see the file without the space, because DOS does not support spaces in its file names. Similarly, when a Macintosh file name is more than the 8-character limit, NetWare shortens the name of the file when it shows the name to DOS users while maintaining the full Macintosh name of the file to show to Macintosh users.

NetWare provides users with a system that works even when file names violate some environments' naming rules, because it maintains an internal database of names for each of the environments that it supports. Table 6-2 shows a chart of the way that NetWare resolves the file naming differences between its client environments. This system sometimes permits different NetWare clients to access the same file by different names.

Table 6-2 File name resolution.

Macintosh	DOS	UNIX
March Expenses	MARCHEX	March Expenses
March $'s	MARCHS	March $'s
Mar. Expenses	MAR.EXP	Mar. Expenses
April Expense (Projected)	APRILEXP	April Expense (Projected)
April Expense (Budgeted)	APRILEX1	April Expense (Budgeted)
April Expense (Actual)	APRILEX2	April Expense (Actual)

Some more creative Macintosh file names end up being relatively obscure to DOS users. In a sense, a mixed client environment is constrained in its file naming practices by the environment's most restrictive client's rules. Macintosh users who work on projects with other computer users should be aware of the file name limitations of the other users so that they can accommodate them. This is particularly true of DOS and Windows users who work under the most restrictive file naming rules.

Using Macintosh application programs on a network

Several issues that relate to the use of application programs in a networking environment are new to users accustomed to working in a stand-alone environment. Macintosh users who switch from a stand-alone applications environment to a NetWare environment should be aware of the possible impact, and modify the way they use their application programs.

One of the issues involves a decision of whether to store only data files on a NetWare server, and store and run application software locally, or whether both data files and application files should be stored on the server. The biggest benefits of keeping everything on the server are convenience, and the possibility

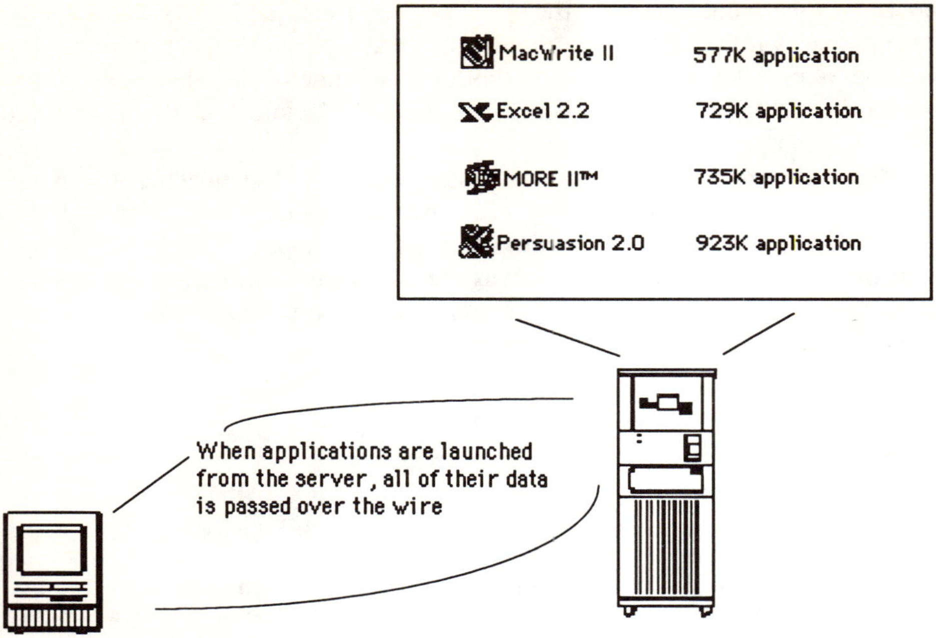

6-13 Large Macintosh applications need high bandwidth to run effectively over a network.

of cost savings, if having the server means an organization does not need to buy hard disks for all the Macintosh clients. The disadvantages include the use of server disk space, and possible effects on performance, if all of a network server's users store and launch their applications on the server. A brief summary of these issues follows.

First, let's summarize the way that application software works. When both a document file and the application program that it came from are stored on your local disk, each time you double click the data file, the Macintosh operating system loads your application program and opens the data file into the application. Both the application program and document are being read into the Macintosh's RAM memory, as shown in Figure 6-13. If you have a hard disk, this happens fairly quickly.

This happens fairly quickly over Ethernet or Token Ring cabling systems, if both the data file and the application program are stored on a NetWare server. If you were connected to the server through a LocalTalk cabling system, however, the process occurs much slower. This is because its bandwidth is unable to move the amount of data from the server to the Macintosh's RAM memory fast enough. Application programs are large files, often 500K or more, take a long time to travel over the wire at LocalTalk bandwidth.

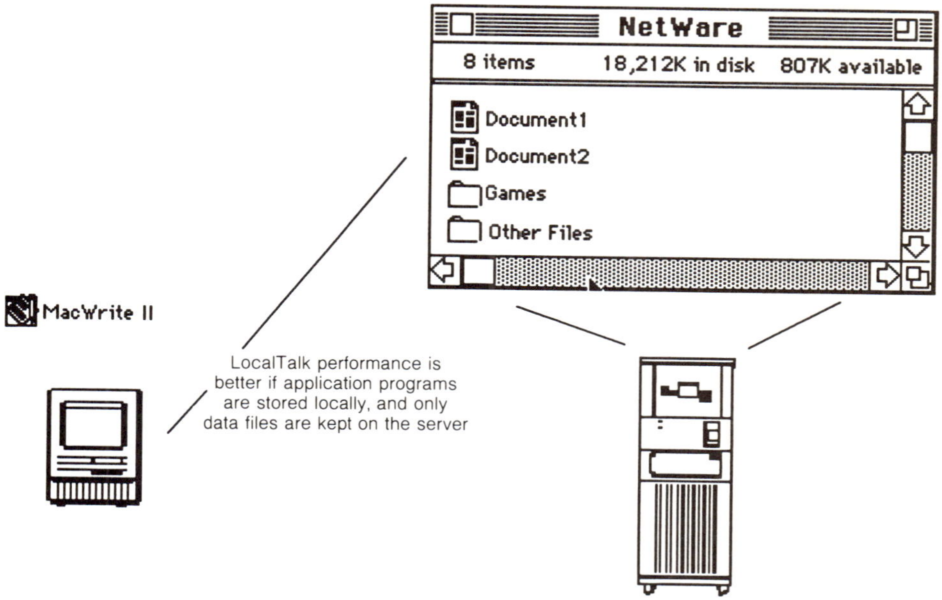

6-14 Efficiency can be improved sometimes by storing applications locally.

The alternative to storing both the application program and the document file on the server is to store the document there, and the application program on your local disk. If your Macintosh has a hard disk, it might solve the performance problem on LocalTalk. You can launch your application program from your local hard disk, and only the document's data will have to travel over the network wire. Assuming your documents are not that large, much less data is transmitted over the network.

This compromise is one that many NetWare for Macintosh users choose. It requires only one adjustment to the way they work in a stand-alone environment, which is using the File-Save As command in their application software's menu to specify the server as the drive to store new documents. Most Macintosh application programs provide a similar interface for this, to what you see from MacWrite II in Figure 6-15. By clicking the Drive button, you can rotate your disk resource between your local disk and the server volume.

If you are on LocalTalk cabling and don't have the benefit of a hard disk, or you don't want to incur the expense, you might decide to put your application programs on the NetWare for Macintosh server anyway. If your Macintosh is on Ethernet or Token Ring cabling, you can do so without any significant performance sacrifices. However, for all users, regardless of the cabling system, a few customs must change when working this way.

When documents and application programs are stored on a NetWare server,

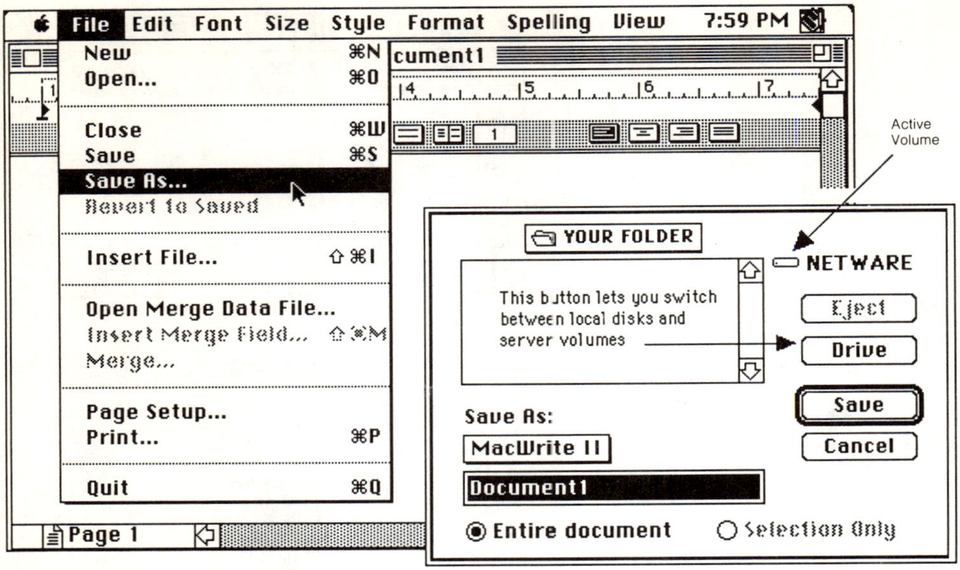

6-15 Macintosh applications can store files easily on NetWare for Macintosh servers.

the isolation you had when you worked stand-alone is lost. Because you were the only one who had access to your local hard disk, there was never any contention from another user for the files you created. If you store a file in a publicly accessible folder on the server, and someone else who has access to it is using it, it might not be available for you to use. If someone else has a file open when you try to open it, you might receive an error message similar to the one in Figure 6-16.

6-16 Some single user applications will display an error message if more than one user tries to launch it.

A worse scenario than that occurs if the application program you are using does not prohibit more than one user from opening a data file. If application programs do not prevent multiple access to data files, then work could be inadvertantly spoiled by another user who had the same file open at the same time. In order to avoid the hassles of intrusion by other users, you might consider keeping your data files on a NetWare for Macintosh server, secure from access by anyone but yourself. This entails making rights settings on your application files or folders that allow only you to access them, which is done with the NetWare Control Center or the NetWare desk accessory (menu item). Figure 6-17 shows a diagram with an example of how that would look to you, if implemented by your organization.

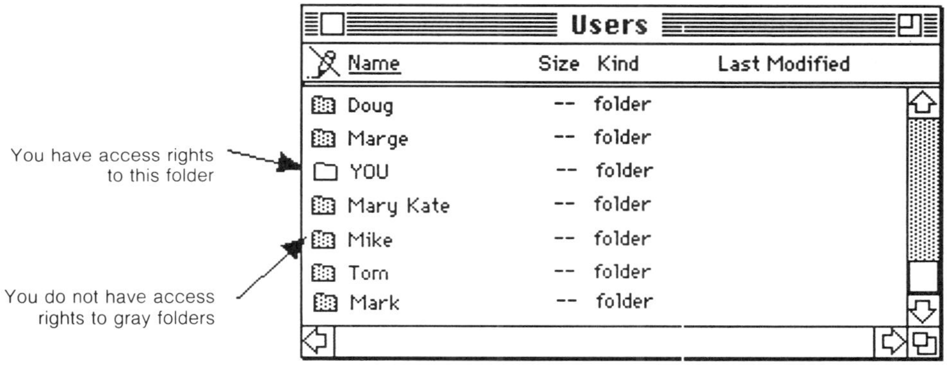

6-17 Folders can be set up to prohibit access by other users.

Fortunately, for the convenience of users, most vendors of major single-user software packages allow multiple users to launch one of their application programs. If they did not, the applications would be difficult to use on a network because there would need to be a separate copy of the application program for each person that used the application. That would take up a great deal of server disk space, and would be very difficult to administer. Generally organizations are required to purchase a copy of the application program for each user or have purchased a software site license, even if users share a copy that is stored on the server. It is not legal for many users to share one copy of a single license application program.

Despite the ability of application programs to support more than one launch, these programs were not neccessarily intended to be shared. They are *single-user* programs. For some end-user applications, single-user programs are a bad choice. For example, if your organzation had a network application that needed to provide access to a database, such as a customer file, single- user applications would not be able to do it. However, some application programs solve this dilemma because they are *multiuser* programs that allow multiple users access to data files.

Multiuser applications

Single-user application programs and multiuser application programs primarily differ in two ways. The first is that multiuser programs were intended to be used by more than one user at a time. When using multiuser application programs and complying with their licensing terms, you are allowed to buy one package of the application for the server and let many clients share it.

The second difference is that when more than one user at a time opens or tries to open the same file, the multiuser application will lock part of the file to avoid conflicts in updating the information in the file. This is called *record locking* or *byte-range locking,* shown in Figure 6-18. These locking schemes allow more than one user to get into the database file, but they prevent the two users of the program from opening the same bits of data at the same time. With record or byte-range locking the program can ensure that one user's changes will not be overwritten by the changes of the other users. Locks on files make sure that a second user cannot access the data until the first user has saved it. The application manages all of this locking, and users only know the difference when they are temporarily denied access to data someone else is using.

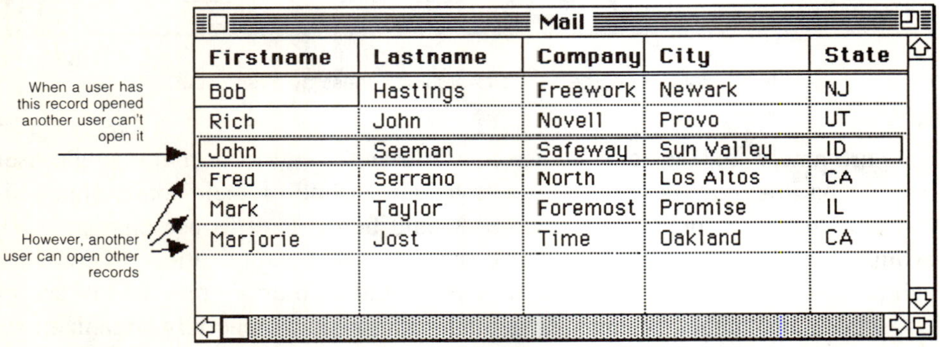

6-18 Multiuser application programs were meant to manage simultaneous users.

Multiuser programs are most often the type that share a common set of data entries. These kinds of programs have files, in addition to the application program itself, that are accessed by multiple users. Macintosh applications include everything from programs that are specifically called database programs (such as Filemaker from Claris, 4th Dimension from Acius, Omnis from Blythe, and others) to programs, such as workgroup calendars and schedulers. Programs such as workgroup schedulers are often referred to as *groupware,* because they were specifically written for collaborative input.

File locking for single user application programs

Single-user applications allow more than one user to open a file, because they do not possess the ability to lock files. They cannot protect users from loss of data if another user opens the file they are working on at the same time. Fortunately, a NetWare for Macintosh server has protections that can prevent that from happening.

One extremely useful feature of NetWare and NetWare for Macintosh is a set of controllable characteristics called *file attributes,* or sometimes referred to as *file flags*. One of the capabilities that these attributes provide is a file locking environment even for single-user applications on NetWare servers. In NetWare v2.x, one of these attributes, called the Non-Sharable attribute, allows you to identify a file that is to be locked by NetWare itself, rather than depending on the application program to do it. In NetWare v3.X, files are automatically flagged this way. When you open a file with an attribute set so that it is not sharable with a single user application program, NetWare will lock the file so no other user can open it until you close it.

There is a set of 13 attributes that control things such as the ability to copy or delete files, hide files, and various other actions. These attributes are discussed further in chapter 7, along with NetWare Rights.

Using features of Macintosh System 7.X with NetWare

Macintosh System 7.X has two features that add new and interesting functionality to networking environments. These features both work with NetWare. One of the features is called *Publish/Subscribe* and is an enhancement for sharing common data among applications. The other feature is called *Aliasing,* which with NetWare works well as a way to automate loggins.

Publish/Subscribe allows you to take data within an application, such as a spreadsheet program, and make that data available to other application programs. This is the publish part of the feature. The subscribe part of the features take that data and incorporate it into another file. Publish/Subscribe creates a link between common data in two different files. The usefulness of Publish/Subscribe is that the changes made to data in the file that published, are automatically reflected in the file that subscribed to the published data. Figure 6-19 shows you a conceptual diagram of two files that are subscribers to data published by another file.

Microsoft Excel 3.0 is a good example of a Macintosh application program that provides publish and subscribe capabilities. In order to publish data, select a range of cells on a Microsoft Excel spreadsheet, and then go up to the Edit menu and pull down the Publish command, as shown in Figure 6-20. When you publish data in a file, a new file is created that is linked to the original data in the

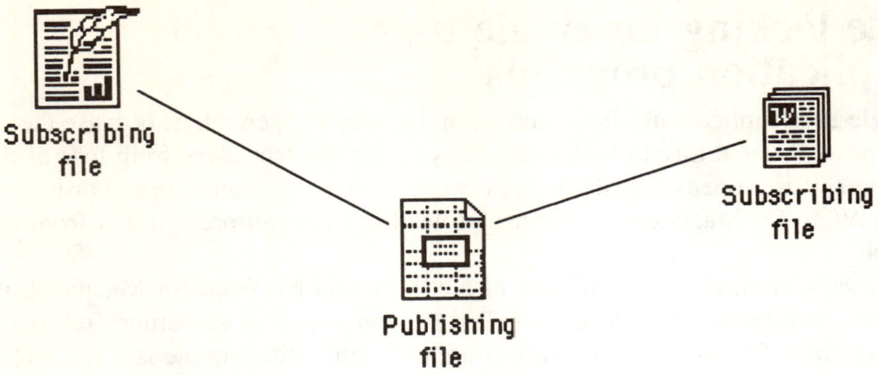

6-19 System 7.X will allow data within different files to be linked together.

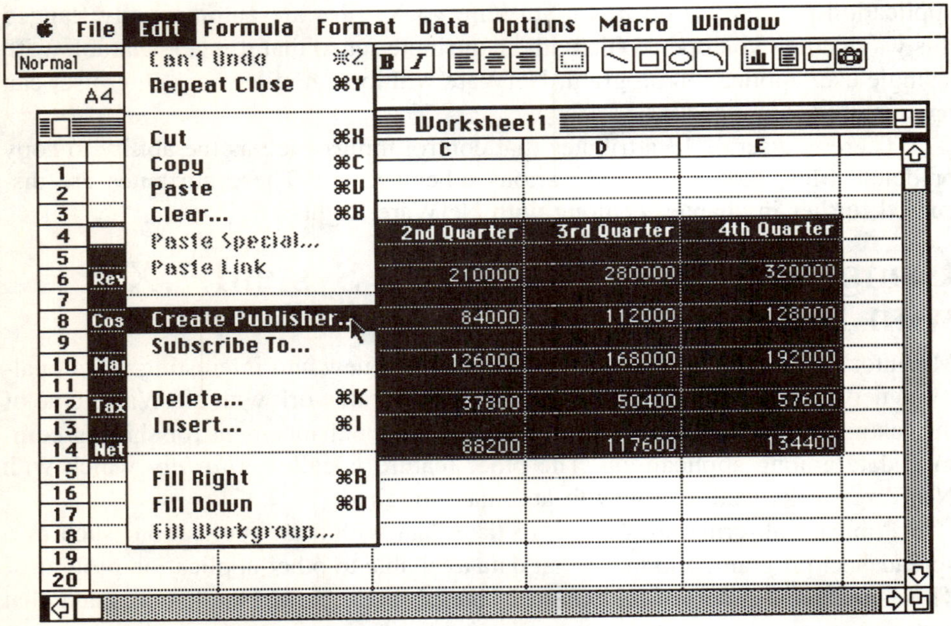

6-20 Publishing data with Microsoft Excel v3.0

spreadsheet. This command asks you to name the file, and then save it to the disk of your choice. If you placed this publish file on a NetWare for Macintosh server, then any networked client potentially can get at it.

In order to subscribe to the published file, a user in the application program that is going to subscribe to the data pulls down the edit menu, and selects the Subscribe command. This command asks the user to select the published file that is being subscribed to. When they select your published file, your data will be pulled into their application. The fascinating thing about the subscribed data is that it retains a link to the original data in your spreadsheet. If you change that data, those changes will be updated in the subscribers file the next time they open the file. This gives significant power to collaborative reports.

Using System 7 aliasing with NetWare for Macintosh

Another Macintosh System 7.X, called *aliasing,* works as a short-cut for logging on to NetWare for Macintosh servers. It also provides a good substitute for the auto-mount feature of AppleShare workstation client software, which gets disabled if you use NetWare for Macintosh's encrypted user authentication.

Aliasing is a method of substituting a file for another file or file server volume. By creating an Alias for a NetWare for Macintosh volume, or even a file that resides on a NetWare for Macintosh volume, you can log into a NetWare for Macintosh server by simply clicking on the alias file.

To create an alias file for a NetWare for Macintosh volume, first log on to a NetWare for Macintosh server by your customary account name, and let the volume sit on your Macintosh desktop. Then, select the volume by clicking on it once, and pull down the Make Alias choice from the Macintosh Finder's File menu, as shown in Figure 6-21.

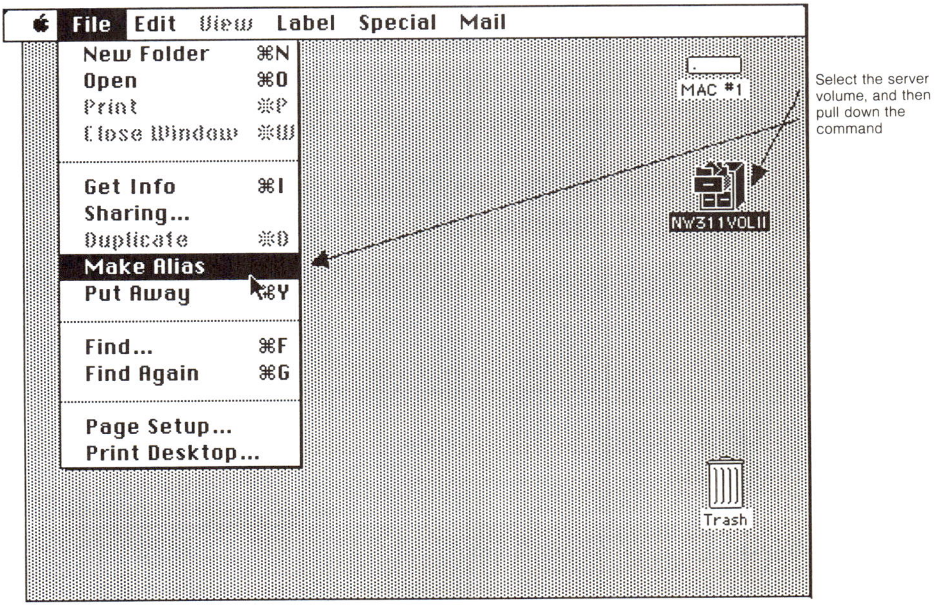

6-21 Making a NetWare volume alias.

In Figure 6-21, you can see that the name of the mounted volume is NW-311 VOL II. When you pull down the Make Alias command with this volume selected on your desktop, System 7. X will create a file called NW-311 VOL II Alias. The Make Alias command always creates a file with the suffix *alias*. The file is tiny, in this example it is 2K. The information in the file is a minimal amount of data that System 7.X needs to link the alias file to the real file it represents, in this case NW-311 VOL II.

An alias is a live link to the real object that it represents. If you double click on an alias, in this example the NetWare for Macintosh volume, it will open the server volume just as if you clicked the server volume. If you are not logged in to the server volume when you double click its alias, the alias will begin to log you in, and take you directly to the AppleShare login screen shown in Figure 6-22. If you create an alias for a file on a NetWare for Macitosh server volume, the alias will begin to login to the server where the real file resides, and then launch the file and the application that it was created in.

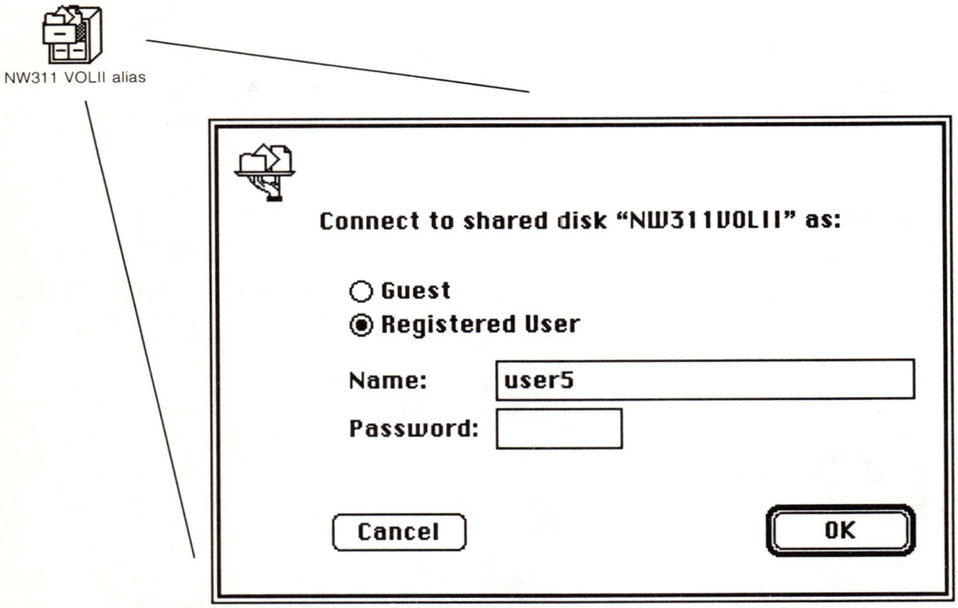

6-22 Double-clicking a NetWare for Maintosh alis will bring you to this window immediately.

Using NetWare for Macintosh print services

Print service access from a Macintosh on a NetWare network is even easier than file service access. Once again, to access this NetWare service, go through the

Macintosh Chooser. When you pull down the Macintosh Chooser, assuming that your Macintosh has the Macintosh LaserPrep and LaserWriter files installed in its System Folder, you will see a LaserWriter icon in the Chooser screen.

After clicking the LaserWriter icon, you are given a list of LaserWriter resources that are available for your selection. NetWare for Macintosh print queues also show up in the Macintosh chooser when a user clicks the LaserWriter icon, see Figure 6-23. In a NetWare for Macintosh environment it is possible that some of the names in the Chooser's LaserWriter list are NetWare print queues, rather than actual LaserWriters.

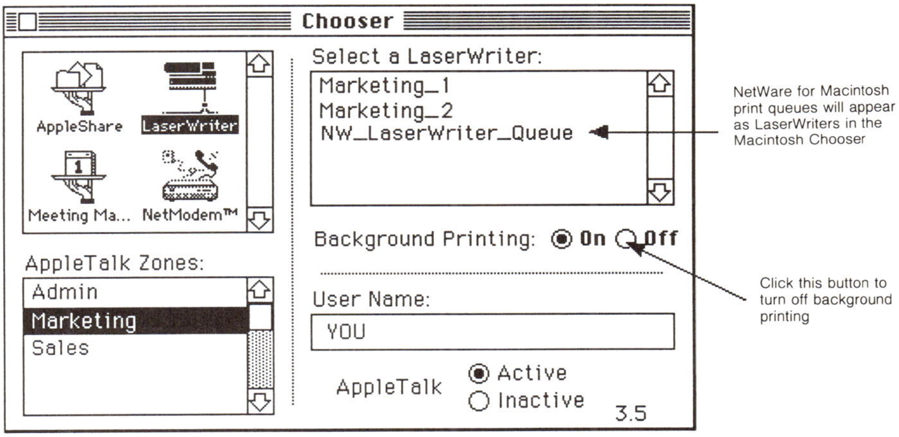

6-23 Print queues spool print jobs to the server, and the server de-queses then to the printer.

A NetWare for Macintosh print queue system is a set of programs that runs on a NetWare server. One of these programs emulates a LaserWriter, which is why users see it in their Chooser. Another program spools and stores the documents that come in, and unspools them according to the order they came in, unless they are rearranged by someone who manages the queue. The functionality that is provided is the same for both NetWare for Macintosh v2.X and v3.X, although the implementation is different. NetWare for Macintosh v2.X uses Value Added Processes (VAPS), and NetWare for Macintosh v3.X uses NetWare Loadable Modules (NLMs).

With NetWare for Macintosh queues running on a server, you can disable the background printing you would probably use if your Macintosh was running MultiFinder in Macintosh System 6.X or Macintosh System 7.X. Figure 6-23 shows how you can use the Chooser to turn off background printing. When you have background printing activated, your Macintosh spools your print jobs to your local hard disk. With NetWare for Macintosh print queues to do the spooling, you are making your Macintosh do processing it doesn't need to do if you keep it on.

Consequently Macintosh print queues often speed a user's printing process, because they are faster than the LaserWriter with its postscript processing. When the server queues the job, it's gone from your computer. Queing also helps the network manager prioritize use of a network's printing resources, as opposed to the first-come, first-served priorities by which network printers accept jobs. In addition, the NetWare for Macintosh print queue permits DOS and UNIX users that have applications with PostScript printer drivers to share the laser printers that the Macintosh computers use. This also benefits Windows and OS/2 users, because Windows and OS/2 have Postscript drivers built-in.

To use a specific NetWare for Macintosh print queue, you must log-in to the server that is running the queue. On any server, multiple print queues can be set up. Generally, a different print queue is set up for each printer that the server hosts. If a single server will be the path to three different printers, that server probably should have three different queues set up. A network server that is the host of many print queues, and also works as a high-demand file server, might at some point begin to degrade in performance because of the burden. The performance problems often can be fixed by installing print queues on a machine separate from the file server if the demands of printer serving cause an unacceptable performance loss on a file server.

In many mixed Macintosh/DOS environments, it is common for another kind of laser printer, such as Hewlett-Packard LaserJet printer and DeskJet printers, to be used instead of Apple LaserWriters. One option that will allow a Macintosh computer to print to HP LaserJets is a PostScript cartridge available from HP. This option makes the LaserJet appear on the network as a LaserWriter, and Macintosh and other clients can access it the same way as an alternative to the LaserWriter through NetWare for Macintosh print queues.

However, in their native modes, printers, such as the HP LaserJet, use a printer language called Printer Control Language (PCL), rather than PostScript, to produce their output. NetWare print services work as a vehicle for Macintosh clients to use printers, such as HP's PCL printers, that are not PostScript, through third-party software that works on top of the NetWare print services.

One example of such a product is called Mosaic, which allows Macintosh computers to print to PCL Hewlett-Packard LaserJet and DeskJet printers. Mosaic was invented by a company called Insight Development Corporation. It consists of software installed on the Macintosh that provides Macintosh clients with a Chooser icon for the HP LaserJet, and a Macintosh printer driver that sends the LaserJet's native PCL printing language to a NetWare print queue. Figure 6-24 shows how a LaserJet appears in the Macintosh Chooser when Mosaic is installed on your Macintosh.

Mosaic is well integrated with both the Macintosh, and NetWare's print

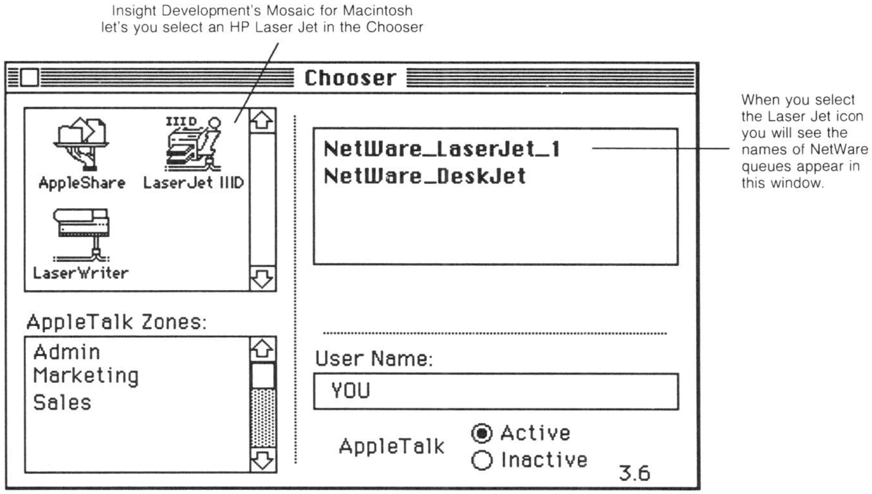

6-24 Insight Development's Mosaic lets Macintosh computers print to Hewlett Packard Laserjets.

queue services. On a Macintosh client, the PCL driver, which is installed in the Macintosh System Folder, takes the images from the screen of the Macintosh and generates PCL code from them. That's basically the same way that the Macintosh's PostScript printer driver works too, except that it generates PostScript. Mosaic even provides Macintosh LaserJet compatibility to the extent that it can allow Macintosh application programs to display LaserJet fonts in their Font menu, as displayed in Figure 6-25.

NetWare print queues allow Macintosh clients using Mosaic's print drivers to access PCL printers that are directly attached to NetWare servers, or even to printers attached to DOS workstations. The combination of NetWare for Macintosh print services and NetWare print queues accessed by Mosaic's printer drivers allows all NetWare clients to share the same printers.

Managing queues with the NetWare desk accessory

The print jobs that you send to NetWare and NetWare for Macintosh print queues are spooled into a queue shared with other users and their print jobs. For you to see where your jobs are ordered in the queue, NetWare for Macintosh provides a tool that you can use to view your spooled documents. The tool, called the NetWare desk accessory, is accessible under the Macintosh's Apple menu, as shown in Figure 6-26.

The NetWare desk accessory actually permits you to do three tasks: you can view spooled print jobs, set and alter the ability other users have to access the

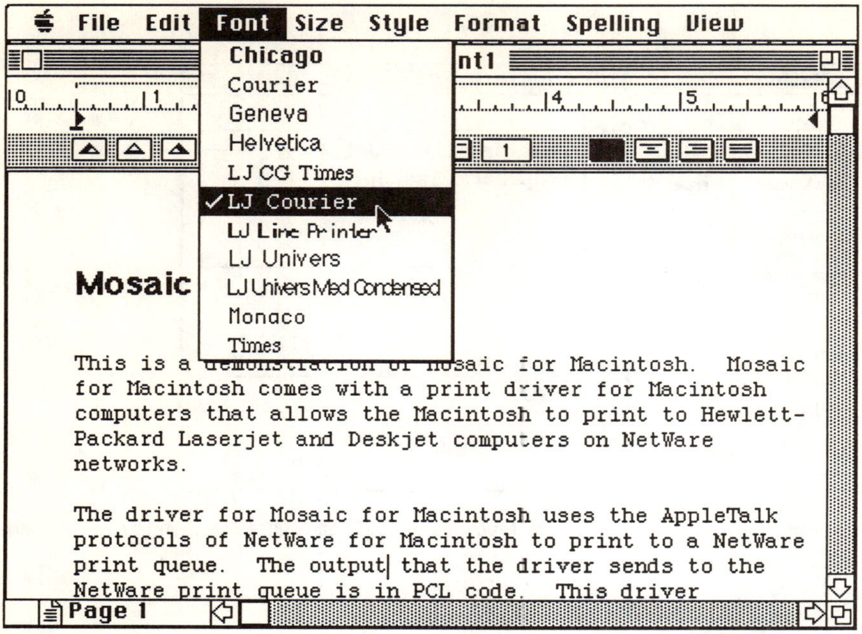

6-25 Mosaic makes LaserJet printer fonts appear in the Macintosh application programs Font menu.

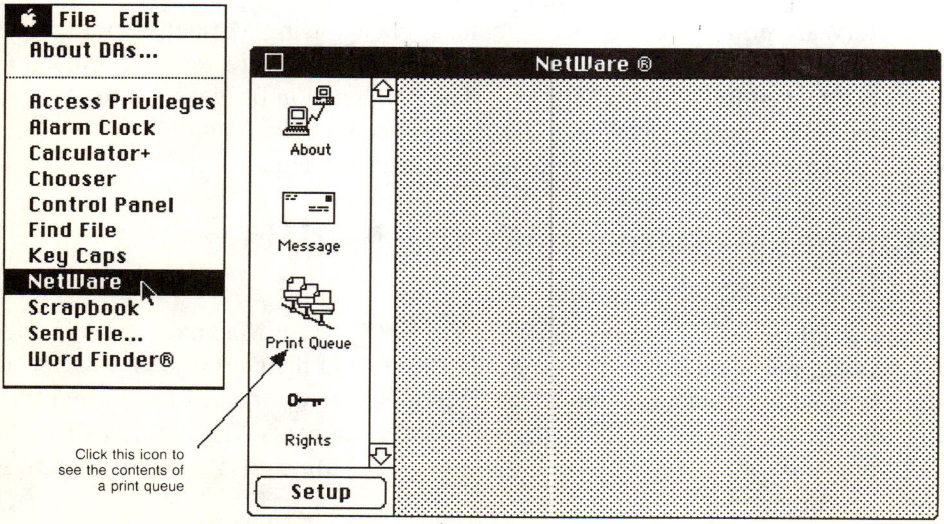

6-26 The NetWare desk accessory is used to view and manage NetWare queues.

data you control, and send messages to other users. In time you will learn about all three tasks, but for now let's stay focussed on print queues. When you pull down the NetWare desk accessory, you receive a window like the one shown in Figure 6-27. The four icons on the window's left hand side represent the operations the DA enables. To view a print queue, click the print icon.

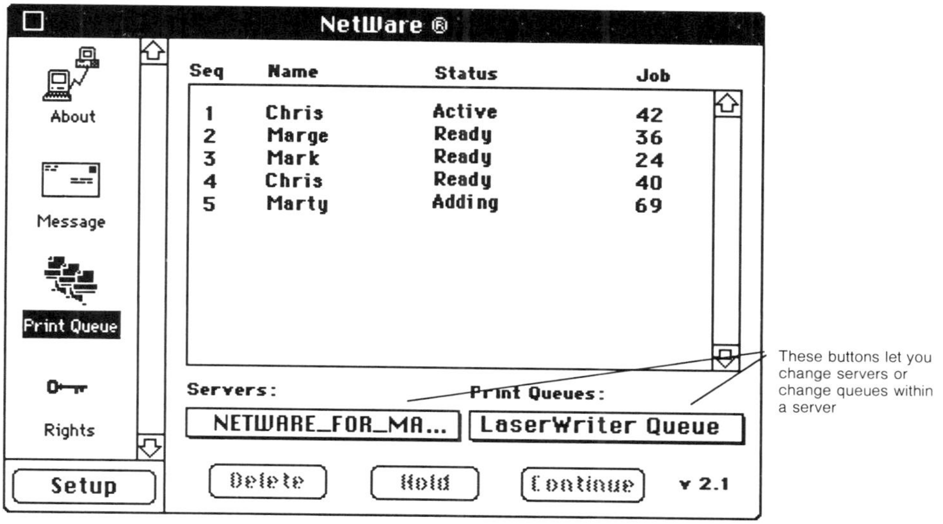

6-27 The NetWare for Macintosh desk accessory viewing a NetWare queue.

Figure 6-27 shows the view the DA provides of a NetWare queue. The names displayed in the queue list represent the users to whom the spooled documents belong. You can see four columns in the list. These four columns, from left to right, are as follows:

Seq This column reports the actual sequence in which queued documents will be printed.

Name This is the user who is printing the document. NetWare displays the account name under which the user is logged in.

Status This is a report on the state of the job. There are five possible messages about the job's status:

Adding. The job is being added to the queue.

Ready. It's in the queue and will be sent to the printer in turn.

Waiting. The job has been set to wait until a certain time to print.

Held. The job is indefinitely postponed, a state in which it stays in until activated again.

Active. The job is in the process of printing or being sent.

Job This displays a number generated by the NetWare queue services that identifies the job. This number is an identifier, and is not meaningful in any context but that. It does not imply the order in which the job will be printed. The print order is explicit by the placement of the jobs in the queue.

In NetWare and NetWare for Macintosh v3.X, print queues are managed by a specially empowered NetWare user, called a *print queue operator*. The print queue operator is a user with the ability to create, manage, disable, and re-enable print queues. Other NetWare users do not have this ability and only can view and alter the print queues placement of their jobs. Print queue operators are assigned by a NetWare supervisor. A supervisor is also a print queue operator. In NetWare and NetWare for Macintosh v2.X, you must be a supervisor to manage print queues.

You will find the NetWare desk accessory very intuitive. In order to delete a print job, select its name and then click the delete button at the bottom of the window. See Figure 6-28. If you want to put a job on hold, select it from the list and then click the Hold button. When a job has been put on hold, you see that status indicated in the Status column. Reselecting the job and then clicking the Continue button changes the jobs status back to Ready. Print queue operators can grab the job they want to move forward or backward in the list and drag it to where you want it to go.

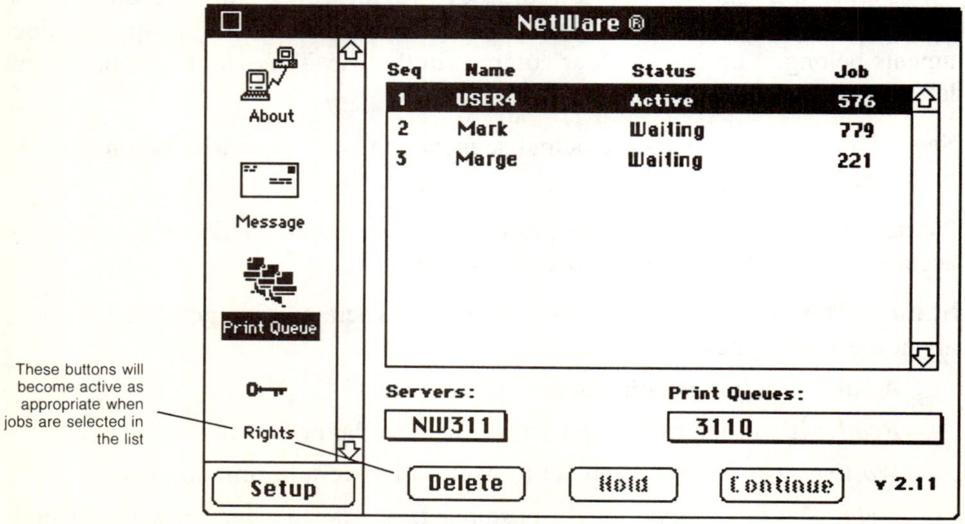

6-28 Deleting a print job with the NetWare desk accessory.

Two selection bars entitled Servers and Print Queues appear above the Delete, Hold, and Continue buttons. The Print Queues bar lets you switch among the queues on a given server. The Servers bar lets you switch servers. Use these bars by holding down the mouse, which makes the lists of choices appear.

Sending NetWare messages

In addition to managing file rights and restrictions, and browsing print queues, the NetWare Desk Accessory allows users to send messages to other NetWare users. The messaging capability of the NetWare desk accessory is not meant to be an electronic mail system. Its 32-character message limit restricts you from sending anything but the most basic notes. Most often the messaging service in the DA is used by people like print queue operators who need to notify all logged in users of some event like a printer that has been temporarily disabled to have toner added. Individual users also could use this feature to try to reach somebody who is on the telephone, and otherwise unavailable. Users can be sent messages only if they are logged in to a NetWare server. If they are logged in and a message is sent to them, they will hear a beep and see the message pop up on their screen.

To send a NetWare message, pull down the DA window and click the message icon, as shown in Figure 6-29. The message window of the NetWare DA permits you to type your message, and then select the user to whom you

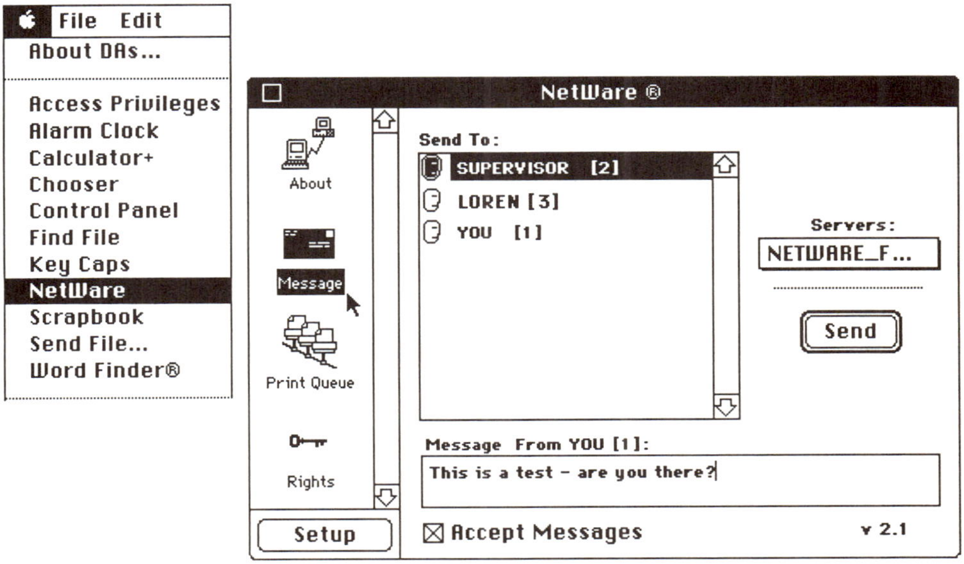

6-29 Macintosh users can send 32 character alerts with the NetWare DA.

want the message to go. The right-hand side of the message window displays a list of the users who are logged in to a NetWare server. You cannot send a message with the desk accessory to a user who is not logged in. To select the user to whom you want the message sent, move through the list and then click the name. Hold down your Macintosh keyboard's shift key while you are clicking names, and multiple names will be selected.

The NetWare for Macintosh Notify file is the reason that messages beep and pop up on Macintosh computer screens of users who are sent messages, as in Figure 6-30. The Notify file is technically called an Init file in System 6.X, and an Extention in System 7.X. It is a program that listens for messages and displays them when it receives one. Init and Extention programs automatically start up when the Macintosh is started if they are in the Mac's System Folder. The NetWare for Macintosh Notify file should be copied into the Macintosh's System Folder when the NetWare desk accessory is installed. In Macintosh System 7.X, it should go into a folder inside the System Folder, called Extensions. If the user who is to be the recipient of the message does not have the Notify file in his or her System Folder, he or she will not get the message.

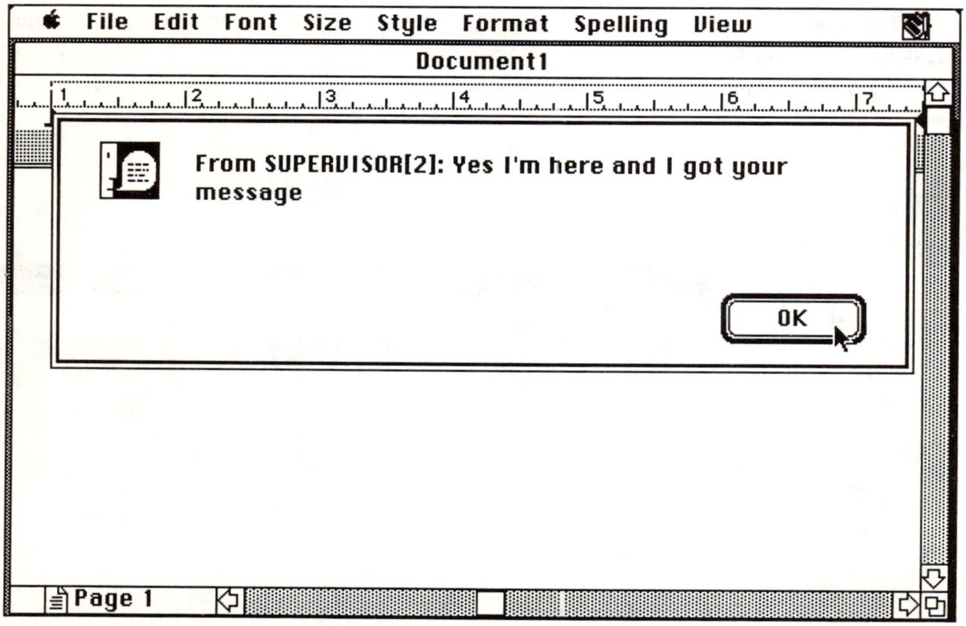

6-30 Messages from other NetWare users will pop up on a Macintosh.

7
Chapter

NetWare security

Discussion of the NetWare Desk Accessory's ability to set and alter file rights and restrictions was postponed in the previous chapter so that the subject could be given proper attention. This chapter provides a detailed overview, and covers the many methods that are used in NetWare networks to maintain security.

Chapters that follow demonstrate practical applications for the security measures explained here. Please feel free at any point to jump ahead to the next chapter, if practical application examples will help you better understand the overviews to some of NetWare's methods for limiting access rights.

What is security and why do you need it?

Security is something every network user should be informed of. In networking, security is a general term for the safegards that protect the quality, integrity, and confidentiality of the data stored and passed on network resources. This includes protections given to data as it is warehoused on the server, and data as it is passed over the network wire.

Security is important because a network is a shared resource that can be accessed by many users. Your computer network is probably a fundamental part of the operation of your organization. The security of the network ensures that none of these users naively, inadvertantly, or deliberately damage the system, the data, or gets access to documents that they shouldn't have.

It's not unreasonable to imagine, for example, that your organization might have an accounting system that runs on the network server. That accounting system would hold your organization's financial records. If they were to be damaged, your organization might have difficulty reassembling the information. If your network couldn't limit access to the accounting system to those users who knew how to properly use it, your system would be at risk. Suppose also that this accounting system did your organization's payroll. Payroll information should be confidential. Only certain people should have access to it. If the network could not ensure this confidentiality, the privacy of the employees in your organization would be compromised.

Security is a positive protection for the organization, and for the user too. Both the organization and the user must be confident that the items they place on network file servers will be used only in the way they were intended to be used. Novell NetWare can help an organization ensure that a NetWare system is secure in several ways.

Secured access and user environments

One kind of security that NetWare provides is access control over the server and its resources, which descends from the requirement that all NetWare users must be assigned an account. A user must login to a NetWare server under the identity of that account in order to use it. Attached to that account is a user password, which helps ensure that no improper account access happens. Optional safeguards can be set so that users must make periodic password changes to minimize the likelihood that any user's passwords is found out. Additional account parameters can limit users by the time of day, and stations from which they login to a NetWare network. NetWare access security is quite comprehensive, as shown in Figure 7-1.

In addition to the initial access restrictions, NetWare accounts allow network supervisors to give individual users their own individual security profile, and to keep audit trails of the login activity of users. These features help supervisors maintain and monitor the continued reliability of the safeguards they put in place.

Types of users

The second form of security is the abilty of NetWare to recognize four primary types of users, each with their own network access privileges and capabilities. These levels are: regular network users and groups, operators, workgroup managers, and network supervisors.

Regular user A regular user is a person who has basic access to the network resource. Assuming that one has access privileges, regular users can store and retrieve files on servers, print to queues, use databases and other applications, send messages, and administer their personal environments. An entity related to regular users is called a *group*. Groups are a category of regular users that can be assigned security privileges collectively rather than individually. For example, everyone in the accounting deparment could be assigned to a group called Accounting. Then everyone in the Accounting group could be given access to the applications and print queues that are set up for their department.

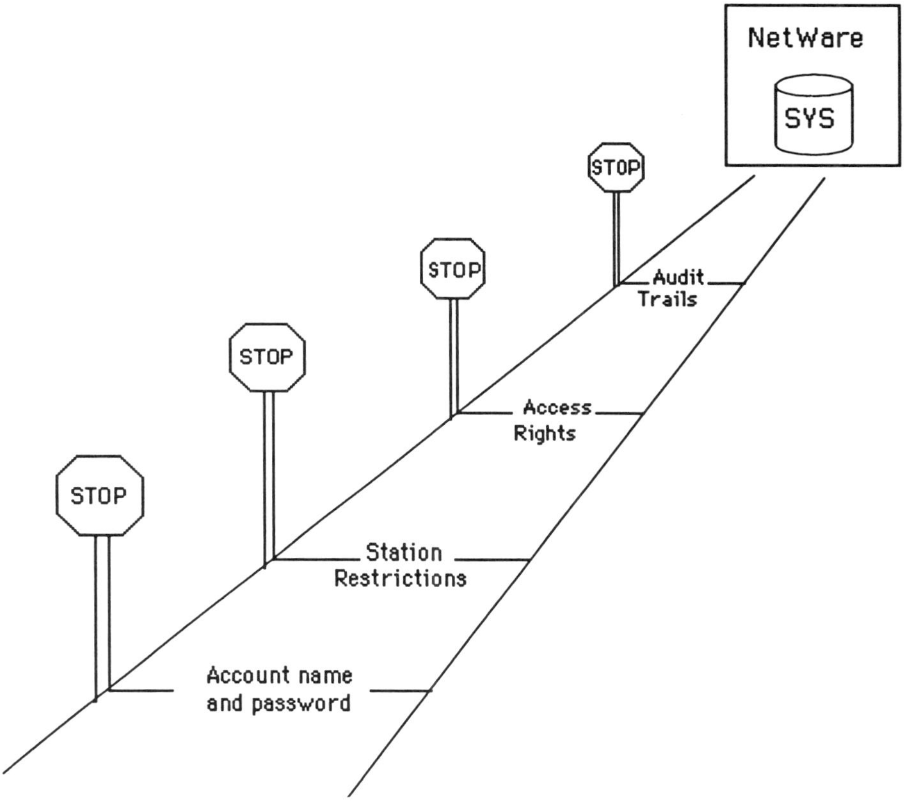

7-1 NetWare has many levels of security.

Operator An operator is a regular network user who is given additional responsibilities over certain network activities. One kind of operator, the print queue operator, was discussed in the last chapter. The print queue operator can reorganize, hold, and delete print jobs from print queues, where a regular user might be able to only view a print queue. Another type of operator, called a file server console operator, might do a workgroup's file backup, because he or she might have the ability to read folders and files that other regular users do not have access to.

Workgroup manager A workgroup manager is a user with broader access rights and responsibilities than either a user or an operator. Generally they have all the same access rights as operators, but in addition, workgroup managers can create new users and groups and manage their accounts. The workgroup manager also can assign users to be operators.

Network supervisor The last type of user, a network supervisor, is the most empowered user on a NetWare network. When an organization's management has determined the access rights that will be given to NetWare users, the network supervisor is probably the one who sees that they are implemented. Network supervisors designate workgroup managers, create and maintain the primary folder structure of the network's servers, and set the security privileges of all other network users and workgroup managers. Network supervisors set the initial password to the system, so that only they will have full access privileges to the entire network system (unless they also give those privileges to others). A network supervisor has ultimate control over the file servers on the network.

The purpose of these different types of users is that a network supervisor can be responsible for maintaining the systems integrity, yet not be the only resource for the day-to-day support of the users. The network supervisor can concentrate on maintaining the global facets of the network. Workgroup managers and operators can be created to help support and maintain the needs of individual workgroups. Users can be assured that they get access to the things they need, yet are shielded from the technical complexity of managing the system.

Limiting access to the server

The supervisor of a system has the right to determine who is given access to the server, and to what extent that access is provided. A supervisor can give a user access to all of the server's resources, or limit the user by criteria, such as the folders they are allowed to see, the number of files they can create, or the amount of storage space they can use.

One way a supervisor can give users shared file access is to create a folder that is accessible by everyone. That method works well for casual exchanging of files, but it isn't very secure. In addition to shared folders that all, or a group of users, access in common, the supervisor often creates personal folders for regular users and lets those users control their own folders. This provides better individual security for users because they have the ability to control the access that other users are given to their files. They can let everybody access their files, let only some other users access them, or prevent anyone else from accessing them. See Figure 7-2.

The privilege to access a server's file system is granted by the assignment of characteristics, called *rights*. Rights security determines which folders and files a user can access, and what the user is allowed to do with those folders and files. For example, users can be permitted to read files from a folder, but not write files to the folder.

A common scenario for the application of NetWare Rights is that a supervisor sets up a folder in which network applications that are shared among users are stored in addition to the shared folder previously illustrated. The supervisor also sets up a folder that contains a personal folder for all of the network users. An example of this configuration is shown in Figure 7-3. Typically in this sce-

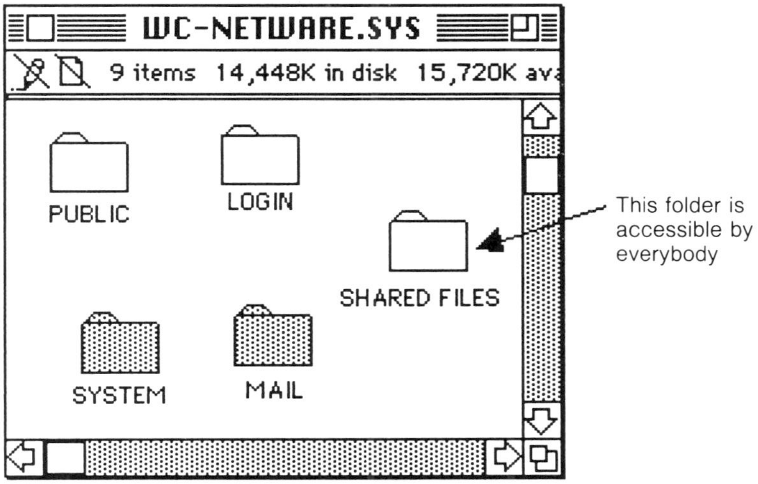

7-2 A publicly shared volume gives all users access to files.

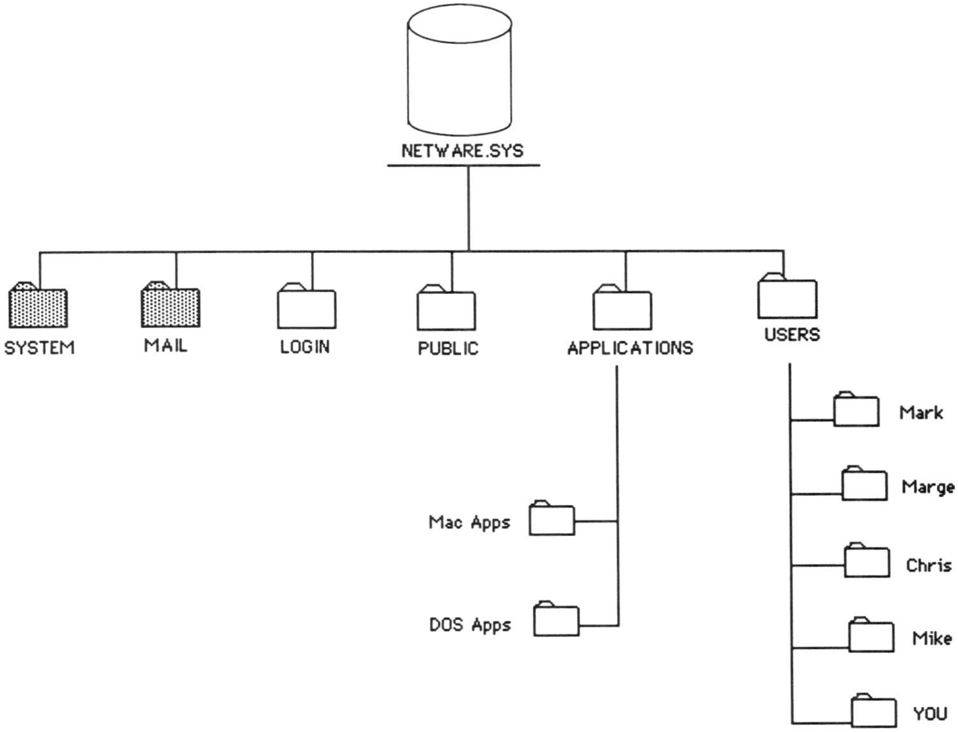

7-3 An example of a file system that is expanded to include user folders.

nario, a user can read and run any of the programs in the applications folder, the user can not write to or delete files from this folder. The Users folder, however, has different rights. The User folder contains personal folders for users who probably have complete access rights to them, including the right to create other folders that branch from them. If this is the case, from the point of their personal folder and beyond, the users themselves are the managers of the file system.

Users must have a basic understanding of the NetWare system of file rights and restrictions in order to manage their own file environments. In a workgroup situation where users often need to collaborate on projects, users often must make some data that they have stored in their personal folders available to other users. Users need to know how to use the NetWare desk accessory to change the rights of files and folders in order to grant others access to files, because users have no rights to another user's personal directory unless that person gives them rights. Sooner or later, every user needs to do that.

Managing and securing files with NetWare access rights

In NetWare and NetWare for Macintosh terminology, to give a user or group rights to a folder or a file is to make them a *trustee*. NetWare has a set of eight potential trustee rights that can be given to a user or group. These rights vary slightly between NetWare versions 2.X and 3.X. One way they differ is that in NetWare v2.X, trustee rights are applied to the entire contents of folders; in NetWare v3.X, trustee rights can be assigned to entire folders or to individual files within folders. For the most part, however, the trustee rights work the same across NetWare versions.

A trustee can be given all trustee rights to a folder or file, or only some of them. For NetWare v3.X versions the rights are:

Create The right to create new folders and files.

Read The right to open and read existing files.

Write The right to save and make changes to files.

Modify The right to change folder names, file names and attributes.

Erase The right to delete folders and files.

File Scan The right to see folders and files.

Access Control The right to make trustee and trustee rights assignments.

Supervisory The right to do everything a supervisor can do in this folder and all of its nested folders.

For NetWare v2.2 and descendents that will follow, the rights trustees can be given are:

Create The right to create new folders and files.

Read The right to open and read files.

Write The right to save and make changes to files.

Modify The right to change folder names, file names and attributes.

Erase The right to delete folders and files.

File Scan The right to see folders and files.

Access Control The right to make trustee and trustee rights assignments.

You might have had encounters with folders or files that had restricted rights already. If you tried to access a folder, such as the NetWare folder called System, which is one of the folders on a NetWare SYS volume, as a NetWare user you were unable to open it. This is probably because you were not a trustee of the folder, and so you had no rights to it.

NetWare rights compared to AppleShare access privileges

The NetWare rights system provides a flexible method of limiting or opening up user access to data . If you have ever been a client to an AppleShare server, you might have used a similar system of data access controls, called Access Privileges. The NetWare system of rights is analogous to AppleShare's Access Privileges, it's but more comprehensive.

There are several major differences between NetWare's Trustee Rights and AppleShare's Access Privileges. One of the differences is that NetWare permits multiple trustees on any file or folder. This feature lets supervisors and users grant folder and file rights to other individual users, and not just to entire groups. It also makes users less dependent on supervisors and workgroup managers for routine rights changes. Another major difference between NetWare Trustee Rights and AppleShare Access privileges is NetWare v3.X's ability to set rights on individual files, rather than just the folders that files reside in. Finally, the set of NetWare rights is much more sophisticated than the relatively small number of AppleShare privileges. Figure 7-4 contrasts the differences between the NetWare and AppleShare systems.

The method that AppleShare workstation client software uses in system 6.X to assign Access Privileges to data on an AppleShare server is a command called *Get Privileges*. The Get Privileges command, which is available under the Macintosh Finder's File menu, opens the window you see in the left-hand side of

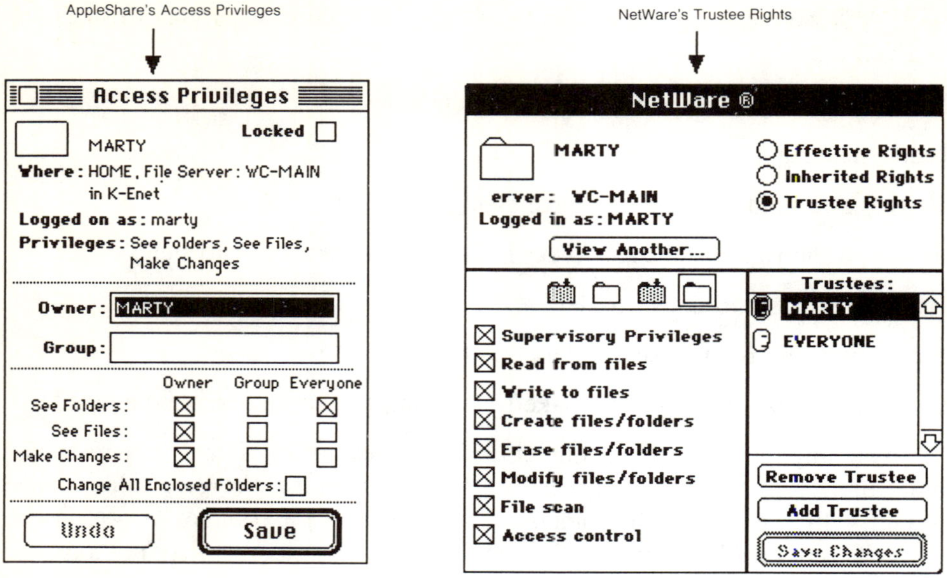

7-4 NetWare Rights vs. AppleShare Access Privileges.

Figure 7-5. In Macintosh System 7.X, a similar command called *Sharing* is also available under the File menu.

The Get Privileges command works with NetWare for Macintosh servers too, because NetWare for Macintosh clients use AppleShare workstation client software. However, to properly set NetWare rights, users should use the NetWare for Macintosh desk accessory or NetWare Control Center. The Get Privileges command is unable to always report the true state of rights on a NetWare server, because it is unable to display the full set of NetWare rights.

However, NetWare will let your Macintosh display AppleShare icons when the NetWare rights settings match AppleShare Access Privileges. Figure 7-6 shows icons that represent common AppleShare settings for Folders, and how they map to NetWare Trustee Rights.

Changing trustee access rights with the NetWare desk accessory

You have two utilities that you can use to set or change NetWare trustee rights. One tool is the NetWare Control Center, the other is the NetWare desk accessory (menu item in System 7.X). The difference between them for rights assignment is that the NetWare desk accessory by its nature, can be accessed from within any application program. The NetWare Control Center, however, is an application program itself, which only can be launched from the Finder.

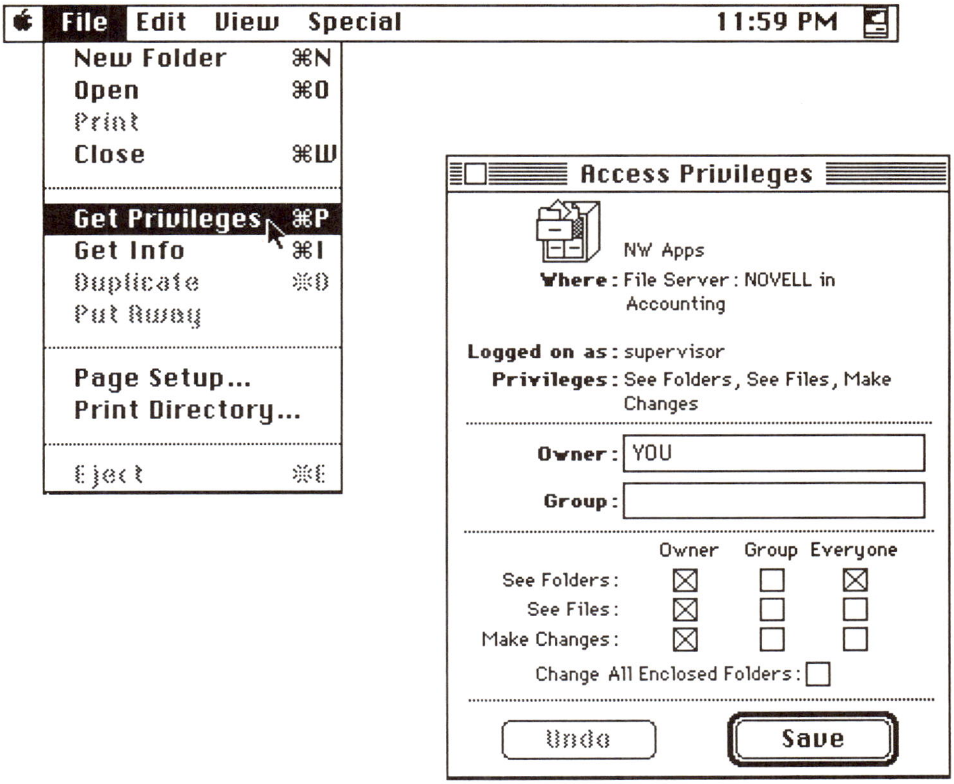

7-5 Get Privileges is under the Finder's File menu.

If you are a network supervisor, you can use the NetWare desk accessory to make changes to anybody's folder rights. With NetWare v2.X, you can make changes to folders even if you are not a network supervisor, as long as you have Access Control rights to a folder. With NetWare v3.X, you also can make changes even if you are not a network supervisor, as long as you have been given Access Control or Supervisory rights. Again, with NetWare v3.X, these rights can be applied to individual files as well as folders.

If you are not a NetWare supervisor, then most often it is your own folders and data to which you are given the Access Control or Supervisory rights. One of the most common reasons you might want to change the access rights that other users have to your own data folders is to make your folder a drop box, so other users can put files into them. To see a file or folder's rights, and alter them if you have that capability, use the Rights section of the NetWare Desk Accessory, depicted in Figure 7-7.

The NetWare DA has the capability to permit its user to create trustees (if they have the Access Control right or Supervisory right to do so), and to alter

Rights Setting	Icon	Explanation
Gray Folder (No access rights)		With NetWare for Macintosh v2.X you see folders that you can't access as gray. With NetWare for Macintosh v3.X, folders to which you have no access rights are invisible.
Drop box (Create right only)		This is a folder in which you have the right to place file into this type of folder, but you do not have the right to open it.
Plain Folder (File Scan right)	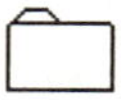	This icon represents folders to which you have, at minimum, the ability to open. You may also have the ability to read files from it, write files to it, and more. If so, the folder that represents it will still look this way. If you do not have read and write access to the files in this kind of folder, when you open the folder you will see AppleShare icons that look like the ones at the left.
(no write)		
(no write & no read)	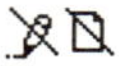	
Black Tab Folder (Access control or Supervisor right)		If you have the right to change a folder's rights settings then it will show up with a black tab.
Drop box with Access Control		You can't see the contents of a black tab, gray folder, but you can change its security so that you can see the contents. There is absolutely no practical use for this, but in NetWare for Macintosh v3.X, if your rights setting ever get put in this state, this is what you would see

7-6 Icons displaying common access rights settings.

rights for either a NetWare v2.X or a NetWare v3.X server. In order to view or make changes to a trustee's access rights to a folder, first pick the relevant folder in the mini-finder window of the DA's rights section, and then click the Folder Info button, as shown in Figure 7-8.

The assignment screen of the NetWare desk accessory's Rights section, shown in figure 7-8, will determine if it is viewing a v2.X or a v3.X server automatically, and show the appropriate sets of choices for rights. This assignment screen has three viewing modes, one to view trustee rights, and two others to view settings that haven't been explained yet, called effective rights and maximum or inherited rights. To make changes to trustee rights, click the Trustee Rights button in the screen's upper-right corner, and then pick the relevant trustee from the list that appears on the right.

Trustees can be users or groups. Suppose you want to make a folder a drop box for all users in the group called Everyone. In Figure 7-9, you can see that the group Everyone is already a trustee of the folder that is being modified. If you want to change one of the trustee rights for the group Everyone, first choose

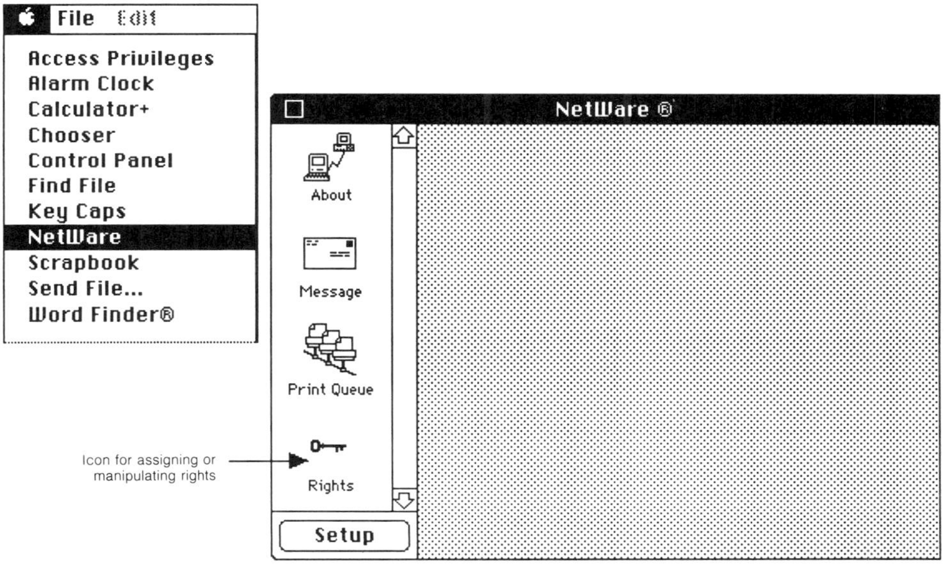

7-7 Choosing the Rights module of the NetWare desk accessory.

Everyone from the trustee list, and then click on or off the rights boxes to set the appropriate rights. When the setting is turned on, an X will be visible in the box.

The NetWare DA's Rights assignment screen provides a feature worth mentioning that sometimes makes rights assignment easier. Again in Figure 7-9, you can see that at the top of the rights list are several icons of folders. These icons are provided as shortcuts for rights assignments. For example, to create a drop

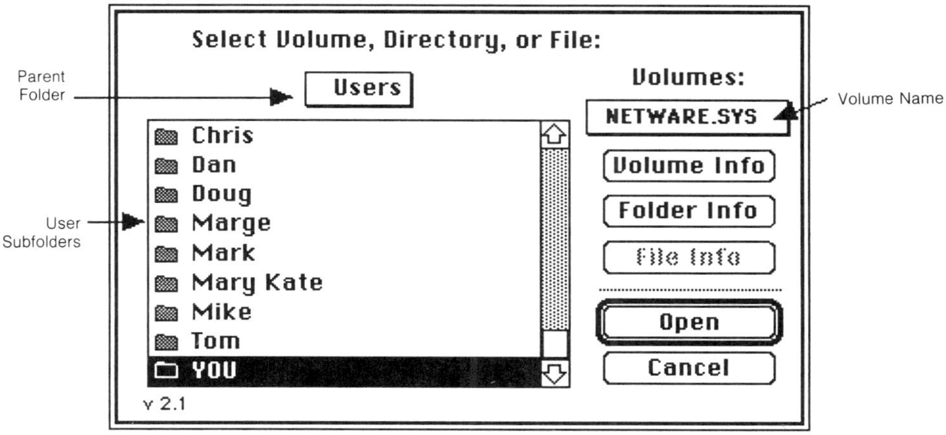

7-8 Selecting a folder to display folder information.

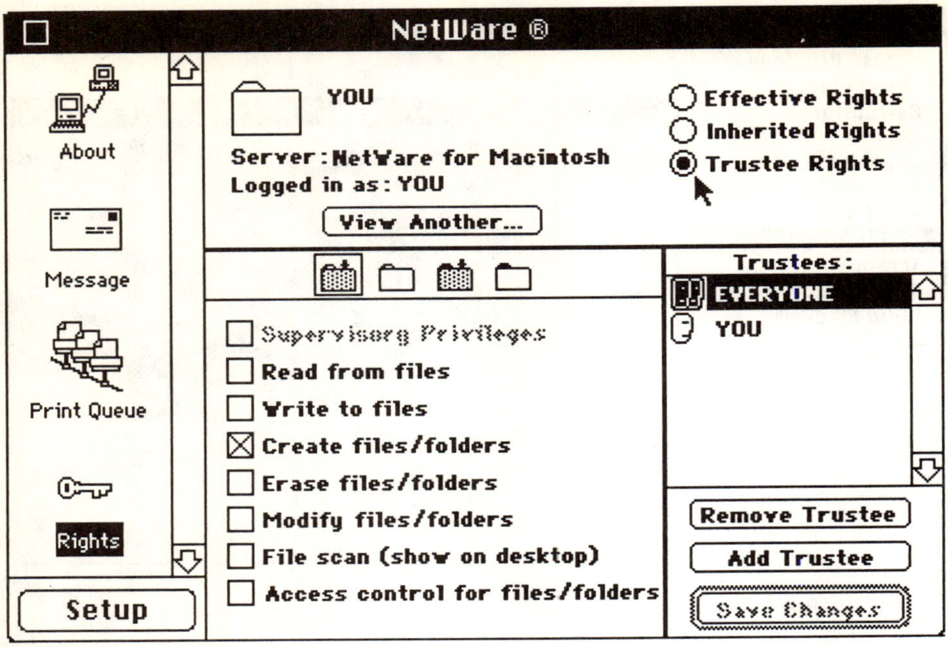

7-9 Setting Trustee Rights with the NetWare desk accessory.

box, you simply can click the box on the far left. The icon looks like a drop box folder. Figure 7-10 shows the sets of rights that map to each icon in the Rights assignment screen.

Assigning trustees

If a user is already a trustee of a folder or file, and you only need to change those trustee rights, then it is simply a matter of clicking the correct boxes to set the rights. If a user or group is not already a trustee of the file or folder, however, you need to make them trustees before you can give them rights. To create new trustees for the folder shown in Figure 7-11, click the Add Trustee button.

Following your command to add a trustee, the NetWare DA shows you a window of the server's users, as shown in Figure 7-11. When you click on the name of the desired user or group, the Add button becomes active. Choose Add, and you are finished. Then you can select the trustee from the folder's trustee list and assign the trustee's rights. Trustees can be removed in a similar fashion.

Exceptions to trustee access rights

Trustees are the way that users are given rights to folders (and files with NetWare 3.X) in the NetWare file system. Although trustee rights are attached to a folder, they belong to the trustee. Each user of a particular folder can be given a differ-

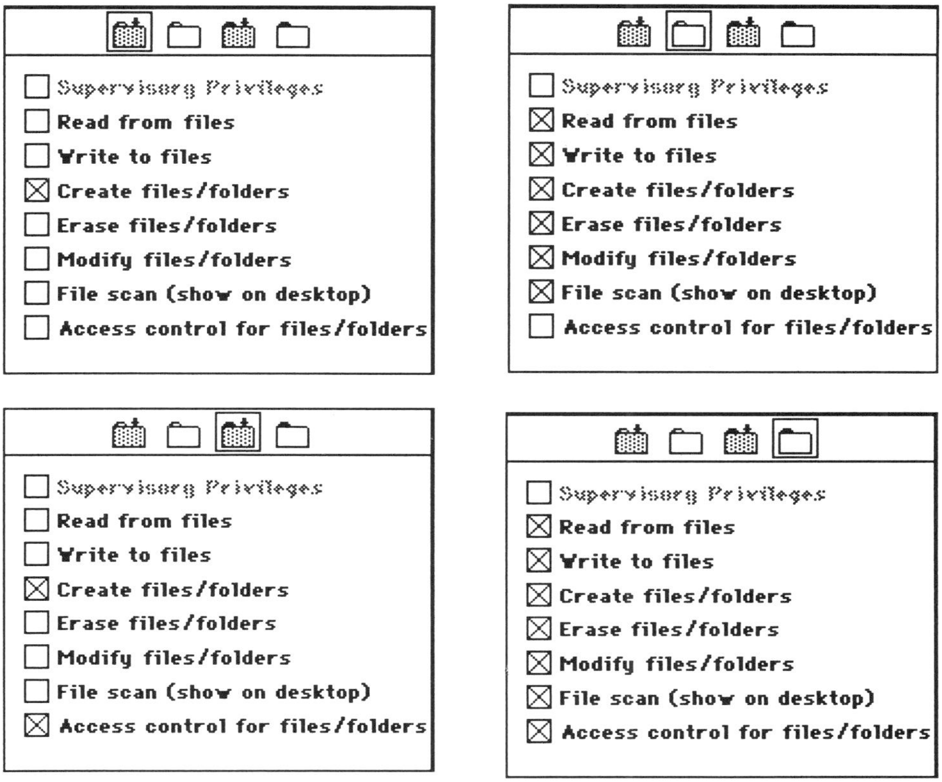

7-10 Shortcuts for assignments of rights.

ent set of trustee rights. Likewise, each user can have different trustee rights to different folders. This is demonstrated in Figure 7-12.

Independent of the trustee rights, which can vary between trustees, folders can be given special sets of rights called *masks*. Masks are sets of rights that can apply uniformly to all of a folder's trustees. In NetWare v2.X, these sets of rights are called a *Maximum Rights Mask,* and in NetWare v3.X, they are called an *Inherited Rights Mask*. Both of these rights masks fulfill the same general purpose, although they work a little differently. They are settings that can override and make exceptions to assigned trustee rights. The advantage of these rights masks is that they provide a way to change the rights of all of a folder's trustees without having to change the rights of all of the trustees one by one.

This example demonstrates the benefit of a rights mask. Imagine a server that contains a folder called Miscellaneous. Suppose that in addition to yourself, the folder had three user trustees (Steve, Dave, and Kathy), and a group trustee called Everyone. Figure 7-13 shows this example, and the rights that are as-

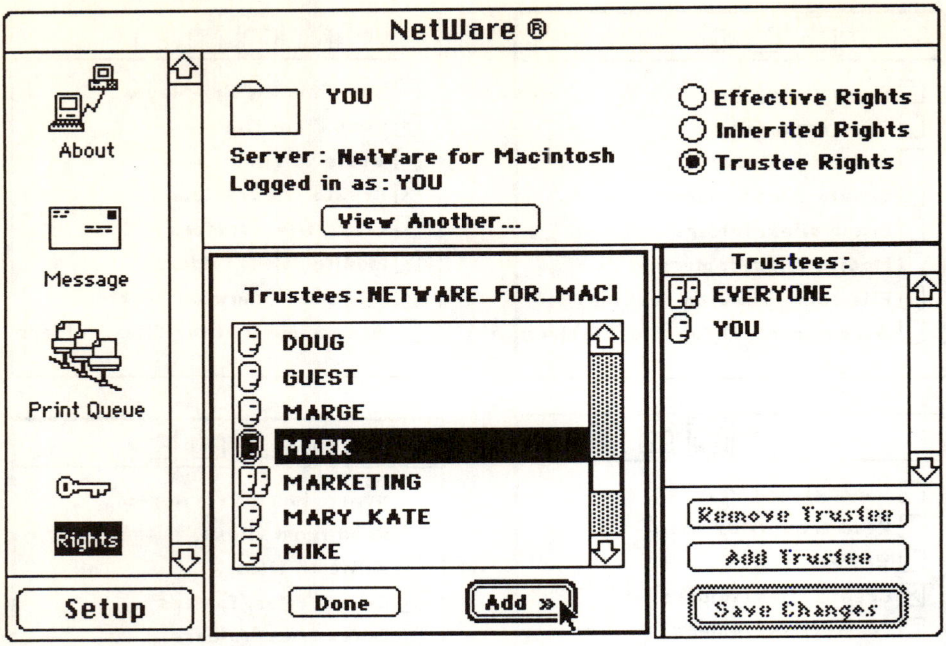

7-11 Adding a trustee to a folder.

signed to the trustees. Without a rights mask, if you wanted to change the rights of all the trustees in the folder so that each could read and write only existing files, and not create new files or erase existing files, you would have to go in and individually change the access rights of each trustee. With a rights mask, however, you can make only one change and have it apply to all of the trustees.

When folders are created on either a NetWare v2.X or v3.X server, they receive a mask that permits all trustee rights to be set. The mask later can take some of these rights away by having some of the permissible rights in the mask modified, so that they are not allowed.

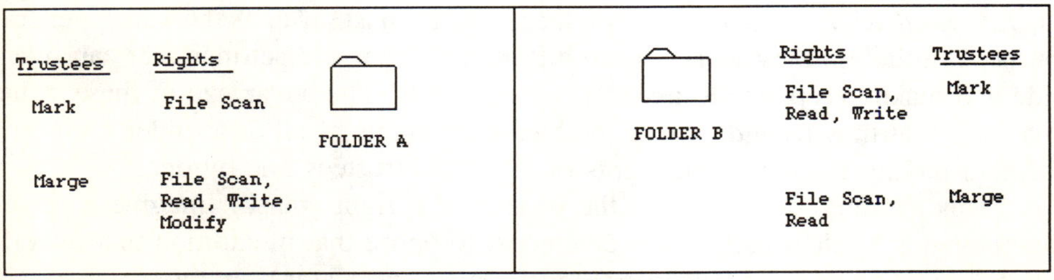

7-12 Folders can have multiple trustees, and any user can be a trustee to multiple folders.

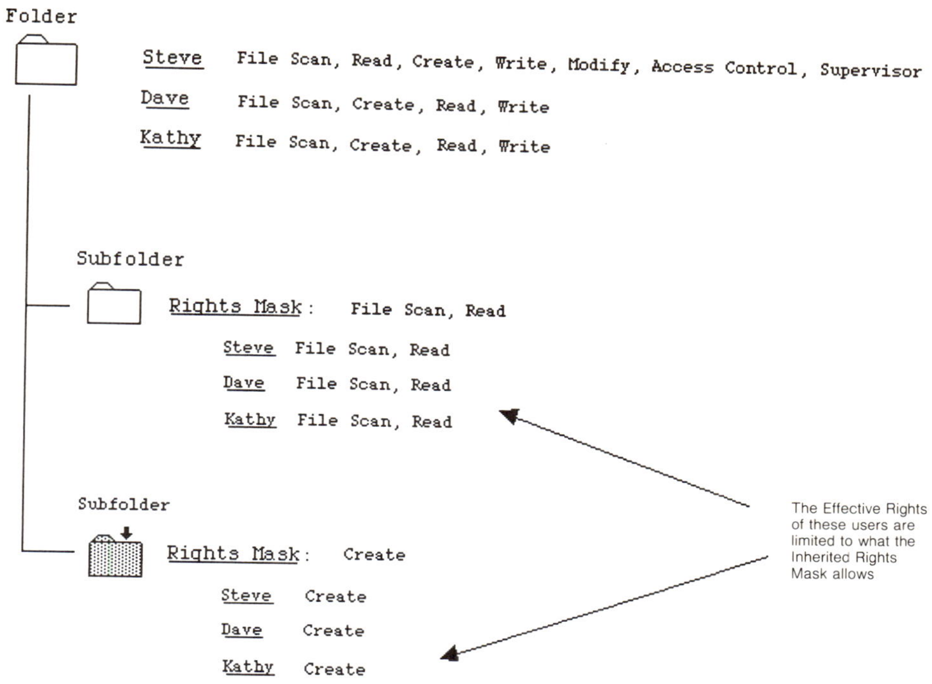

7-13 Rights Masks make exceptions to trustee rights.

The set of rights that the folder is left with in this example are referred to as the folders *Effective Rights*. Any user's effective rights to a folder consist of the trustee rights the user is given to the folder minus the rights that the rights mask has taken away. An example of how this formula is applied is shown in Figure 7-14. If users or supervisors never want the rights mask to make exceptions to trustee assignments, they should leave the rights mask in a state that always permits all rights.

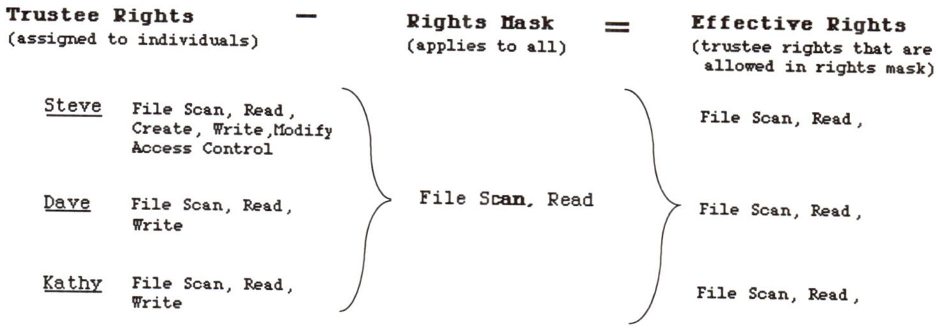

7-14 How Effective Rights are derived.

The Maximum Rights Mask for NetWare v2.X and the Inherited Rights Mask for NetWare v3.X differ in a couple of ways. The biggest difference is that a NetWare v2.X Maximum Rights Mask applies to only a single folder. In contrast, a NetWare v3.X Inherited Rights Mask applies not only to a single folder, but all folders nested within it, shown in Figure 7-15.

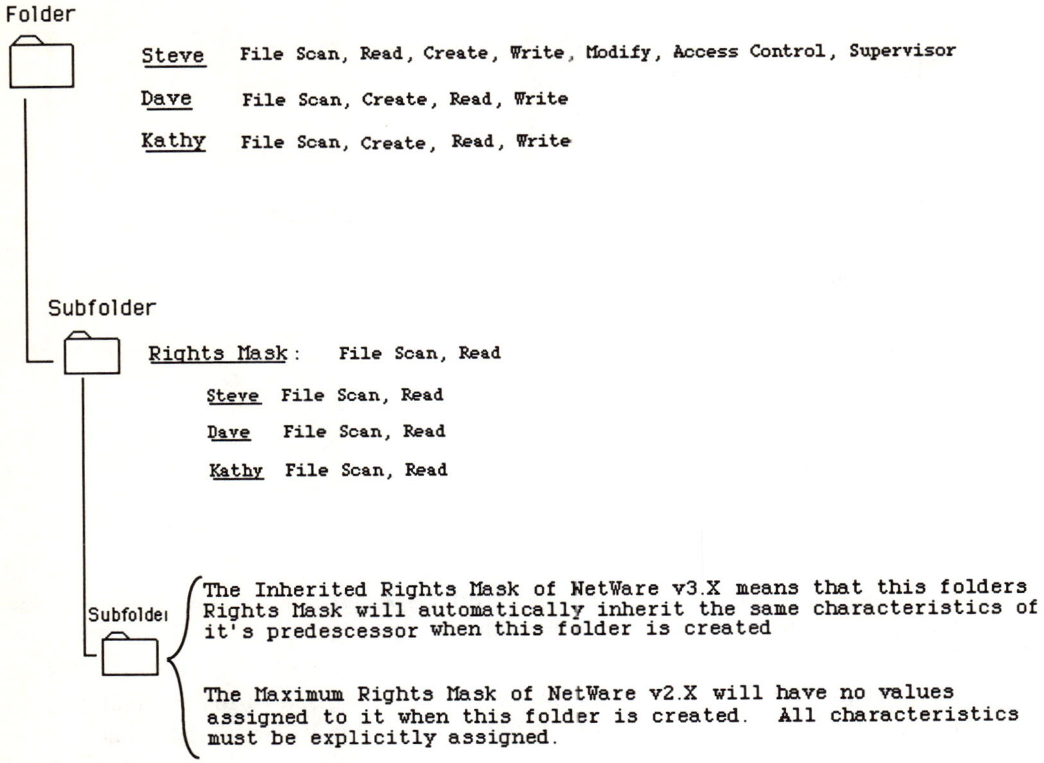

7-15 The Inherited Rights Mask versus the Maximum Rights Mask.

The second difference between Maximum Rights Masks and Inherited Rights Masks is that Maximum Rights Masks are absolute, and no trustee can ever be given more rights than the mask allows. The Inherited Rights Mask of NetWare v3.X, on the other hand, can be overridden in nested folders by assigning new trustee rights. The Inherited Rights Mask is in effect through a server's nested folders, until either the mask is changed or new trustee assignments are made.

Rights that were taken away on one level of a server's hierarchy by an Inherited Rights Mask can be restored through a new trustee assignment in a nested folder. If that sounds confusing, maybe Figure 7-16 can clarify it for you.

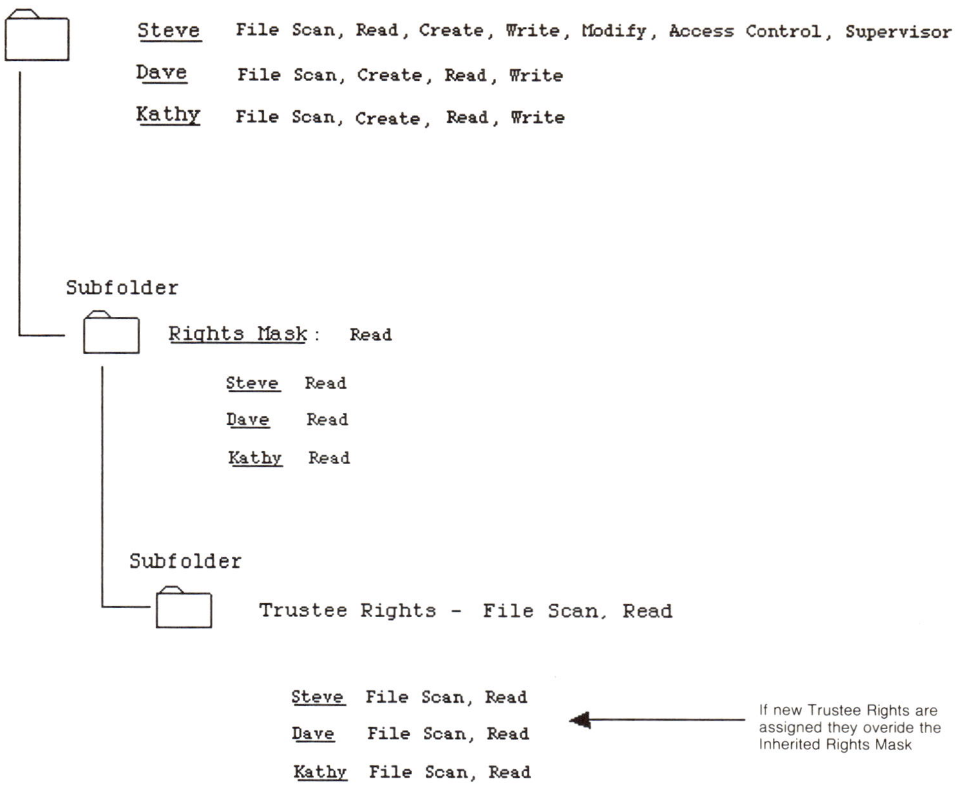

7-16 NetWare v3.X's Inherited Rights Mask is over-ridden by making new trustee rights assignments.

It shows that trustee rights in a folder are passed down in the branching of a server's file structure, until they are revoked by a change in the Inherited Rights Mask. Then the Inherited Rights Mask is passed down from folder to folder, until new trustee rights override them. These trustee rights are then in effect until a new modification is made to the Inherited Rights Mask. Then once again the Inherited Rights Mask overide the trustee rights.

Figure 7-17 revisits the screen of the DA's Rights section, so you can see how to use the DA to view the rights masks of folders or the effective rights of trustees in those folders. By modifying the rights masks, you can alter a trustee's effective access rights in those folders.

Attribute security

Beyond Access Rights, both NetWare v2.X and NetWare v3.X have a set of file and folder attributes that give files and folders special characteristics to make

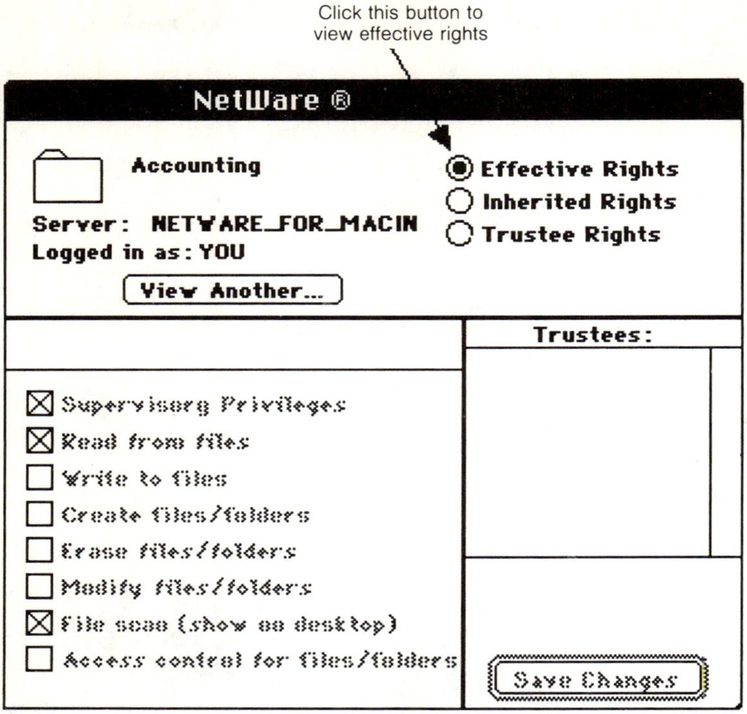

7-17 The NetWare desk accessory can set an Inherited Rights Mask, or view Effective Rights.

them even more secure. Attribute security, like the Inherited Rights Mask, overrides trustee rights assignments. Attribute security complements a folder's or file's effective rights, because attributes can prevent tasks that effective rights would otherwise allow. Both NetWare v2.X and v3.X servers permit attributes to be set on files as well as folders. Attribute security can be used to:

- Control whether files can be shared so that only one user can access the file at a time. This provides protection for data that is being used by an application that does not have file locking written into it.
- Protect files from data corruption by ensuring that all transactions are completed when files are being modified, it also prevents file corruption by prohibiting files from being modified.
- Prevent files from being copied. Among other things, this keeps sensitive data from being carried away on floppy disks.
- Mark files as modified so that backup utilities can select those files that have been modified for backup only.

There are, of course, many other situations for which NetWare attribute rights will solve a problem for you. The set of attributes available are summarized in Table 7-1.

Table 7-1 File attributes.

Sharable (Multi-user)—Allows the file to be used by more than one user at a time. It can be assigned only to files, and not folders.

Copy Inhibit (Mac)—Restricts the rights of Macintosh users to copy the file. This does not apply to other users, such as DOS users. This can only be assigned to files.

Execute Only (DOS)—Prevents files from being copied. This attribute can sometimes protect against viruses attacking files. Only the supervisor can assign this attribute. This attribute, once assigned, can't be removed. Backup utilities will not backup the files to which this is assigned, and some programs will not execute properly when flagged with this attribute.

Rename Inhibit—Restricts users from renaming folders and files even if they have the modify right.

Delete Inhibit—Prevents users from erasing folders and files even when effective rights might permit it.

Read Only—Prevents a file from being modified and cannot be assigned to folders. When the Read-Only attribute is assigned to a file, NetWare automatically assigns the Delete Inhibit and Rename Inhibit attributes as well. Consequently, users cannot write to, erase or rename the file even if their effective rights permit it.

Modified Since Last Backup—Provides information that the file has been changed since the last backup. This attribute is used primarily by backup software. When a backup is done, the attribute is turned off. NetWare will automatically set the modified flag back on when a change gets made to the file by a user.

Hidden—Makes files not appear in the listing when viewing a folder

Indexed—Improves disk access to large files by a method called indexing the File Allocation Table (see the NetWare manuals for further explanation).

Purgeable (NetWare v3.11 only)—Ensures that NetWare makes the file unretrievable even with file salvage utilities once the file is deleted.

Transaction Tracking—Protects transactional files from harm. If a change is not completed when a transactional file is being saved, the file is returned to its previous condition.

System—Indicates a file that is being used by the operating system. To a Macintosh user a System file behaves the same as a Hidden file.

Setting and changing attributes

Attributes can be set by any user that has the Modify right to a file or folder. To change those attributes, however, you must use an application program called the NetWare Control Center.

Anyone can use the NetWare control center to change file attributes. NetWare supervisors can use it to manage user accounts in addition to changing attributes. It allows them to create NetWare accounts for new users, NetWare groups, and to assign users to those groups. Figure 7-19 shows the icon for the NetWare Control Center application. It can be found on the same NetWare disk that you used to install your Netware desk accessory.

If you are not logged into a NetWare for Macintosh file server when you first launch the NetWare Control Center, you will receive the window shown in Figure 7-18, which shows an icon for every server that it finds. To have the NetWare Control Center program log you in, double click on the appropriate server icon.

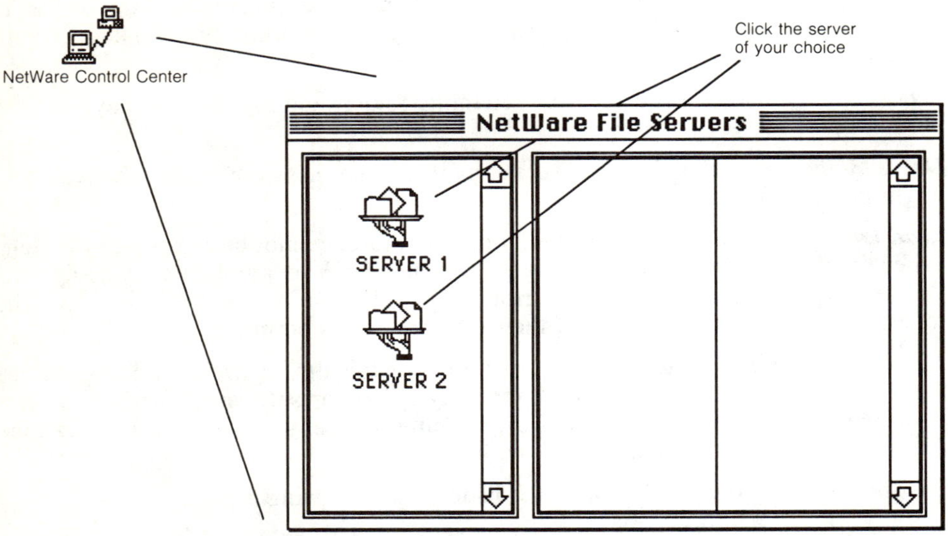

7-18 The first step when using the NetWare Control center is to selct the server.

Once logged in, you will see the NetWare Control Center user interface that is displayed in Figure 7-19. Items to note are the two icons in the middle that allow you to view information about the server's users and groups, the command menu at the top of the screen, and the Volume icon at the far right.

The first step in using the NetWare Control Center to set file and folder attributes (also referred to as *flags*) is to double-click the Volume icon at the right to open the window where you will see its files and folders, as shown in Figure 7-19. You can open other folders in the windows until you reach the files or folders with attributes you want to change.

Next, pull down the selections for Folders/Files from the menu at the top of the screen. If the item you have selected to change the attributes of is a folder,

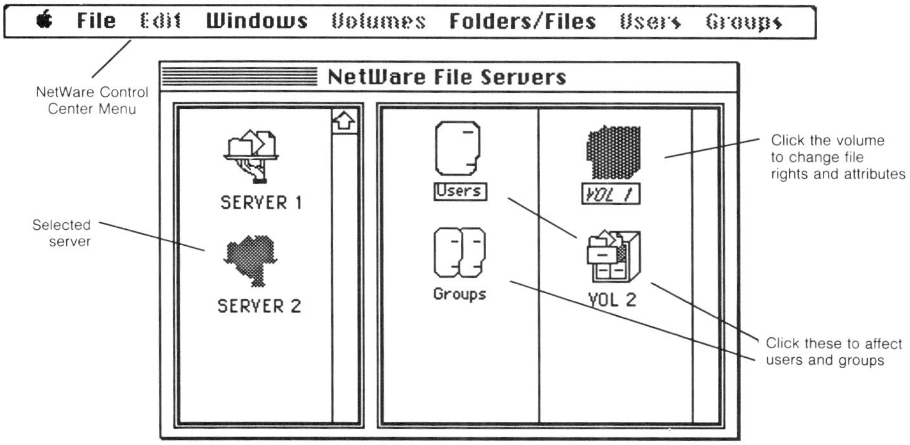

7-19 Selecting the server brings up your other options.

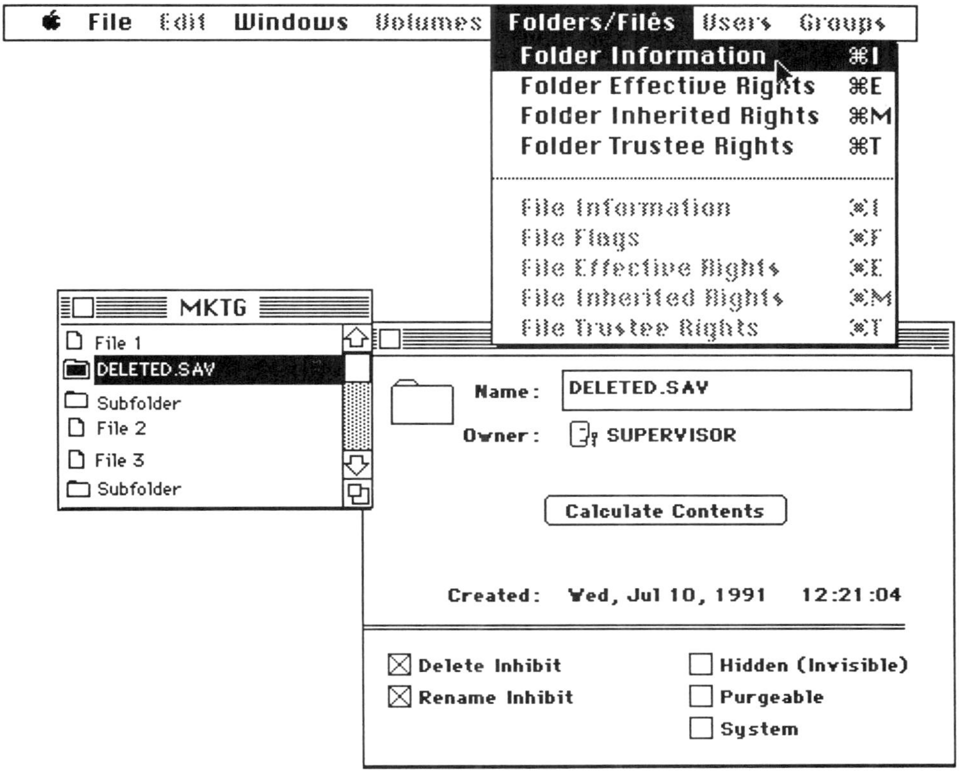

7-20 The Folder Information command sets the attributes of a folder.

you will see the Folder items as active. In Figure 7-21, the items from this menu are grayed out because the object selected is a folder and not a file.

To modify a folder's attibutes, select Folder Information from the menu, which will open up the Folder Information window that you see in Figure 7-20. To set flags, click the boxes for the attributes you want, then close the window.

When setting attributes for files instead of folders, first select your file after clicking the Volume icon, and then again choose Folders/Files from the Control Center's Folder menu, as shown in Figure 7-21. Now you will see the folder selections grayed out and the file selections as active.

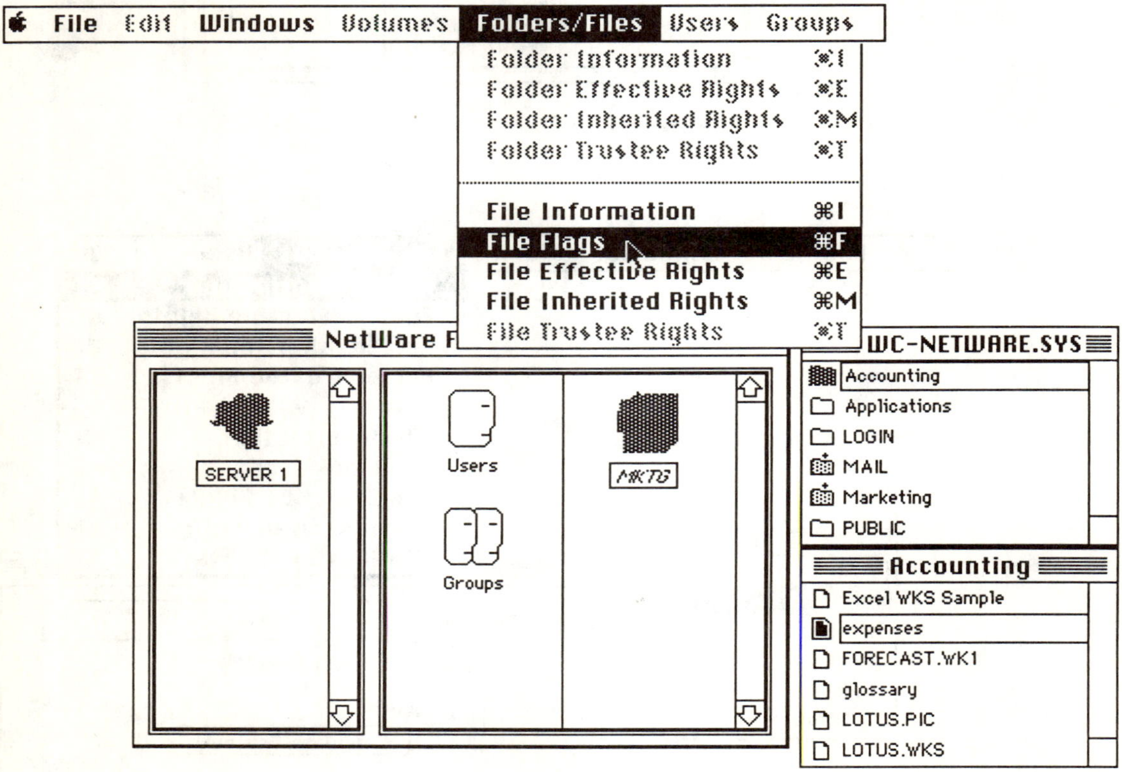

7-21 The File Flags command sets attributes for files.

When you select the File Flags item from the menu, you will get a window that allows you to set or change attributes for the file, as shown in Figure 7-22. The attributes shown in this figure are for a NetWare 3.X server. In NetWare 2.X, Delete Inhibit, Hidden, Rename Inhibit, and System attributes are not available.

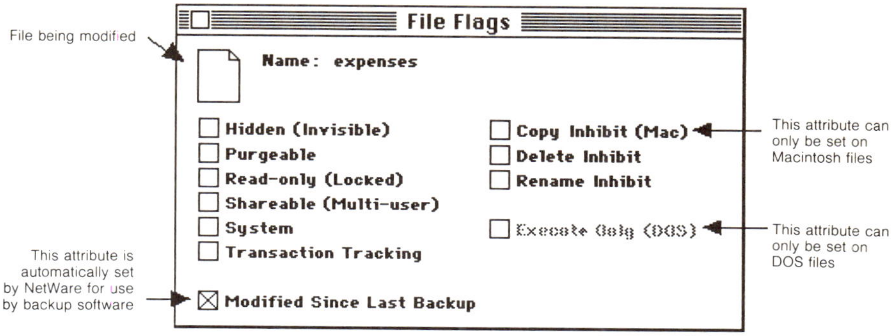

7-22 The File Flags Window.

The NetWare Control Center also can be used to set access rights to files and folders. In this respect, it duplicates what the Netware desk accessory could do for a user. To use the NetWare Control Center for setting rights, select the folder or file rights choices from the Folders/Files Menu. Refer to Figure 7-21, and you will see rights items in the File menu along with the Flag items.

Using the NetWare Control Center to change your encrypted password

If your Macintosh is set up to use the NetWare User Authentication Method (NetWare UAM), then you won't be able to change your password from your Macintosh's Appleshare client login screen. The NetWare UAM is a login method that encodes users passwords when a Macintosh sends them to a NetWare for Macintosh server. It provides a higher level of security than an AppleShare client gets in its native mode. When the NetWare UAM is installed, the Set Password button on the AppleShare login screen is deactivated, so you can't change your password with it.

You must use the NetWare Control Center to change your password when using the NetWare UAM. First select the server you want to change the password for and then double click the Users icon, which will open up a users window, as shown in Figure 7-23. To change your password, find your name in the users list and select it by clicking on it once. This will make the Users item in the NetWare Control Center menu at the top of the screen become active. Pull down the Users menu, and select User Information from the menu, as shown in Figure 7-24. The User Information window that the menu item summons is shown on the right-hand side. To change your password, click the Change Password button.

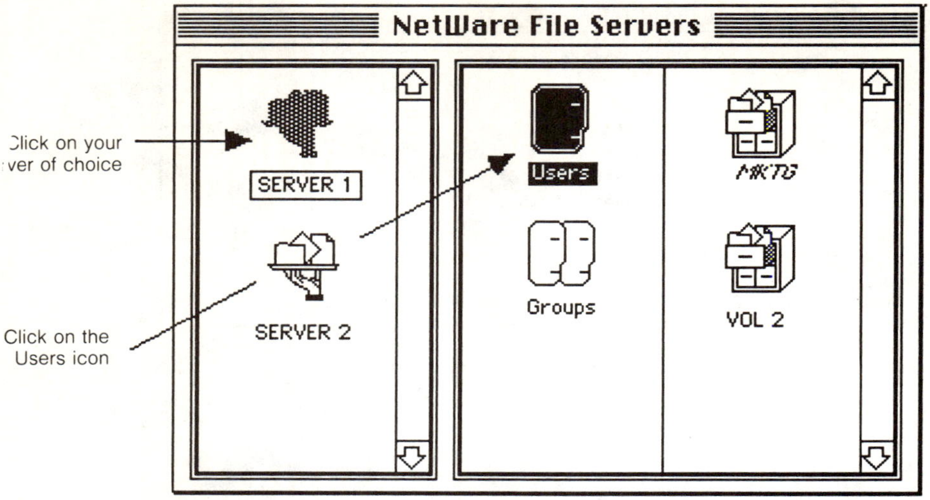

7-23 Click on the Users icon to change your encrypted password.

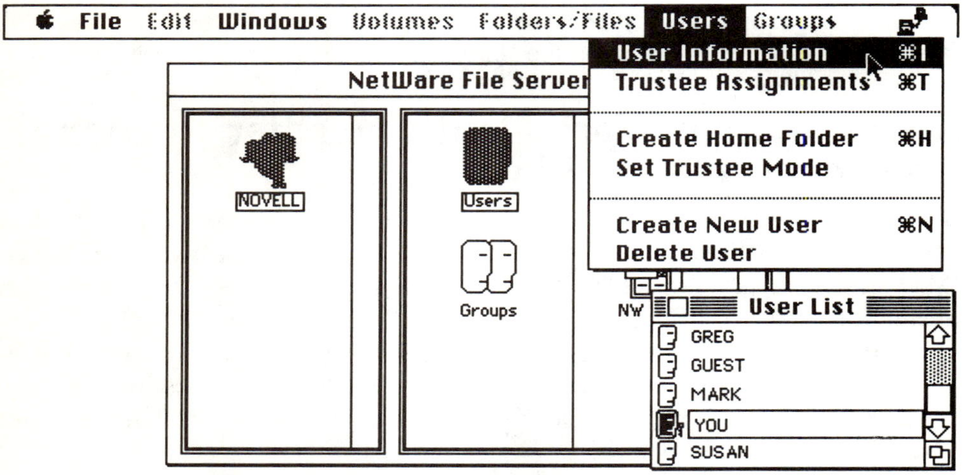

7-24 Selecting your user name, and then pulling down the User Information command.

A series of dialogue boxes follow instructing you to enter first the old password and then the new one. After you enter your new password, and then re-enter it to verify your change, the NetWare Control Center will save it. The other information on this screen tells you the groups that you are a member of and the type of group or individual security rights you have been given the eqivalent of. Most regular users have the same equivalency that you have in this

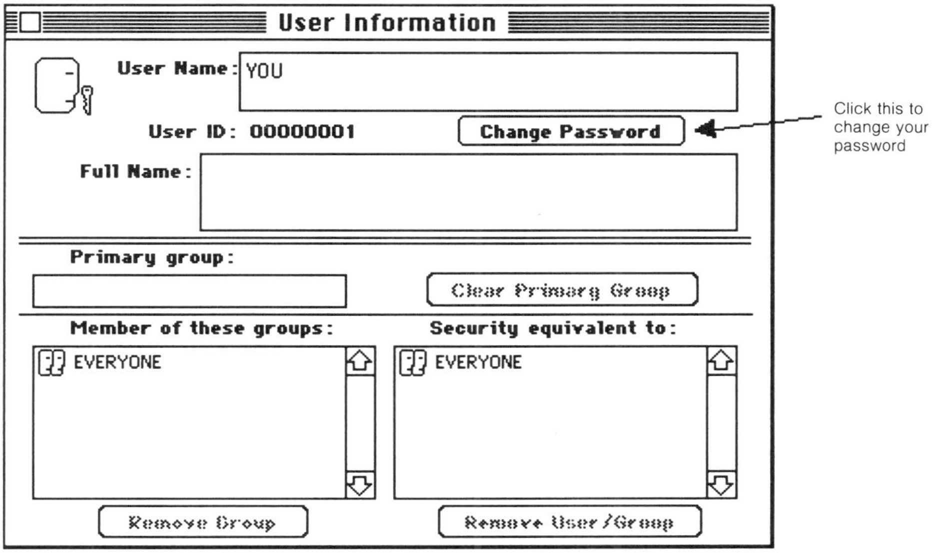

7-25 The User Information Window.

example, which is equivalency with the group Everyone. The *ID number* that you see is a number used by NetWare in a file called the bindery, to equate your account name with an identity in the operating system.

8

Chapter

Setting up a user environment

You have been given a run through of the basic capabilities and security levels you have with NetWare. It's time for a more detailed look at using NetWare tools to set up and real-world applications to get your work done. This chapter discusses how to create folders and assign useable rights to the folders, how to use applications to create and store documents on the file server, and how to view the print queues to which you are sending your documents.

Practical applications for access rights

As stated in the last chapter, your ability to access and store data on a NetWare server depends on the trustee assignments, rights masks, and NetWare attributes that are assigned to the server's files and folders. It is an extremely comprehensive system. When you are exposed to this security system for the first time, it can appear a little overwhelming; however, it will make more sense as you use it.

Assume you work for a company called Tryit, that has a sales department, a marketing department, and an accounting department. The Tryit company has assigned group names of Sales, Marketing, and Accounting to members of the respective departments. It also has a group called Everyone, to which everybody in the company has been made a member. Table 8-1 contains a table of users for the Tryit company, and the groups to which they belong.

Also assume that the Tryit company's server is a NetWare v3.X server whose volume is set up in a way similar to the file system shown in Figure 8-1.

Table 8-1 Employees of the Tryit Corporation.

Sales	Marketing	Accounting	Everyone
Dan	Bill	Mary Kate	YOU
Barb	Doug	YOU	Dan
Marge	Tom	Mark	Bill
		Chris	Mary Kate
		Joe	Marge
		Mike	Mark
			Chris
			Doug
			Barb
			Mike
			Tom
			Joe

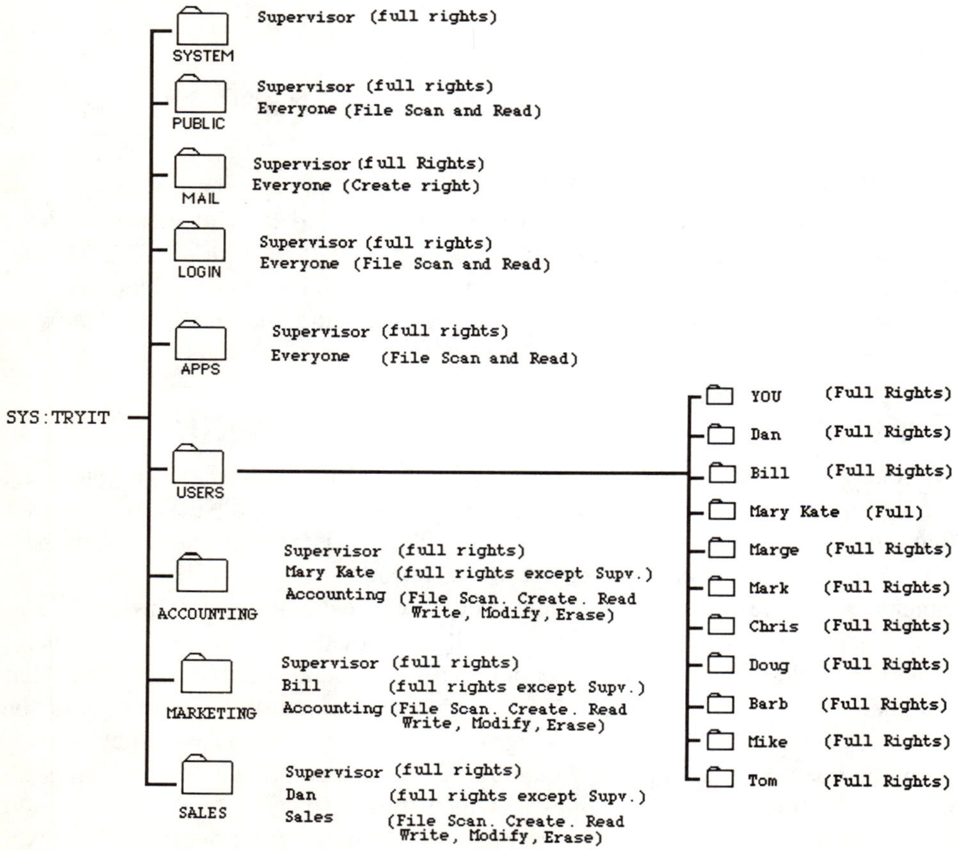

8-1 The rights settings for the Tryit Company's server.

Next to the folder names in this example are the individual and group trustees, and the rights that they were given.

One of the folders on the NetWare server is called System, not to be confused with the folder you have on your Macintosh called the System Folder. The NetWare server's folder called System contains the core of the NetWare operating system, and as shown in Figure 8-1, only the supervisor has full rights to it. The other users are not trustees, so they don't have rights to it. They don't even have the File Scan right, which would allow them to see it, so it is invisible to them. On a NetWare v2.X server, users who did not have the File Scan right to the folder would see it, but it would be gray to them and they could not open it.

The folder called Public, on the other hand, has the group Everyone as a trustee, so all users have some set of rights to it. The set of rights that the group Everyone is assigned gives all users the right to scan and read from the files in the Public folder. However, they cannot create, write to, modify, or erase files in the folder. Similar trustee access for the group Everyone is given to the Login, Mail, and Apps Folders. In the case of the Apps folder, these same trustee rights are passed down to the DOS and Mac folders. Figure 8-2 shows how you would see this file system from your Macintosh.

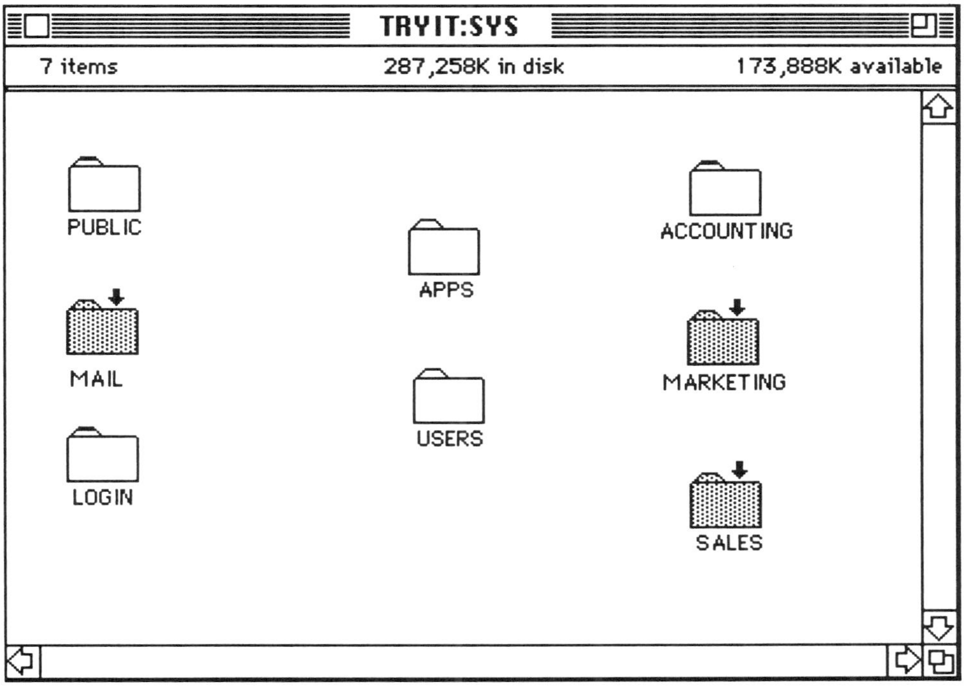

8-2 Your view of the server.

The scenario described so far is a common one. Folders, such as Public, have NetWare utilities in them that DOS users run to set access rights to their files in the same way that Macintosh users do with the NetWare desk accessory. Folders such as the one in this example, called Apps, might have application programs such as word processors and spreadsheets that users need to get their work done. In general, users would not need to modify the application files in these folders, or to create new files. Therefore it's a common practice, just as in the Tryit company's example, that the supervisor would restrict the access rights to the folders to prevent a user from inadvertently doing damage.

Self directed use of rights

In the Tryit company's folder called Users, an environment has been created where each user is the exclusive trustee to a folder that carries the user's own name. This is shown in Figure 8-3 as a branching diagram. As opposed to the other folders discussed so far in this example, each user has full rights to their folders. In their folders, they can create new files (and folders), delete them, modify them, or do anything they want. They can use the NetWare desk accessory to assign another user as a trustee to their folders, and determine the rights that the new trustee will have. However, unless they assign a new trustee, they are the only users with rights to their folders.

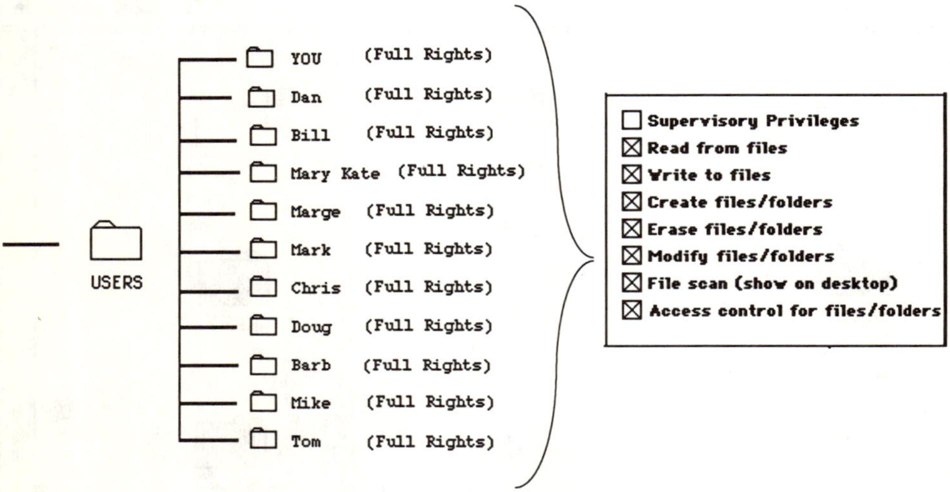

8-3 Each user has full rights to their personal folder.

If you were a NetWare user in this company, and all of the users had maintained themselves as exclusive trustees, you would not see any of the other user's folders. They would not be visible because NetWare v3.X, which is what the Tryit company is using, does not show you folders to which you have no rights. You would see only the folders to which you had been made a trustee, which would be only your own folder at this point. If you were a NetWare v2.X user, you would see all folders, except for your folder as grayed-out folders (indicating no access rights).

By providing an exclusive user folder, the company allows employees to keep the documents they create private. Even though other users have access to the folder named Users, they have no access to somebody else's folder, unless they are given it by that somebody. A similar environment is set up in the company's folder that is named Departments, except that in the case of the Departments folder, the trustees are groups rather than individuals. Figure 8-4 shows the folders and their trustees. Naturally, the individuals that are in the groups are the members of the actual departments. An arrangement such as this one allows all of the group members to access common files that they need to share, but prohibits access by the members of other departments.

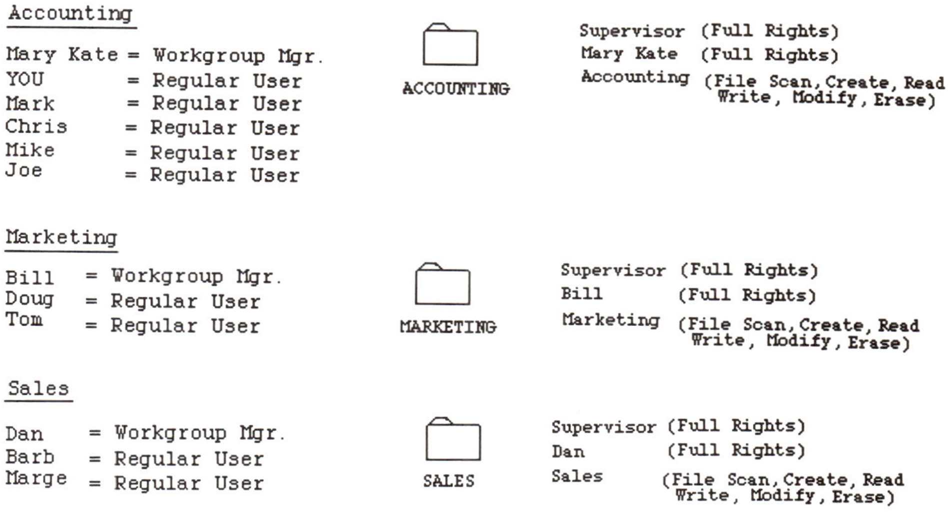

8-4 The groups that have access to folders.

A special circumstance and application of Netware rights has been implemented in the departmental folder called Accounting. In this folder is a file called Payroll. The Payroll file contains company confidential salary information. Chris is the payroll officer, and Mary Kate is the department manager. They should be the only persons authorized to see the contents of that folder.

In this example the access rights to the file called Payroll should be set with only Chris and Mary Kate as trustees. The easiest way for the supervisor to make those settings is to first set a rights mask on the file so that all trustee rights are revoked, and then overide the rights mask with new trustee rights assignments for only Mary Kate and Chris. Figure 8-5 shows this file's trustee and rights settings.

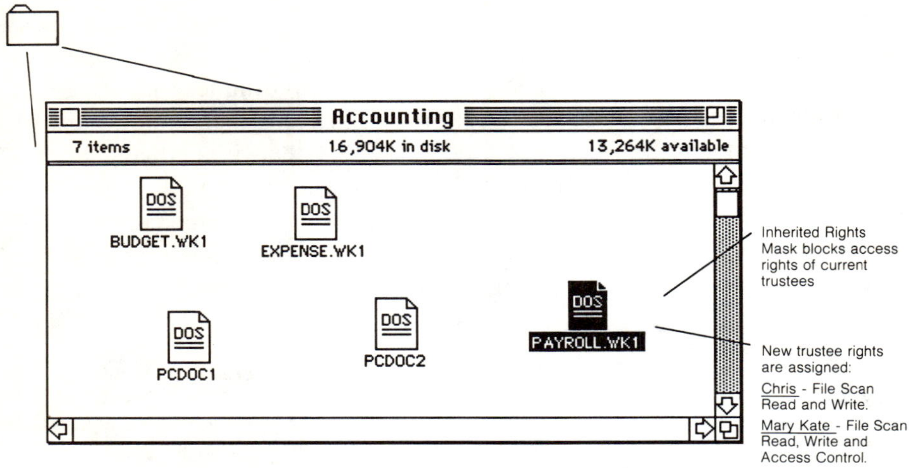

8-5 Only Chris and Mary Kate have access to the Payroll file.

The members of departments other than accounting will never be able to see the Payroll file, because they don't have any kind of access to the Accounting folder. Even the other members of the accounting department cannot access the Payroll folder. All users except Mary Kate and Chris lack the proper NetWare rights to access that file and do not even have the rights to see it.

Mary Kate has been granted supervisor rights and Access Control rights to the Payroll file. This permits her to assign other users besides Chris with trustee rights. As manager of the accounting department, Mary Kate will need this capability so that she does not have to make a special request of the supervisor every time a new user or a trustee assignment must be changed. For example, if Chris should leave the company, Mary Kate would probably want the ability to create a new user when Chris's replacement is hired, and to give the new user the same rights that Chris had.

Finally, because the Tryit company does not want the information in the Payroll folder to leave the building and because there is really no reason why it needs to be anywhere but on the server, the Payroll folder has had the NetWare Copy Inhibit attribute set. Copy Inhibit makes the folder (or file) incapable of being duplicated so that the contents can't be copied to a floppy disk and carried away. Also set is the NetWare Delete-inhibit attribute, so that it can't be accidentally erased.

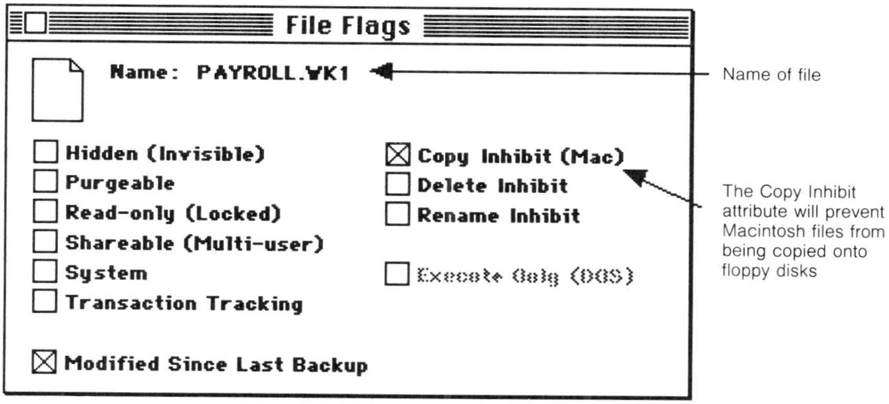

8-6 Preventing a file from being copied.

Creating folders and assigning rights

In the example so far, you have observed situations where the user was working with an environment already set up by the supervisor. It was the supervisor who created the User and Department folders, and assigned the access rights that Tryit's management had decided were appropriate for its users and groups. It's time to extend the examples to show you how users might set up their own environments. For these examples, assume that each user has the Access Control right for their user folder on the server, as shown in figure 8-7. Assume also that Mary Kate is a NetWare workgroup supervisor for the accounting department.

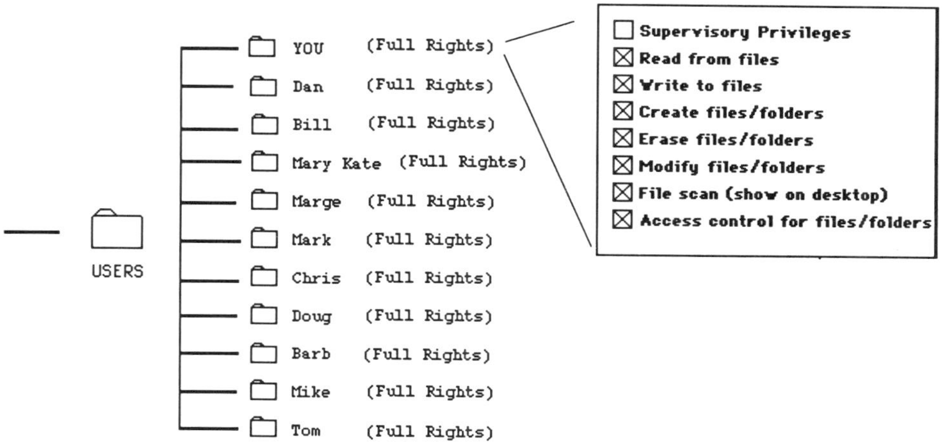

8-7 Each user has full rights to their personal folder.

In the Tryit company, each user was given a folder of which they were originally the only trustee. Users will use these folders in the same way that they do their own local hard disks or floppy disks. One of the advantages that the network disk has over a local hard disk is that on the network disk, the users can make files and folders sharable by other users. The following example shows how a user can create a trustee and assign that trustee rights of access to a file in either NetWare v2.X or v3.X.

Suppose that you, as a member of the accounting department, are working with the Sales and Marketing departments to forecast sales for the upcoming business year. You might start by summarizing last year's sales on a Macintosh spreadsheet program and storing it in your personal data folder on the server, as shown in Figure 8-8. Next, you want to have the sales manager, Dan, and the marketing manager, Bill, look at last year's numbers, and use them as a basis for their new forecast.

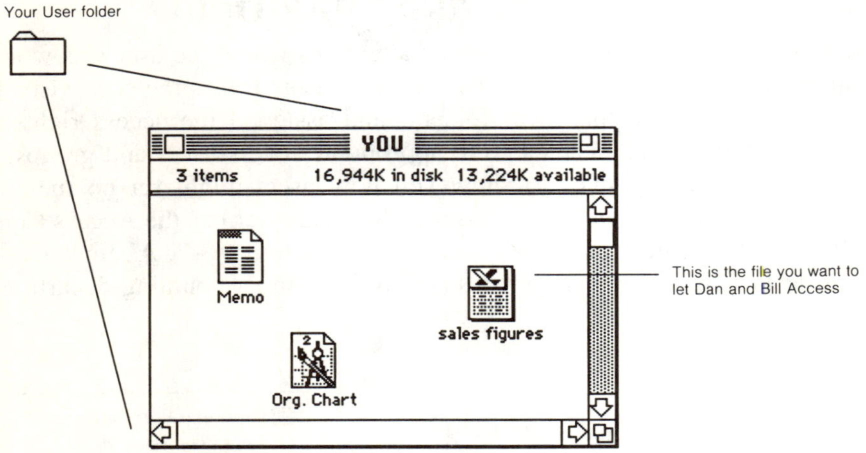

8-8 A file is created in your folder.

In order to make working with them more efficient, you might want to give Dan and Bill access to the file. To do that you must make Dan and Bill trustees of your folder, which is where the file is stored, and give them the access rights to read, write, and modify the file. Then Dan and Bill can use their copies of the same spreadsheet application program that they have stored on their Macs to make changes to the file. How they handle the task if they use some other computer, like a DOS machine, rather than a Macintosh, will be addressed in chapter 9.

You can create trustees, and change NetWare access rights to your folders by using the NetWare desk accessory, as shown on the left-hand side of Figure

8-9. Your first step is to select the folder you want to make changes to, in this case your own user folder. Then click the button on the right that says Folder Info. After that selection, you will see the main Rights window as shown in Figure 8-10.

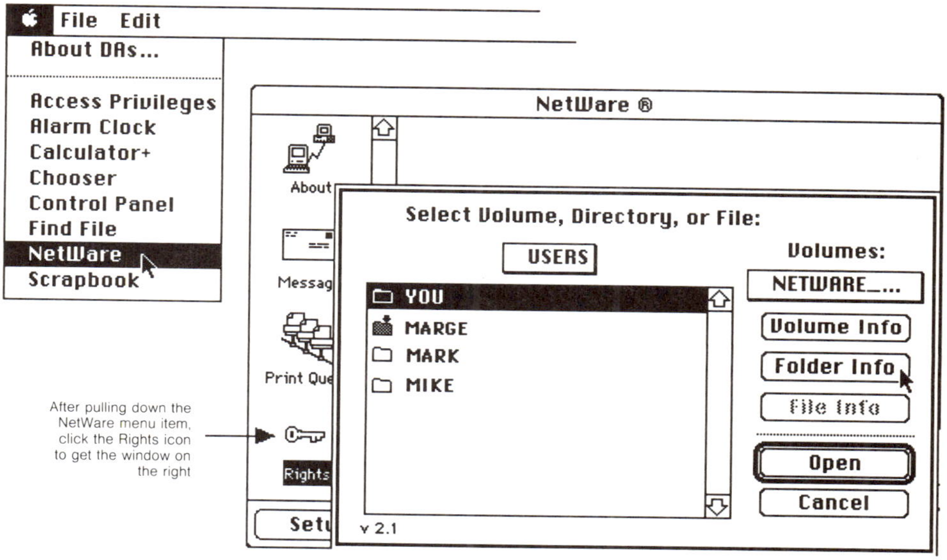

8-9 The Folder info button will display a folder's rights settings.

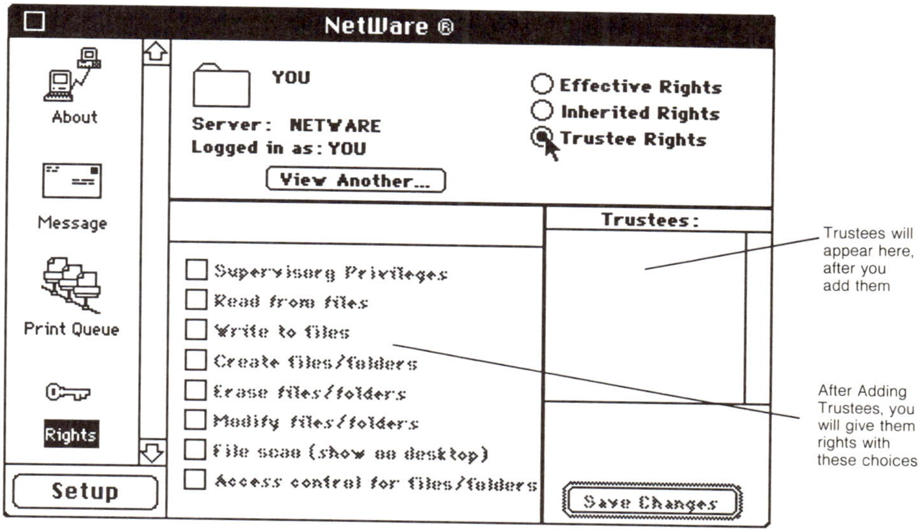

8-10 Clicking Trustee rights to assign new Trustees or to change rights for existing trustees.

After making the selection for Trustee Rights at the top right corner of the Rights window, the button to add a trustee will become active. When you click the Add Trustee button, a list of the users appears. Select Dan and Bill from the list, and the trustee assignment is done. See Figure 8-11.

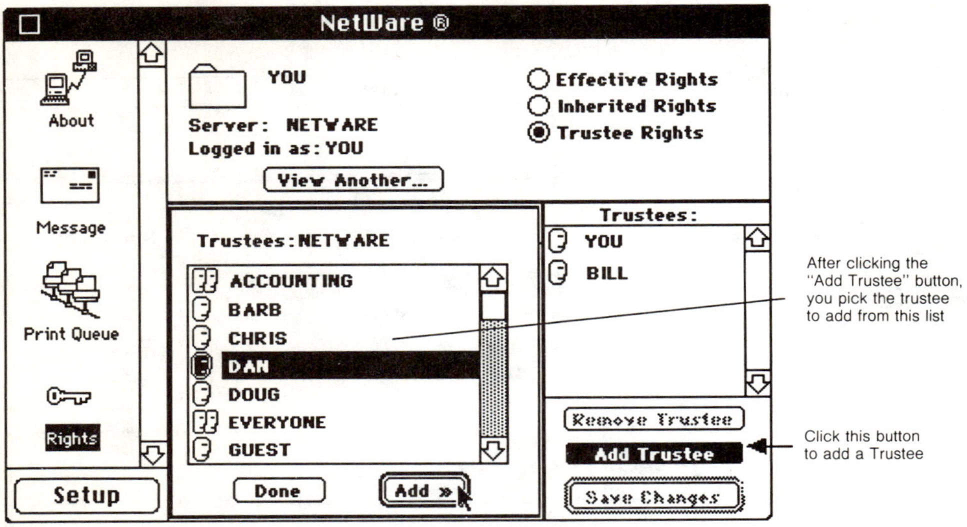

8-11 Selecting the user who will become a new trustee, or whose rights will be modified.

Next, you need to select the rights that you want Dan and Bill to have. The possible choices for rights are displayed in the center of the window. This rights list will vary slightly, depending on whether the server is NetWare v2.X or NetWare v3.X. These differences were documented in chapter 7. Figure 8-12 shows the Rights window for a NetWare v3.X server. Click on the appropriate boxes to give Dan and Bill those rights.

By giving Dan and Bill the rights you selected to your folder, you have given them access to all of the files and folders that are nested within your folder. On a v2.X NetWare server, because you cannot assign rights to just a file, you must either permit trustees access to all of your files in a folder, or nest files within other folders that they can't access.

On a NetWare v3.X server, exclusivity of access is easier to assign. With NetWare v3.X, you don't have to make Dan and Bill trustees to your whole folder, you can make them trustees to an individual file. With NetWare v3.X, you could have made them trustees to only the spreadsheet file. Dan and Bill would be unable to see the other files in your folder that they were not made trustees to, as shown in Figure 8-13.

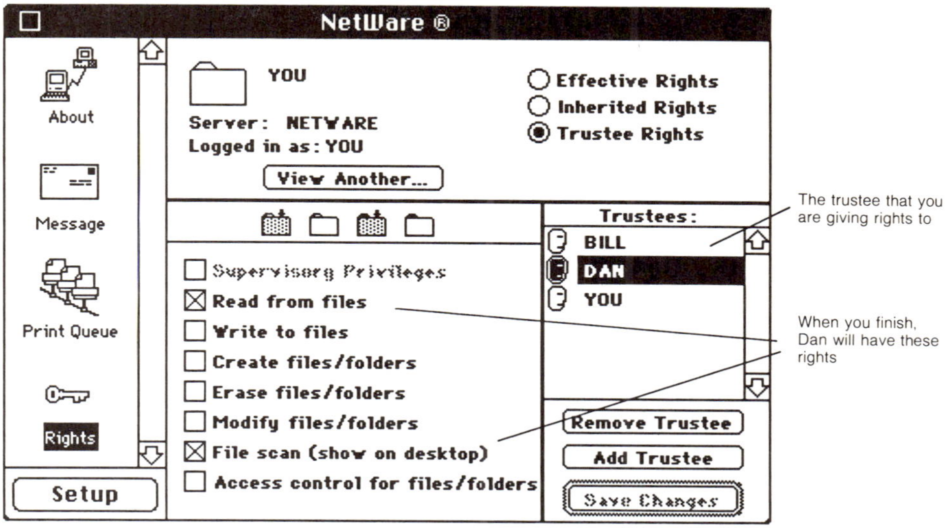

8-12 Assigning Dan's Trustee Rights.

Printing documents

When Dan and Bill go back and forth in their editing exercise, and eventually come up with the sales forecast for the next year, they will want to print it out. The final example covered in this chapter is how you can print via NetWare print queues, and how print queue operators and supervisors use the NetWare desk accessory to manage print queues.

The accepted company procedure for printing at the Tryit company is to use NetWare print queues, because it's common for people at Tryit to print large documents, and NetWare queues makes the printing of those documents easier to manage. At Bill's request, Dan sends the job to the print queue for the printer in your department. Figure 8-14 shows the print window Dan gets when printing to the NW_LaserWriter_Queue for the LaserWriter in the accounting department. Its name appears at the top of the window.

Suppose that Dan's timing is bad, and he happens to print the document to the queue at a time when a number of other large documents have entered the queue before his. If he wants to expedite the job by having it moved up in line, he needs to ask a print queue operator, a workgroup supervisor (which is unique to NetWare v3.X), or a NetWare supervisor to move the job up. A print queue operator would first pull down the NetWare desk accessory, and click the Print icon to access the Print Queue window, as shown in Figure 8-15.

The Print Queue window shows you a list of the jobs currently in the queue, the user who sent the job, its priority, and its job number. As you can see in the list, Dan's job is currently last in line. If his need to print the job is urgent, you

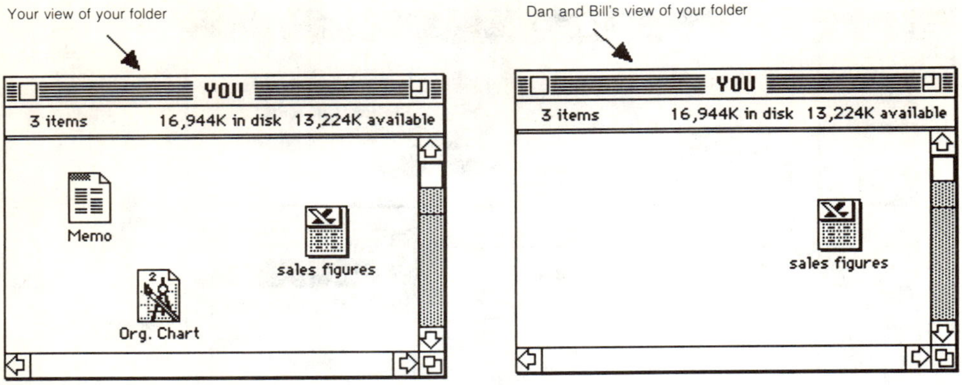

8-13 The results of limiting and providing access to files.

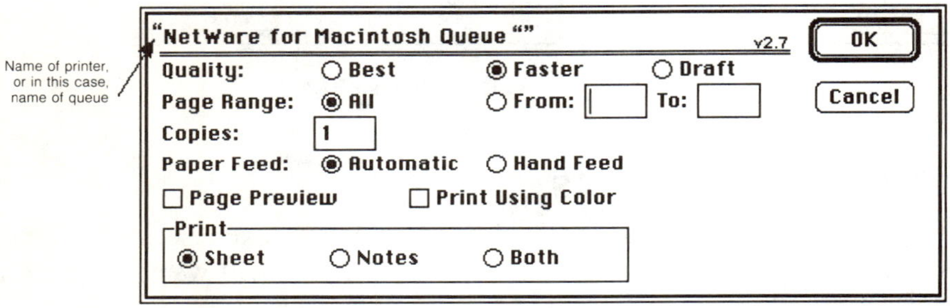

8-14 Macintosh applications think the NetWare queue is a LaserWriter.

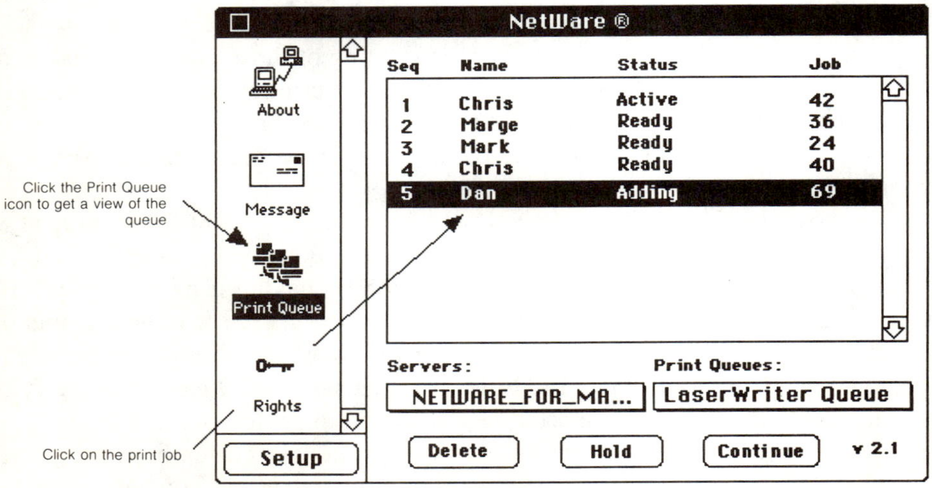

8-15 Viewing and managing print queues.

can move it up to be the first in line by clicking on the job to select it, and dragging it to the top of the list. It's that straightforward. You also can change a job's queue status to hold, or delete print jobs, by selecting the job and then clicking the buttons at the bottom of the Print Queue window.

9
Chapter

Integrating Macintosh, DOS, and Windows applications

As explained in the previous chapter's file exchange with Bill and Dan, it's easy for a user to change the access rights of a file to let others get at it with the same word processing tool. What would happen though if Bill used Microsoft Word for the Macintosh, and Dan used MacWrite or WordPerfect for Macintosh? What if Bill used a Macintosh, and Dan used a DOS PC? These scenarios are very real in many, if not most, office environments, and users clearly need solutions for these situations where another user has a different kind of application or computer.

Fortunately, many software solutions abound for these problems. Some of these products are not Novell NetWare products; they are the products of other software manufacturers. NetWare is in the middle of the problem, however, because the network is what brought these different users together. These products are all NetWare compatible, and do a good job of bridging the differences between other Macintosh, and even DOS PC applications.

DOS coprocessing

NetWare and NetWare for Macintosh act as facilitators that allow Macintosh users to see the files of DOS, OS/2, and UNIX users, and vice versa. However, what they do not do is allow the Macintosh to run application programs written for another computer's operating system, such as DOS, or allow a user of a DOS or other computer to run Macintosh application programs.

However, some other NetWare products and some products from third-party software companies do allow Macintosh computers to run DOS applications. One such product is called SoftPC, from the company Insignia Solutions. Soft PC allows a Macintosh computer user to bring up a program for a DOS computer by emulating a DOS environment within the Macintosh operating system.

SoftPC is a Macintosh application program that can sit on a local disk or a network server, and is started up like any other Macintosh application program. Figure 9-1 shows the program icon for SoftPC in the left frame. In the right frame, you can see the startup window that it displays when launched. SoftPC treats the Macintosh local disk resources as a DOS A: drive if it is a floppy disk, and a C: drive if it is a hard disk. It also can recognize disks over a network to communicate with NetWare resources, just like any DOS client would.

This network connectivity lets SoftPC run DOS based NetWare administrative utilities, or any server-based DOS application program. The result is not

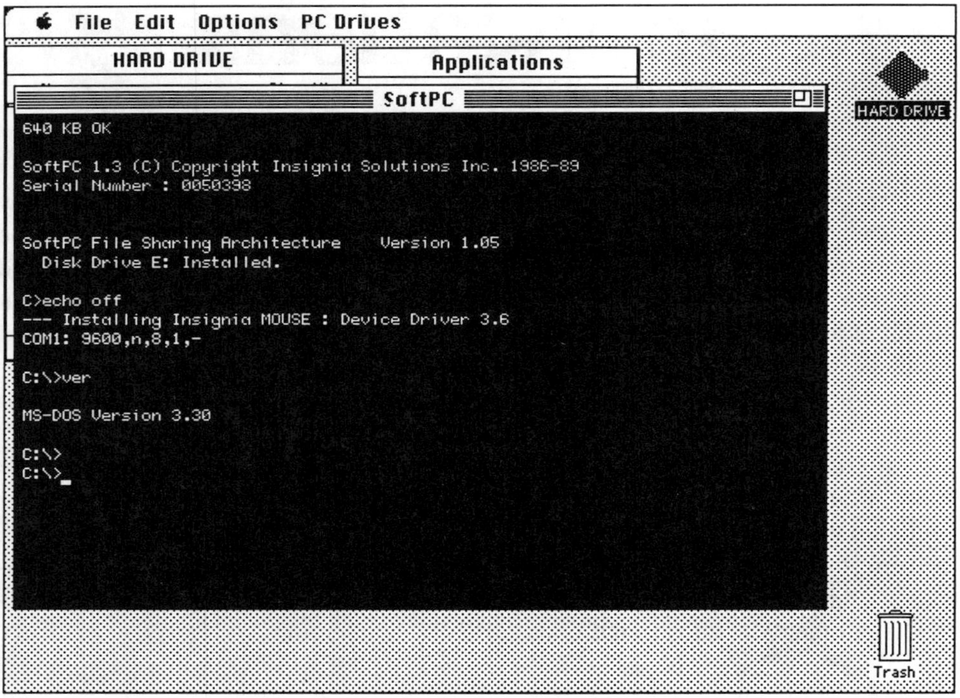

9-1 SoftPC shows a DOS session in a Macintosh window.

Mac-like; Macintosh users will not get a Macintosh interface. They will see the program just as the DOS user would, but it will allow the Macintosh user to type in data and give commands. You can see how SoftPC would display a session running Lotus123 in Figure 9-2.

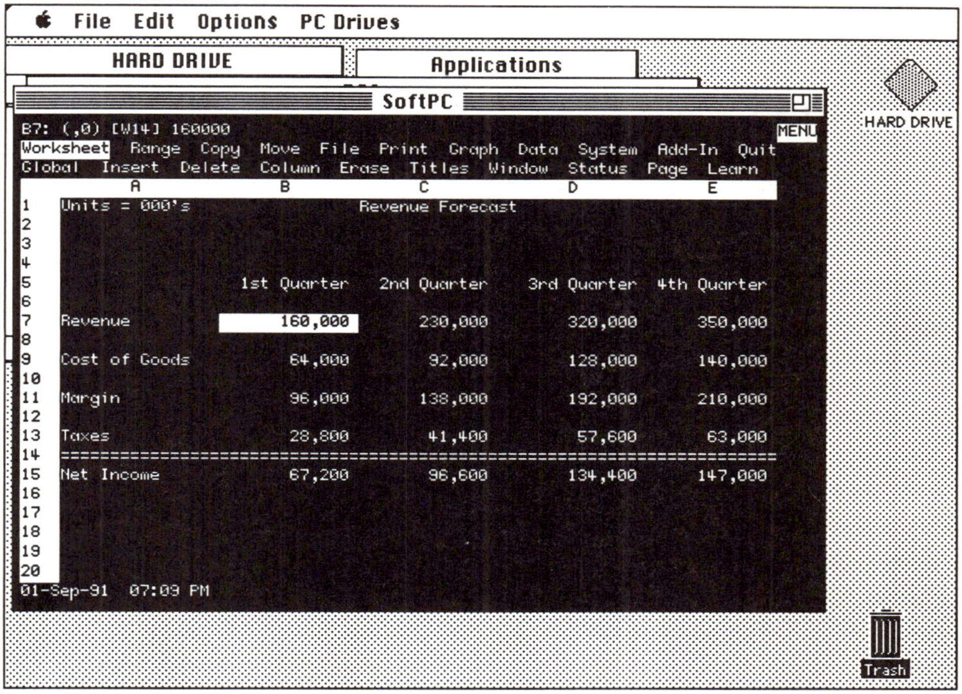

9-2 DOS emulators do not take advantage of the Macintosh interface.

Another product that provides a little more functionality than SoftPC is the NetWare Access Server. Like SoftPC, the NetWare Access Server allows Macintosh users to run DOS applications in a window on the Macintosh. One distinguishing feature of the NetWare Access Server is that the Macintosh can emulate DOS sessions either over the LAN, or from remote locations. The configuration options for the NetWare Access Server are depicted in Figure 9-3. Another characteristic of the NetWare Access server is that the actual DOS processing happens on the Access Server, and not on the Macintosh client. This saves a Macintosh from the burden of translating Motorola CPU instructions into Intel CPU instructions, and enables better performance.

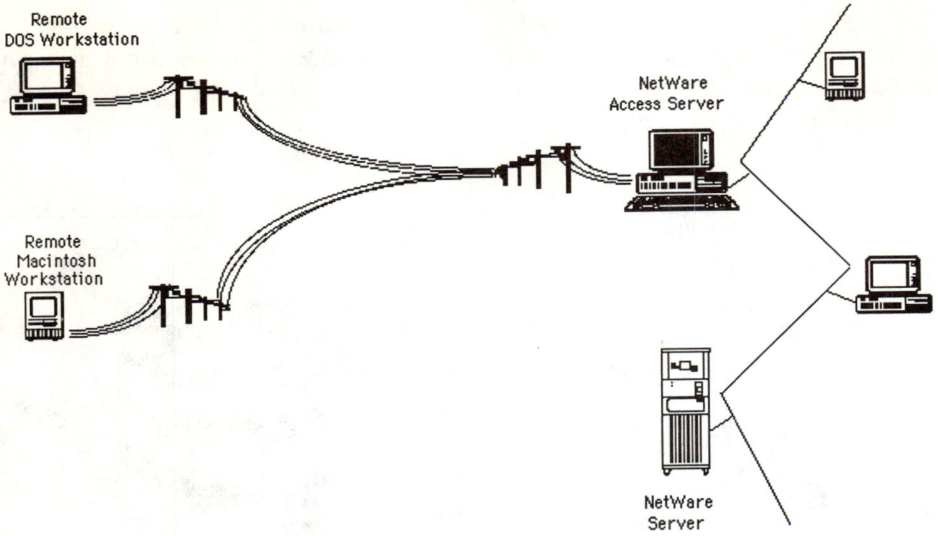

9-3 The NetWare Access Server allows Macintosh clients to run remote, as well as local DOS sessions.

Sharing data across platforms

Products, such as SoftPC and the NetWare Access Server, are good solutions for organizations that occasionally need their Macintosh computer users to access an application program that only works on DOS. However, the majority of Macintosh users who are interacting with the users of other computers have no desire to run the other computer's application programs. They often would prefer to run their own Macintosh application programs, and access only the data created by those other programs. NetWare for Macintosh makes the data available to them so they can do it.

One of the simplest solutions for exchanging data between Macintosh users and the users of other computers is to directly import it into a Macintosh application. Many application programs now have file importing features that let them read the files of other application programs. The competitive nature of the computer software business has precipitated a trend toward this functionality. It makes good business sense for a software company to permit its application to import another program's files, because it permits the application to be compatible in an environment where its competitor might be dominant. NetWare for Macintosh users who use the network to access files of other Mac users, or of DOS PC users, are big beneficiaries of this functionality.

A partial list of some of the most popular Macintosh applications noted for their ability to import the files of other Macintosh applications, and in many cases even the files of DOS PC applications, is displayed in Table 9-1. It is not

Table 9-1 Cross platform applications.

Product	Vendor	Imports from
Word processing		
WordPerfect 2.0	WordPerfect Corp.	WordPerfect (DOS) 4.2, 5.0, 5.1 Microsoft Word (Mac) 4.0
MacWrite II	Claris Corp.	WordPerfect (DOS) 4.2, 5.0, 5.1 Microsoft Word (DOS) 4.0 WordPerfect (Mac) 1.0, 1.1 Microsoft Word (Mac) 4.0, 3.1
Spreadsheets		
Lotus 123 for Mac	Lotus Corp.	Lotus 123 (DOS)
Wingz	Informix Corp.	Lotus 123 (DOS), Wingz (DOS), Microsoft Excel (Mac), Wingz (UNIX)
Excel	Microsoft Corp.	Lotus 123 (DOS)
Desktop publishing		
Pagemaker	Aldus Corp.	Pagemaker (DOS)
FrameMaker	Frame Technology	Framemaker (Unix & Nextstep)
Client/server databases		
NetWare SQL	Novell, Inc.	Macintosh Data Access Language NetWare SQL for DOS and OS/2
Oracle	Oracle Corporation	Oracle for DOS, OS/2, and Unix
File server databases		
Foxbase (Mac)	Fox Software Corp.	Foxbase (DOS), Dbase III (DOS)
Omnis (Mac)	Blythe Software	Omnis (DOS)
Dbase (Mac)	Ashton-Tate	Dbase (DOS)

a complete list, or up to date; it is only an attempt to list a number of helpful examples.

The advantage of a solution that allows for the direct importing of files is that the Macintosh user has few adjustments to make. There is one small, yet important adjustment, however. In general, the user importing a file from another application program will not be able to do it by double clicking on the file that is to be imported. Microsoft Excel is an exception to this rule, because double clicking will work on Lotus 123 files. Most of the time, however, double clicking to import files does not work for one of two reasons: if the file is a Macintosh file from another application, and the other application is available, double clicking will launch the application program it came from instead of the one that was intended to be used; if the application program of the file's origin is not present, or if the file is a DOS PC file, double clicking will yield a box with the error message "Application is busy or missing."

Instead of double clicking files when you are importing files from other applications, you first should open the application you intend to use, and then use the File menu to access the file. With the Open command from the file menu, you can retrieve the file the way it is intended. A quick example of how file importing works, either from a different Macintosh application or from a DOS PC application, is provided by MacWrite II for the Macintosh. MacWrite II has the capability to read files from other Macintosh programs, or from some DOS PC programs, such as WordPerfect for DOS.

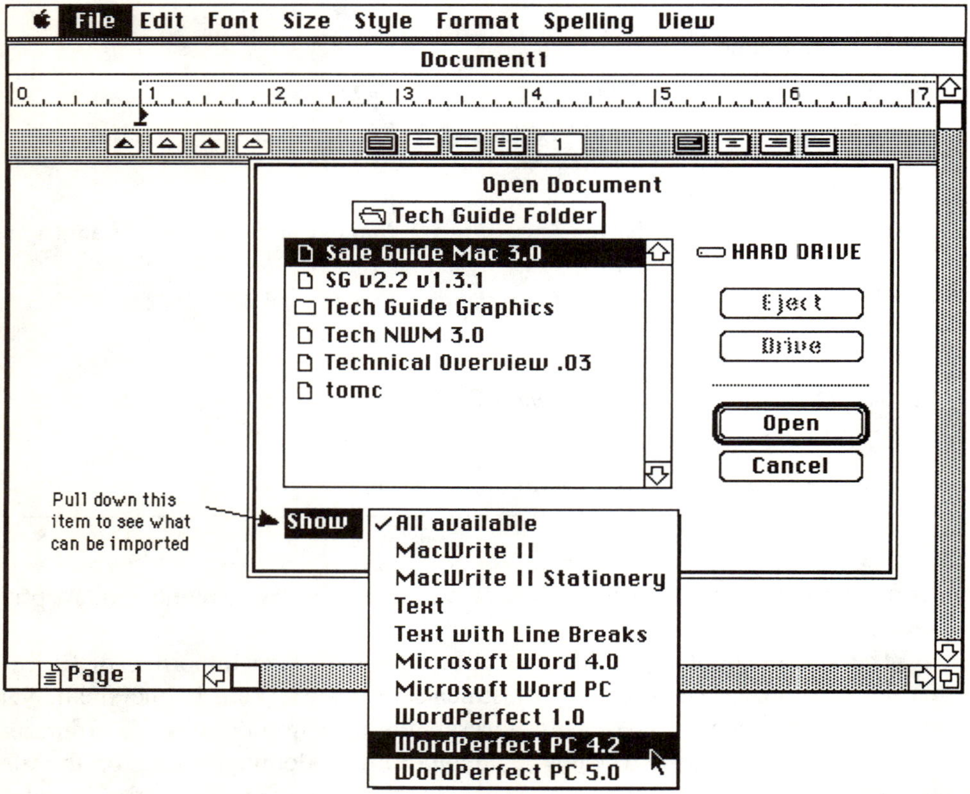

9-4 MacWrite II can read the files of many other applications.

In MacWrite II, you can see a special dialog box when attempting to open a file that was created by another application. This box asks you to indicate the format of the file you are opening. This dialogue box is displayed in Figure 9-5. Other Macintosh programs with file importing capabilities usually work basically the same way.

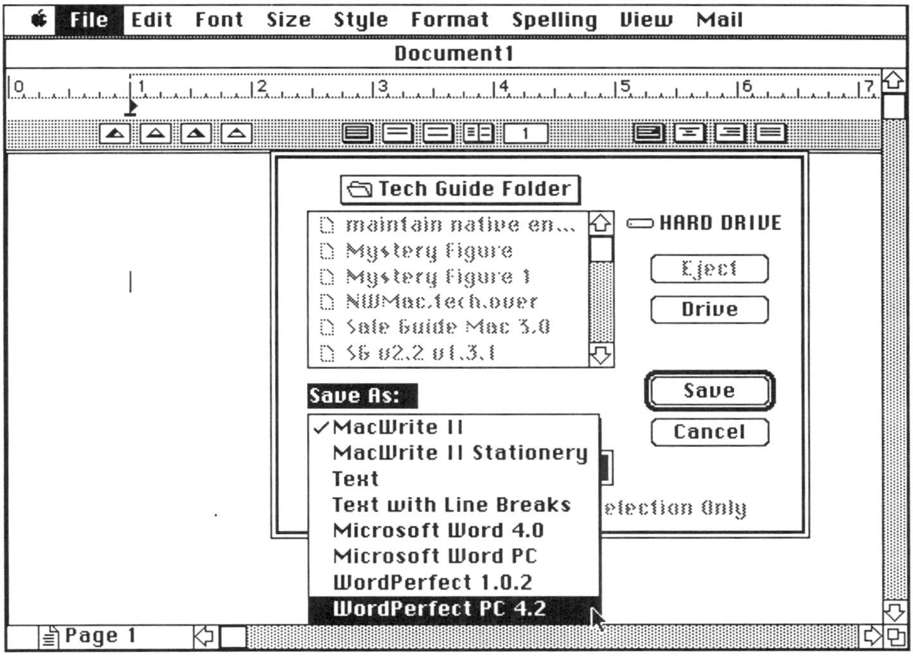

9-5 A dialogue box to be specific about the format of the file being imported.

Knowledge of the proper format is needed so that MacWrite II can convert not only the files text content, but the attributes, such as boldface and underline, as well. If you are not sure of the proper format, you can guess. If you guess wrong, the file might be refused, or you might have odd characters scattered in with the text when it appears on screen. Ordinarily, a wrong guess will not damage the original file, but as a safeguard it might be prudent to make a copy of the file before guessing.

A complement to a Macintosh program's file importing ability is its ability also to export files to different application formats. MacWrite II, for example, can export files to the same programs it imports from. Exporting to different application formats is done through the application's File menu with the Save As command. The Save As command for MacWrite II brings up the window shown in the left hand side of Figure 9-6. After clicking the File Format button in this

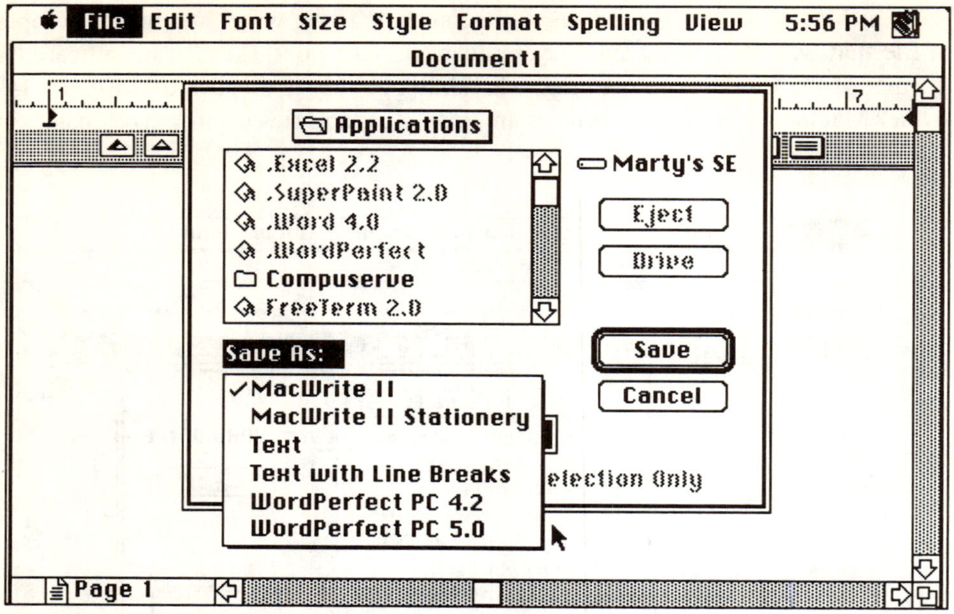

9-6 MacWrite II can export various file types.

window, users get the window on the right hand side of Figure 9.x, which allows them to specify an export format. Most other Macintosh programs with exporting capability export files in the same way.

Organizations that standardize their users on application programs that work on multiple platforms, or easily exchange data with other applications, will find that their users adjust to performing the exchanges fairly easily.

Translating files

When import capability for a file type is not part of a user's application program, users must find a way to translate the file. One method is the Apple File Exchange utility that comes free with the Macintosh System software. Beyond this, some commercially available translation programs extend what Apple offers.

Apple includes Apple File Exchange (AFE) with Macintosh System software versions 6.0 and later. Apple File Exchange consists of an application and translation files that work with the application to do the translation. Figure 9-8 shows the AFE application, and one of the translation files Apple provided. The one pictured here is for the conversion of DCA-RFT files to MacWrite. DCA-RFT is a common standard in IBM environments. Apple includes some translation files with the AFE application. Additional translation files are available from third-party software vendors, such as DataViz.

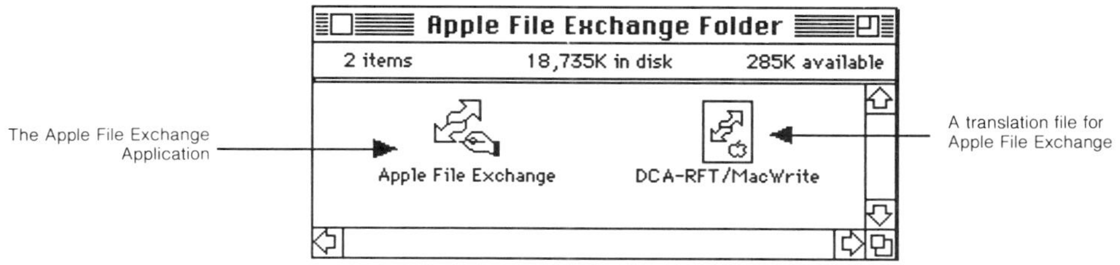

9-7 The Apple File Exchange application program.

When you launch the AFE program, you see a screen like the one in Figure 9-9. AFE, with the proper translation files, allows you to translate and convert files from different Macintosh programs, as well as DOS, Windows, and other application environments. To perform a translation, first select the file to be translated by clicking on its name. Figure 9-8 demonstates a DOS WordPerfect file being selected for translation.

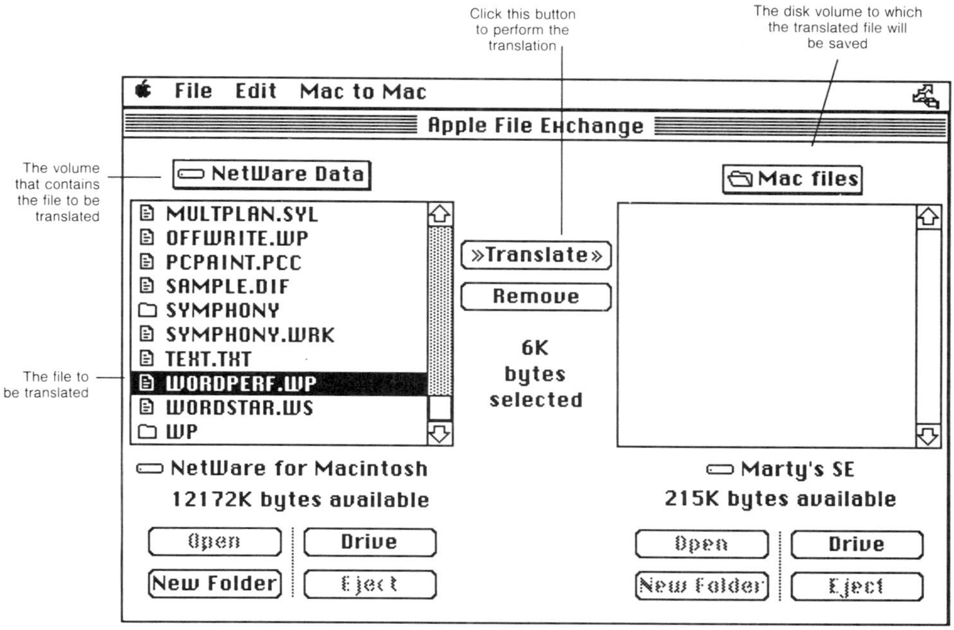

9-8 The Apple File Exchange interface.

In the tranlation process, a new file is created (the working copy in the translation process) with a name of the user's choice. To activate the translate button, you are required to select a destination for the translated file, which can be a different disk or the same disk as the original file. Figure 9-8 shows a file being translated from a NetWare for Macintosh server onto a user's local hard disk. When the destination drive is selected, the Translate button becomes active, with its arrows pointing in the direction that it will be copied (from the left window to the right, or vice versa).

Before selecting the translate button, you must tell the AFE program what translation you are doing. Figure 9-9 shows the selection made to specify a WordPerfect file being translated to MacWrite.

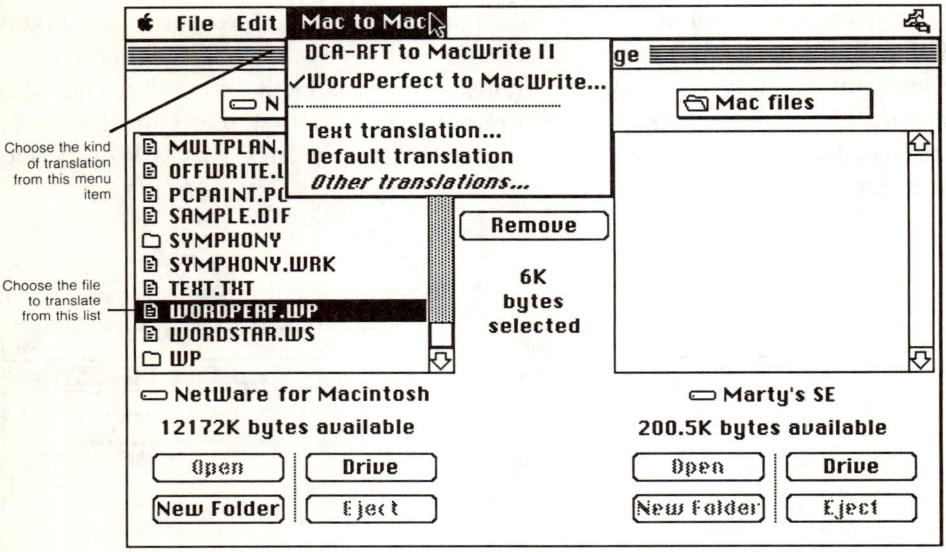

9-9 The menu to choose a translation.

The AFE program makes a working copy of the orginal file it is to translate, does the translation, and stores it in translated form. As the AFE program creates the new translated file, it checks to see if the name the user chose already exists, and if it does, it notifies the user of the name conflict. AFE uses the name of the original file for the translated file unless you specify a different name as shown in Figure 9-9. To select a different name, pull down the AFE file menu and choose a new name, as shown in Figure 9-10.

Adding new translators

In addition to the translators that come with it, the Apple File Exchange utility supports translation files written by third-party software vendors. After copying translation files to your Macintosh system, you must add these translations to the

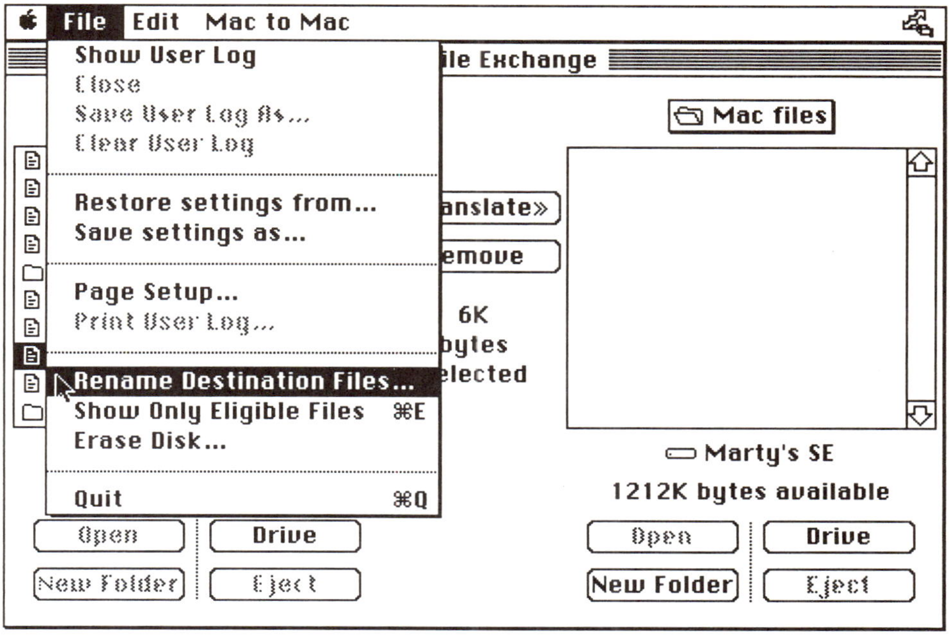

9-10 You can specify a new name for the destination file.

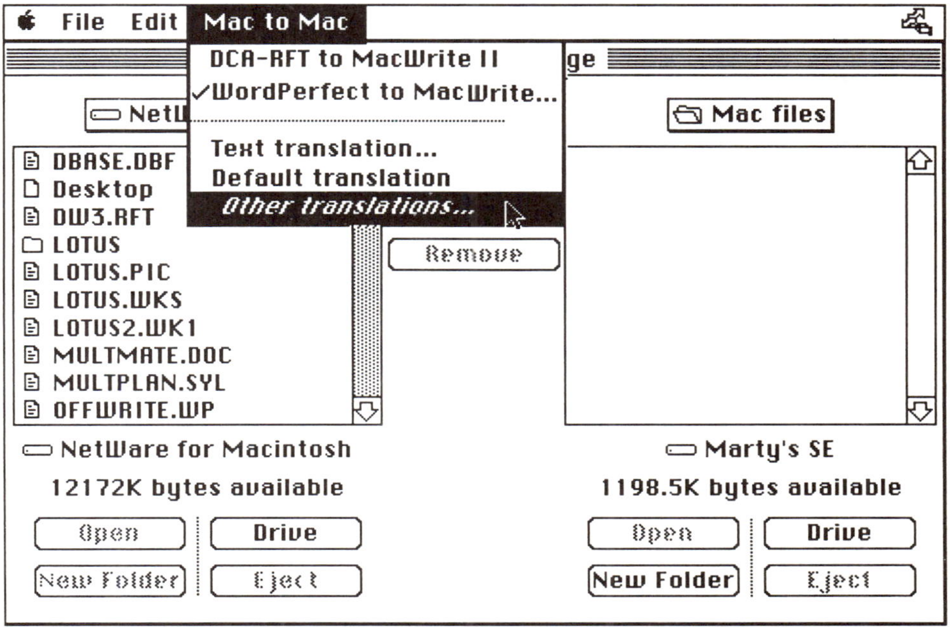

9-11 Choose Other Translations to add new translators to the menu.

AFE menu in order to use them. This is done with the Other Translations choice in the AFE Mac to Mac menu item, shown in Figure 9-11.

After choosing Other Translations, you will see a window, as shown in Figure 9-12. In this window, select the translation files you want, and away you go.

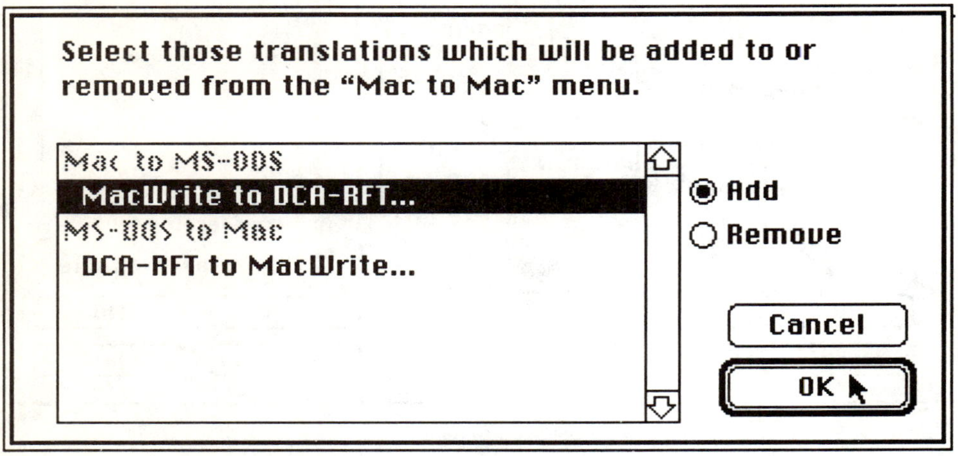

9-12 The menu to choose a translation.

Using DataViz's MacLink

DataViz, the company who makes translation files for Apple File Exchange, also makes a file translation program of their own, called MacLink Plus. MacLink plus is another good method for translating files from DOS and other computer

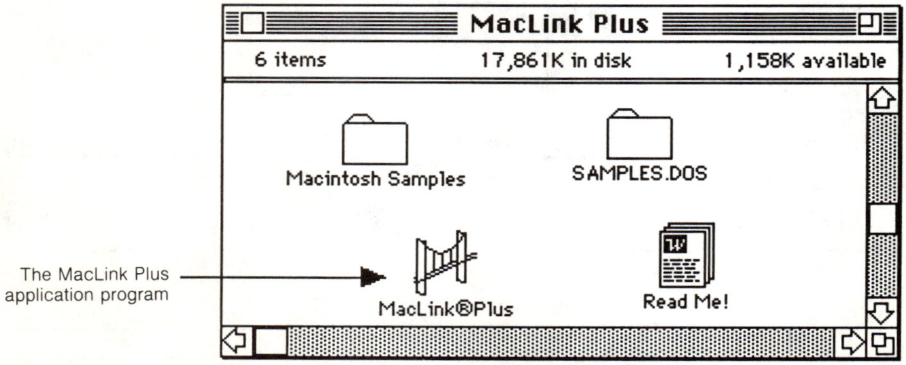

9-13 The MacLink plus applicaiton program.

application programs into formats for Macintosh application programs. One of the advantages of MacLink is that MacLink comes with a fairly large, built-in set of translations.

MacLink Plus can translate files from Macintosh format into some other format, and translate formats into Macintosh format. Figure 9-14 is showing a situation where a file from a DOS application, called Wordstar, is being converted into MacWrite format for a Macintosh. After making the fomat selections, you need to click the file selection button.

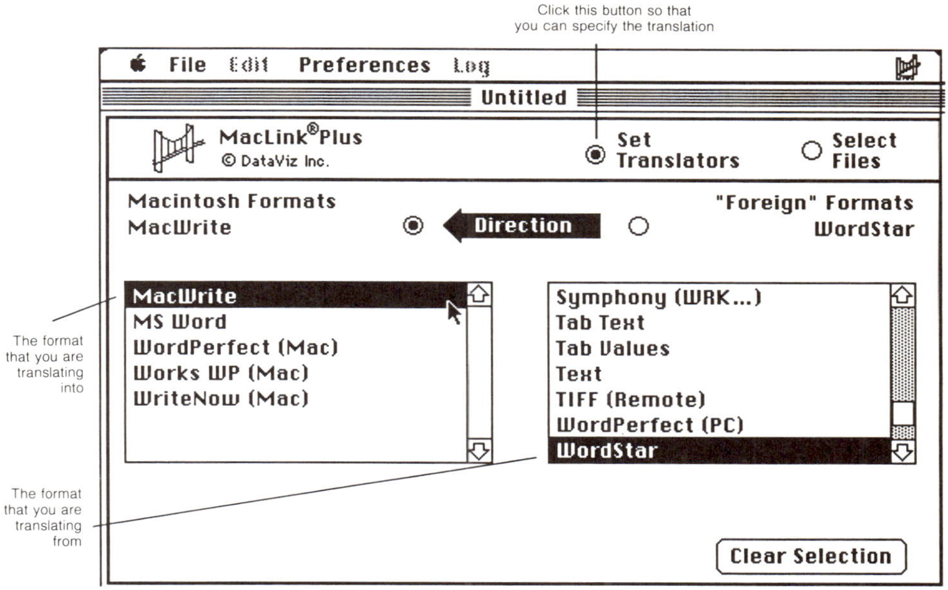

9-14 The interface for MacLink Plus to select translations.

Figure 9-15 shows the screen you use to select the files to be converted. Like the Apple File Exchange program, MacLink Plus makes a working copy of the file it will convert, and then saves the converted working file under a new name. The file can be saved on the same drive, or to a different drive. The example in Figure 9-15 is copying and converting a file stored in a folder called Accounting, which is on a NetWare for Macintosh server, into a folder on the user's local hard drive called Business. When the file is converted, it will be in MacWrite format.

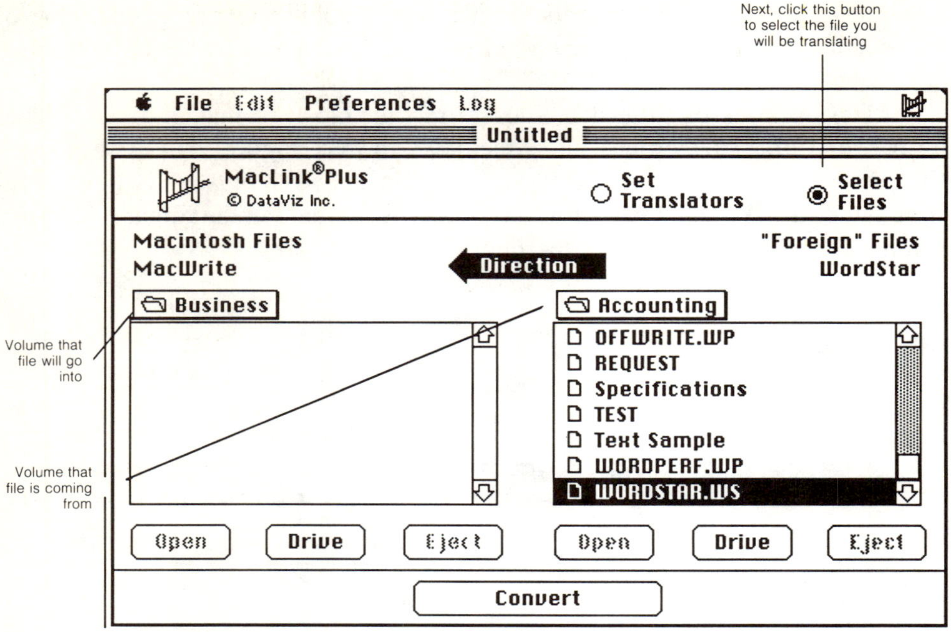

9-15 The screen to select files and the destination of the translated file.

Plain text conversion

In the absense of having the proper translation file for the applications that must exchange data, a generic method of file exchange exists through a format called ASCII text. ASCII stands for American Standard Code for Information Exchange. ASCII formatted text is often just referred to as text; the word ASCII is dropped to shorten the term. In any case, ASCII text is readable and writable by virtually any application.

The first user screen encountered when running MacLink Plus is shown in Figure 9-16. The window that designates Macintosh file formats is on the left-hand side, and the window for the format of the other file is on the right-hand side. This screen requires that you select the format the file is in currently in one of the windows, and the format that the file will be translated to in the other window.

For a Macintosh to store a file in text form, the user must pull down the Save As item in the application's File menu. Figure 9-16 shows this choice, along with the format screen that would follow if this choice were made in MacWrite II. In the format screen, the choice of Text Only is used if the text is bound for another Macintosh application. If the text is bound for a DOS or Windows application, the proper choice would be Text With Line Breaks.

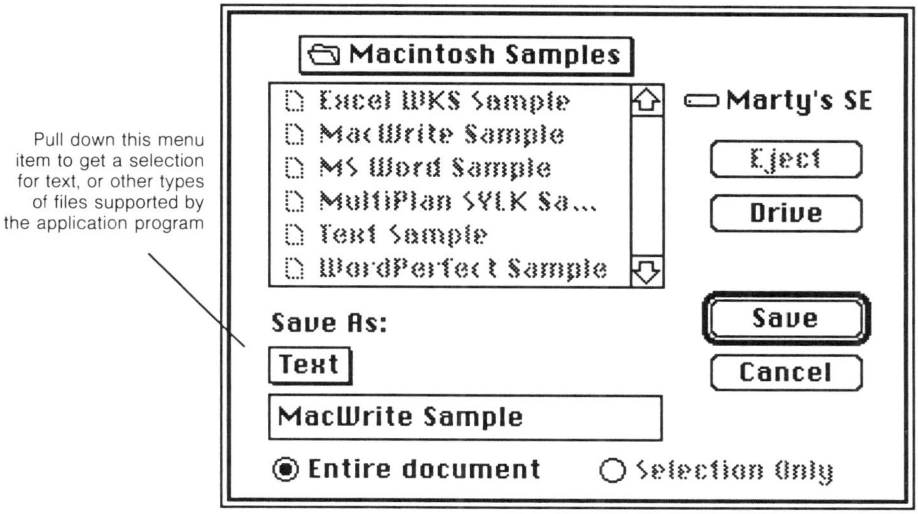

9-16 Saving a file as text.

The example in Figure 9-16 shows the process for Macintosh users to store a file as text so that DOS/Windows, or OS/2/UNIX users can import it into their applications. Sometimes a DOS or other user needs to save the file as text, so it can be imported into a Macintosh. When a file is being saved by a Windows or OS/2 user, the Save As item in the File menu also will have a choice for saving as text. For DOS applications, however, there is no standard method. The process varies from application to application. Refer to your application user's manual for instuctions on the procedure.

If the text is inbound to the Macintosh from a DOS application, then depending on the Macintosh application that will receive it, some additional work might be required. This is because DOS and Macintosh versions of ASCII differ. The DOS version of ASCII has a line break character at the end of each line that Macintosh text does not have. That is why Text with Line Breaks was specified in MacWrite II when saving the file for a DOS user. In order to remove the Line Break character from DOS text bound for Macintosh applications, you must use the Apple File Exchange utility to strip those characters away.

The choice for text translation falls under the *Mac to Mac* item in the AFE menu, as shown in Figure 9-17. What you intend to do is convert DOS text to Mac text. The Text Translation menu item calls up a screen, shown in Figure 9-18. This screen contains a choice for MS-DOS (DOS) to Mac.

After clicking the MS-DOS to Mac button, a list of selectable character options appears for parts of the text that might be variable, such as foreign characters or tab settings. This list is pictured in Figure 9-18, on the left-hand side of the window. The list in the figure is set to parameters that work for most

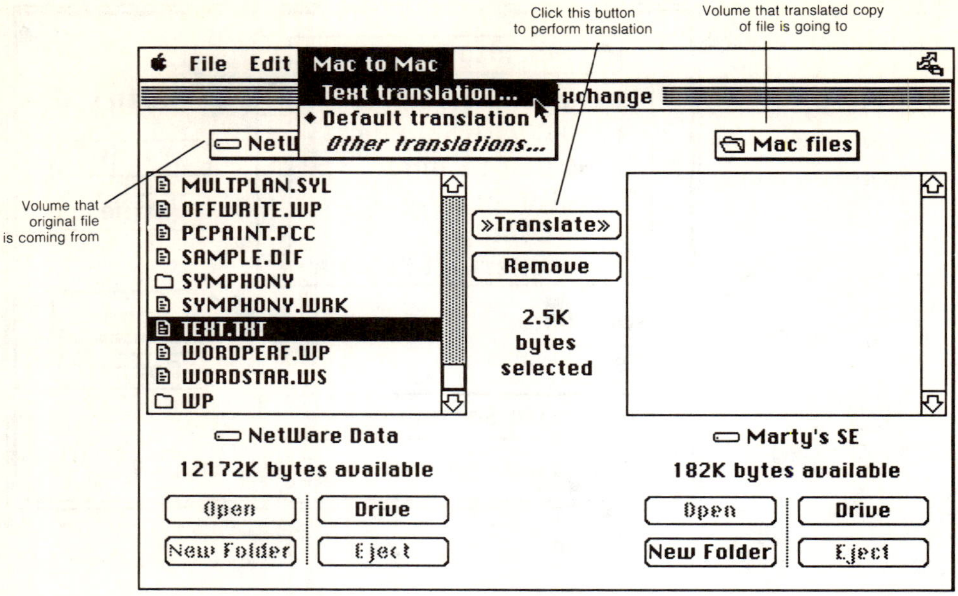

9-17 Converting DOS text to Macintosh text.

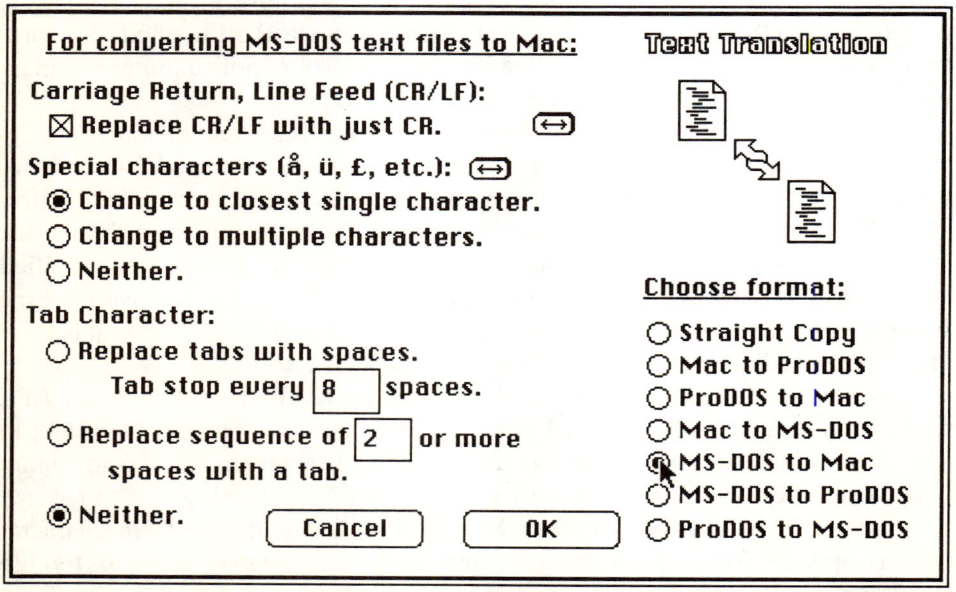

9-18 The settings for DOS to Macintosh text conversion.

people most often, but feel free to experiment with these choices to make them work better for you.

Clicking the OK button causes the Apple File Exchange utility to copy the file from the network drive to another network drive, or to your local hard disk. It also filters out the DOS Line Break characters, and converts tabs as it copies. What is left is a file that your Macintosh application can cleanly read.

However, to make your application see the file when you give the File menu's Open command, you might need to click the button in the Open window's finder box, so that text files appears in the list. Figure 9-19 shows how to do this with MacWrite II.

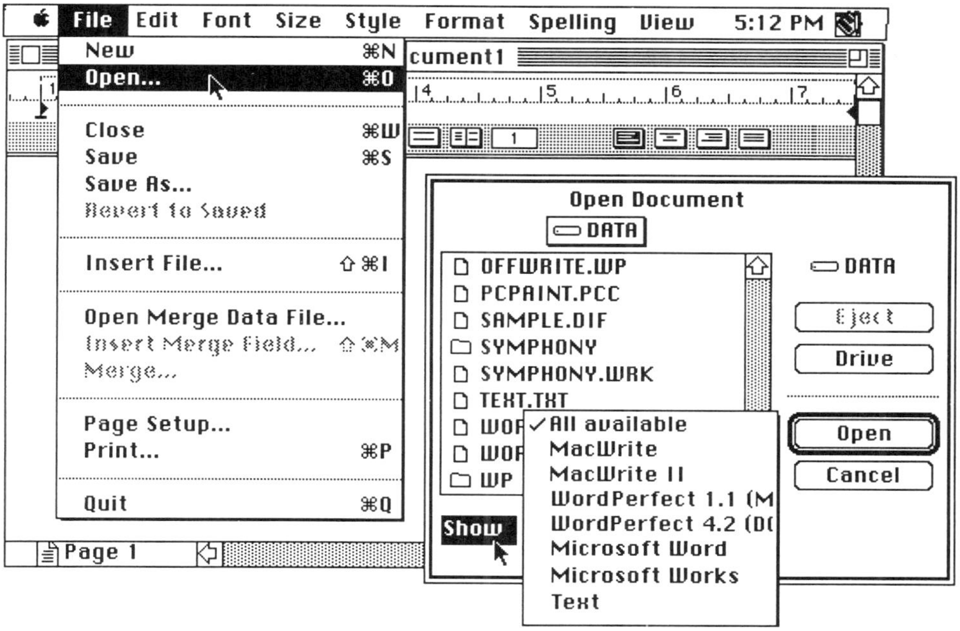

9-19 MacWrite II is able to import text.

10
Chapter

Troubleshooting with NetWare for Macintosh

Occasionally in your day-to-day interaction on a network you might experience a problem. Server or client network interface cards go bad, network wires break, and various other unpredictable things happen from time to time. In those cases, if your organization is fortunate enough to have support people who can assist you in finding and solving the problem, all you have to do is report it. If your organization is not deep in support resources, however, you might need to help diagnose or solve the problem yourself.

This final chapter is a guide to help point you in the right direction if you are experiencing problems with NetWare for Macintosh networks. It is not a comprehensive trouble shooting guide, but it will provide you with some information that can get you started. The assumption made in this chapter is that you are working on a previously installed NetWare for Macintosh server that is now experiencing problems. If you are installing NetWare for Macintosh for the first time, the most complete source of information to help you is the NetWare for Macintosh Installation and Maintenance Guide.

Troubleshooting basics

If you are the only user on the network who is reporting a problem, your report of the problem might not have a lot of credibility with those supporting you, unless you first take a few steps to diagnose whether the problem is with your computer.

Step one is to verify that your computer is properly attached to the network. This is not suggested as an insult to your intelligence. This is suggested to encourage you to do more than a visual inspection. Remove and re-attach the network connection, tighten the screws, and make yourself comfortable that all is well. Even if it looks OK, when you shift your computer on its desktop or when maintenance people clean up in your area, connections can get bumped and come loose.

As you are conducting your inspection, make sure that the only network connection you unfasten is the one that attaches to the network interface card of your computer. Do not unfasten the other connections if they look anything like the one displayed in Figure 10-1, because if you do, you might disconnect other users in the process. Many network topologies, such as LocalTalk and Ethernet buses, use your connector as links in a chain, and if you undo some of those connections, you break the chain.

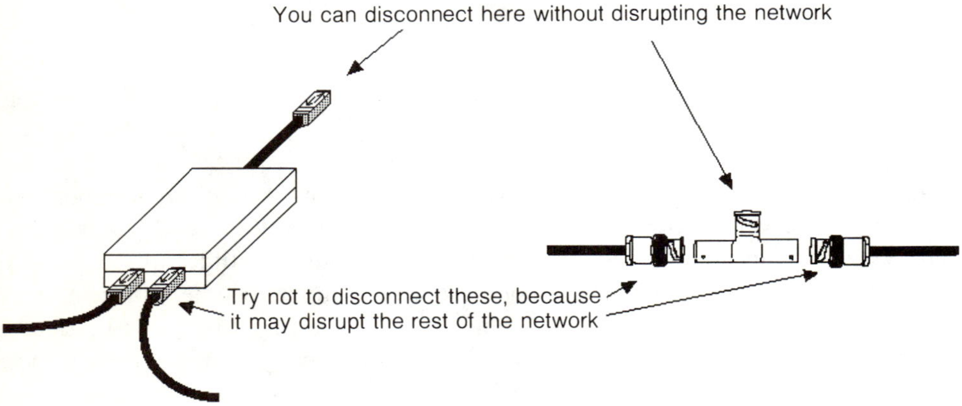

10-1 Checking your network connection.

When you are satisfied your connection is OK, you can begin to narrow the problem down to other factors. Can DOS workstations, or other computers see NetWare services? If so, the problem could be with your computer, or with NetWare for Macintosh.

If you have lost contact with NetWare for Macintosh File services, then use the Chooser to make sure you are looking in the right zone. Select the Laser-Writer icon to see if you can find a printer or print queues. Likewise, if you lost print services, see if you can find network file services. If you see one, but not the other, you probably have discovered that the problem is with the service programs that reside on the NetWare server, or with an AppleTalk router (assuming your network includes one).

If those tests don't tell you anything, you need to examine things a little closer. Next, look in your Macintosh Control Panel to verify that the appropriate drivers are selected. Figure 10-2 shows you the Control Panels for both System 6.X and System 7.X that were explained in chapter 5. You must make sure the right driver is selected for the cabling media that you are using, and that you are using the right version of AppleTalk. If your server is using AppleTalk Phase 2, and the driver that you have active is AppleTalk Phase 1, you won't see the server.

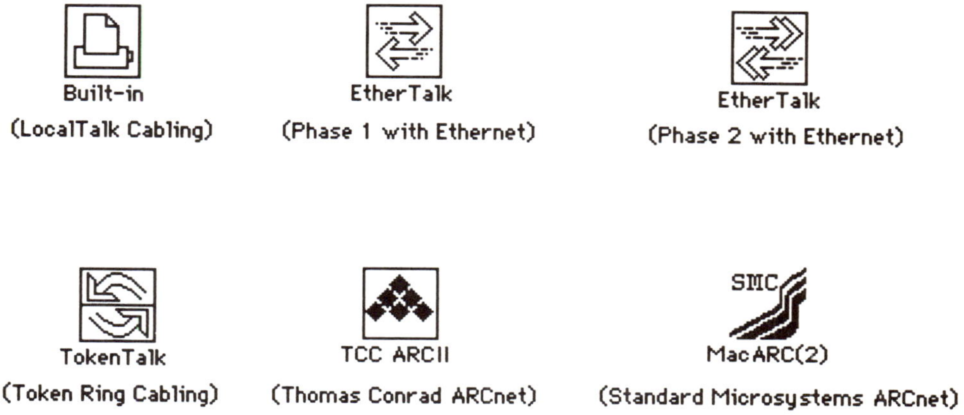

10-2 Checking various AppleTalk Drivers.

Checking your computers cabling and interface

If your driver selection is OK, then you should check and see if the problem is with the network cable, or the network interface card in the computer. First, do a visual check of the cable. On twisted pair cabling, look for crimps in the wire or loose leads that might have been caused by the wires being pulled too hard. If you are electrically inclined, temporarily disconnect the network fasteners and use an ohm meter to complete the circuit and see if you get a reading. If you suspect that you have a cabling problem, an easy way to validate your suspicion is to move your computer to a different location and see if it can attach to a LaserWriter. If it works there, then your cabling is bad. If you still can't see any services, then the problem might be a result of your network interface.

It's very easy to check the health of your computer's Ethernet network interface card with a straight-forward network utility called Echo. Echo is a public domain program that sends data over to another node on the network and back again, verifying that it got back the same data that it sent. The echo utility is shipped on the driver disks that come with most Ethernet cards. Figure 10-3 shows the icon for this utility.

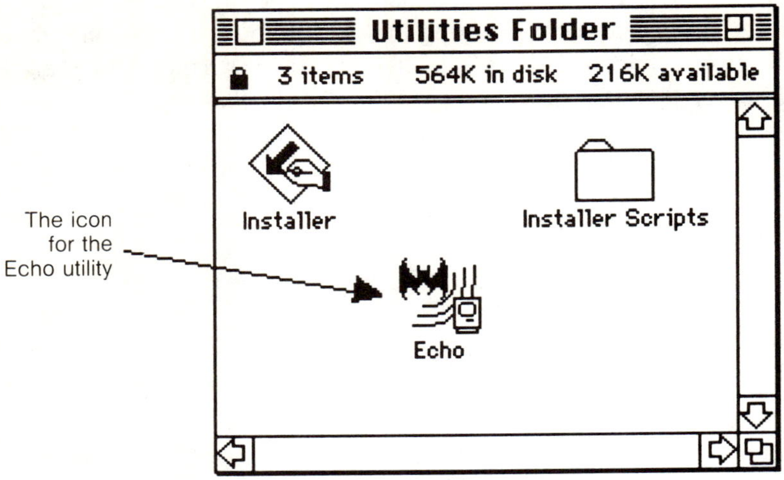

10-3 The Echo utility's icon.

When you launch the Echo utility, you are presented with the window that you see in Figure 10-4. In this window you must fill in the instructions for the echo test that you want conducted, which is a lot easier than it might look at first. At the top of the screen; you can see the AppleTalk node number for your Macintosh, and the network number that it resides in, if you are on an internetwork with routers. Even if there are no AppleTalk routers on your network, you can see a network number of zero.

In a box on the left-hand side of the window that is labeled Hosts, appears a list of other nodes on the network, when you click the button labeled Find hosts. These nodes are called hosts in this program because of the historic use of the word for network nodes that provide services, which they are doing in this case by providing their addresses for echoing tests.

To perform the echo test, select one of the node numbers from the list, and click the button at the bottom of the window. When you do so, the Echo utility sends out 50 premeasured data packets and counts them as they are returned by the other node. The counters for these data packets are displayed on the right-hand side of the window. If fewer than 50 data packets are returned, it might indicate the inability of your network interface card to read data off of the network wire. It also might indicate a problem with the card of the other node. Repeat the test with several different nodes. If the test comes up short each time,

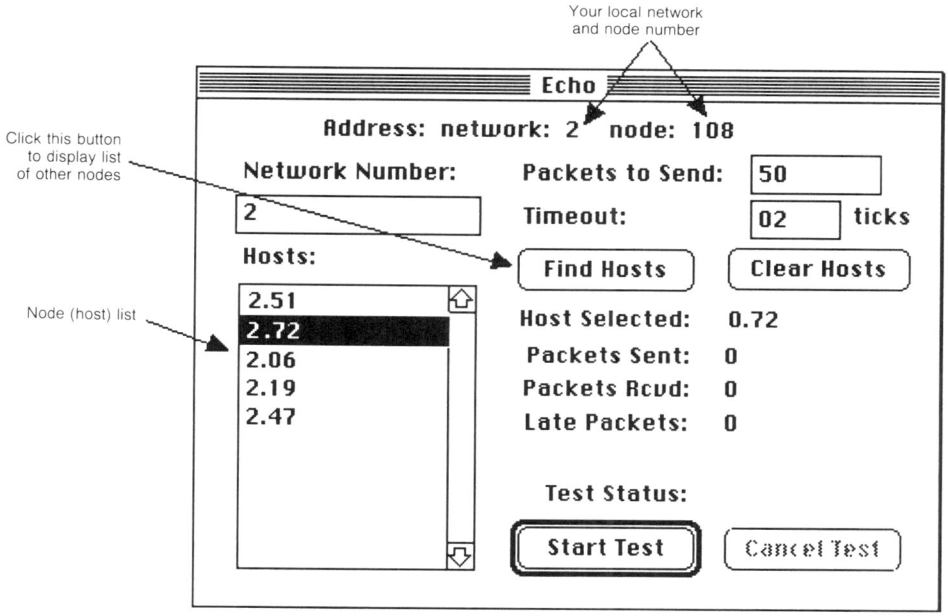

10-4 The Echo test program.

you have a bad card or network cable. Try the test with a new cable to pinpoint the problem conclusively to the card.

If you are on a LocalTalk network, Echo's tests still will help you, but you need to find a copy of it. You might be able to secure one from your local Macintosh reseller, or from the Macintosh sections of electronic bulletin board services, such as CompuServe. If you can not get one, on NetWare for Macintosh v3.X servers, you can perform the echo test form the console of the server.

Comprehensive testing from a Macintosh client

If you are a nontechnical computer user, then the steps recommended in the previous section might be as far as you can go towards locating and solving your organizations network problem. If you have a more technical knowledge about networking, or an inquisitive nature, however, there are other diagnosing methods you can use to get closer to identifying or solving your networks problems.

The Echo testing utility is a simple tool that you can use to test one part of the operation of a network interface. Although it is effective, it does not give you very descriptive information about the problems your network is experiencing. Another tool called Inter · Poll contains a set of tests that can do a little more to help you find problems and monitor and analyze network performance. It also should be available through Macintosh resellers.

Inter · Poll performs a sequential series of tasks designed to isolate the location of a problem. It begins with a zone and device listing and proceeds to local testing at the device or network level. Optionally, individual devices can be checked to assure network integrity by testing for data loss and network path changes resulting from router malfunctions. Inter · Poll is a tool not often used by an individual trying to solve a personal problem, but by a supervisor or administrator trying to solve it for them, or perhaps for a whole group of people.

The tests that Inter · Poll performs can be used to:

- display listing of zones, networks, and active network devices
- test the integrity and response of the network path to a specific device
- isolate possible problems

On a NetWare network, Inter · Poll provides information about only the AppleTalk network. This AppleTalk network, which is made up of all the AppleTalk devices on the NetWare network, coexists with other networking and is sometimes referred to as a *virtual network,* because it exists within another network. The network it exists within is the composite NetWare network, which includes SPX/IPX devices and possibly TCP/IP devices.

Inter · Poll can list the devices within zones, sorted by network number, node number, devices name, device type and a few other criteria of the operators choice. The criteria are specified in an easy-to-use window menu that appears as Inter · Poll is launched. When the search begins, Inter · Poll broadcasts the network for respondents to its criteria and displays them in a window, as shown in Figure 10-5. One obvious conclusion that can be drawn should a sizable group of devices not be found in this search is that either a router or a segment of cable that connects them is malfunctioning.

Having identified the devices and their network and node numbers, a user can then perform more rigorous tests. Inter · Poll's other tests are available through its command menu. One of these tests devices by initiating loopback tests similar to those performed by Echo, which checks connection paths and response times between the device and the workstation running Inter · Poll. Data, such as response times of specific devices, can be compared to averages of other devices to identify slow responding nodes. Slow responses often signify malfunctions that can be detrimental to overall network performance because in a particular network interaction, other devices must wait to use the network until the slow responding node is finished. This is particularly troublesome when the slow responding node is a server. The window that displays this test result is shown in Figure 10-6.

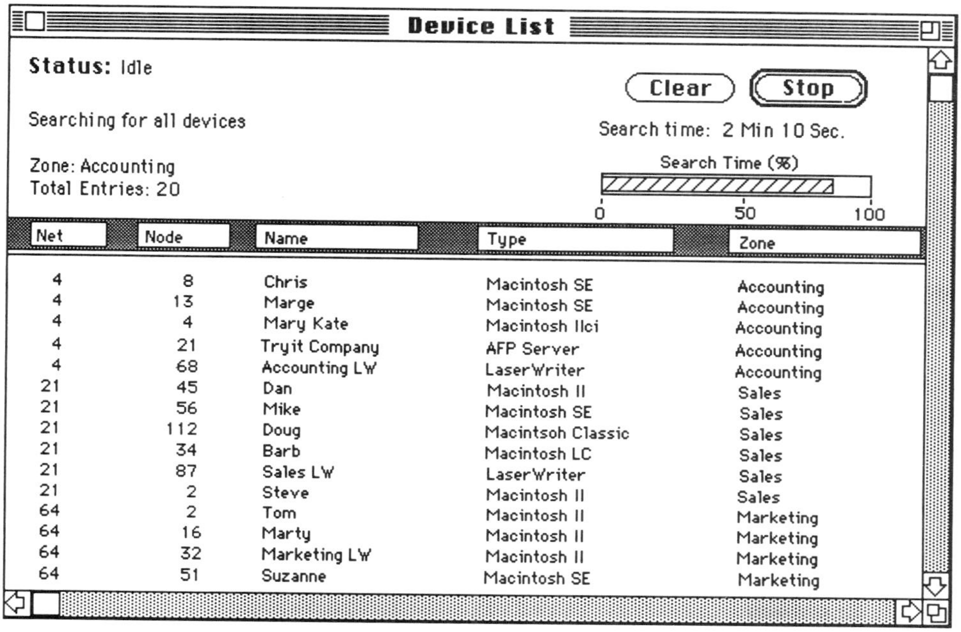

10-5 InterPoll's device list window.

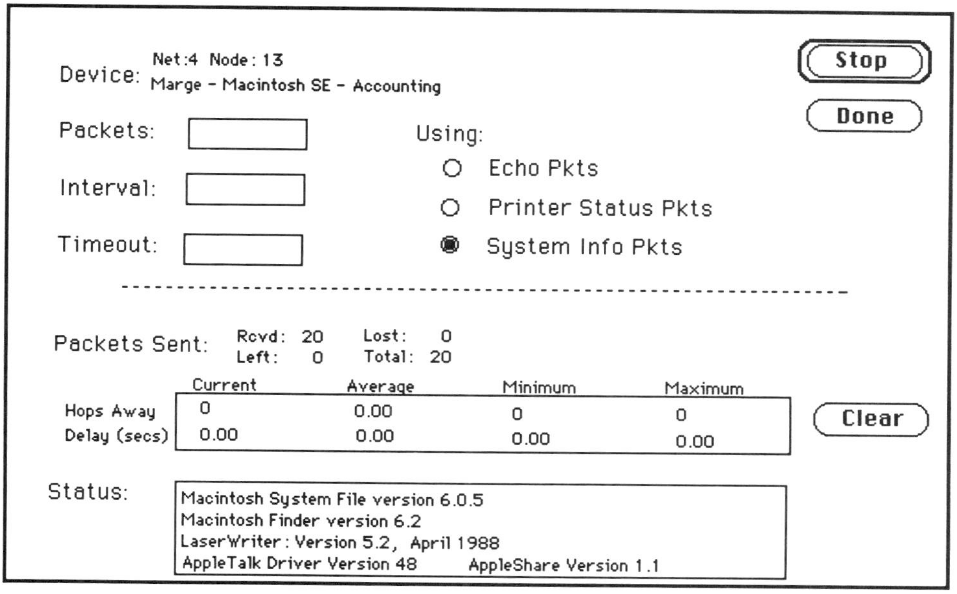

10-6 InterPoll's device test window.

In addition to the loopback tests, The Inter · Poll test window can be used to test LaserWriters, and to query individual workstations for the verisons of Macintosh system files, and the LaserWriter drivers that they are using. The information about LaserWriter drivers is especially helpful when users are experiencing conflicts with other user's who have different versions of the drivers.

Several third-party software vendors have developed useful AppleTalk and EtherTalk tools that do more sophisticated packet analysis of data on AppleTalk, or NetWare networks than does Inter · Poll. Among these tools are GraceLAN from Technology Works, Inc., EtherPeek from the AG Group, NetMinder from Neon Software, and some NetWare products called the LANAlyzer and the LANtern Network Monitor. They acutally can look inside data packets and determine the nodes sending out bad ones.

Troubleshooting AppleTalk routers

Many times, problems like the disappearance of servers are a result of problems with AppleTalk network routers rather than the server. If your network uses routers, one sure way to find out if your network is having router problems is to check whether the zones that used to appear in your Chooser are gone. If your zones have disappeared, it could mean that your router has failed.

Other than failure, the most common router problem is a mismatch of network numbers. In an AppleTalk network, two different segments of physical cable should not be given the same network numbers. This is demonstrated on an AppleTalk Phase 1 network through Figure 10-7. If this ever happens, the network will start to behave erratically. To fix the problem, remove the duplicated net numbers from one of the routers. This requires a painstaking search of the numbers for each router interface to identify the offenders.

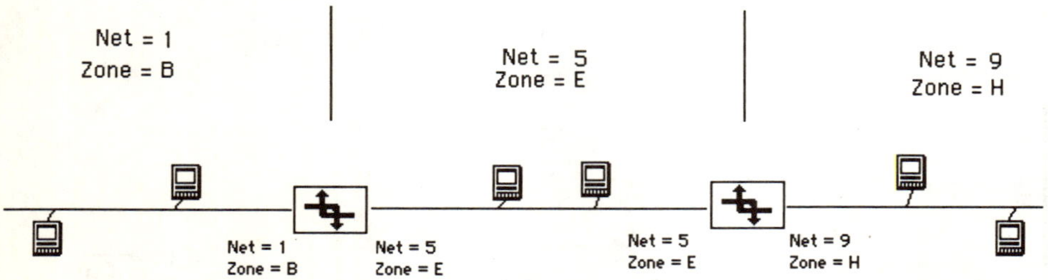

10-7 Troubleshooting routers.

Troubleshooting on a server

If you are a support person, the network supervisor, or system administrator for your organizations network, you will find yourself doing a fair amount of network troubleshooting from the console of the network server. The *server console* is simply the interface you are presented with as you give commands and interact with the server's operating system. The rest of this chapter assumes that you are somewhat familiar with giving commands at the server console, and you are the NetWare supervisor or have supervisor equivalence. Only the supervisor, or someone with supervisor equivalence, can perform most of these operations.

Both NetWare v2.X and NetWare v3.X have server consoles from which you can configure, modify, and troubleshoot the particulars of your network server. The server consoles are different for the respective NetWare versions, but the basic processes used to operate them are the same. There is a certain amount of testing you can do from menus provided by the console, but the rest you must do from a command line. Sometimes these commands are the same for both verisons, and sometimes they are different.

In both versions of NetWare for Macintosh, the first step in diagnosing problems with file or print services is to make sure all the NetWare for Macintosh VAPs or NLMs are still running, and then check if the servers AppleTalk LAN drivers are loaded for the network interface through which Macintosh clients are attempting to reach the server. Beyond that, the procedure will vary depending on the symptoms of the problem you are having.

Volume names are grayed out

When the file server is located in the Chooser, but the volume names are in gray in the Volume window when you try to select one as they log in to the server, it could mean that you already have a volume mounted on that server. If you do, you must unmount that volume by dragging it into the trash, and then log in over again. During your new log in, you can mount multiple volumes. A security feature in NetWare for Macintosh will not allow a Macintosh user to select new volume on servers that already have one mounted.

However, if an unmounted volume is not the source of your problem, then try these steps:

- Issue the FLAGDIR command from a DOS workstation to verify that the volume is not flagged as PRIVATE. It should be flagged as NORMAL.
- On a NetWare for Macintosh v3.X server, issue the command Set Allow Unencrypted Passwords = On.
- Use a DOS workstation to issue the USERLIST command to see if the server thinks the Macintosh is logged in. If it does, then the cause of the problem might be that files are missing from the DESKTOP directory of the server. Look into the NetWare DESKTOP directory (a directory hidden from most users) and make sure that the right files are present. Refer to your NetWare for Macintosh Installation and Maintenance manual for

the file names and information for the version you are using. If any are missing or damaged, replace them.

- From a DOS workstation, try to create a new directory at the root level, if the directory cannot be made, the volume might be damaged.
- Also from a DOS workstation, use the SYSCON utility to view the rights for the group EVERYONE at the root level of the volume in question. If an error message is returned, there is damage to the volume, and VREPAIR should be run (after first backing up the data).

Users get messages that minor repairs need to be made on the volume

This error message is often accompanied with the symptom of allowing users to log into the server, but the icon never showing up on their desktop. This is normally a problem with the servers Desktop files.

It might be that some of the files are missing or that they have been damaged. Look in the NetWare DESKTOP directory, a directory hidden from most users, and make sure that the right files are present. Refer to your NetWare for Macintosh Installation and Maintenance manual for the file names and information for the version you are using. If any are missing or damaged, replace them.

If they are all present, but you are not sure if any are damaged, you can try using your Macintosh to rebuild them. To rebuild the server's desktop files, hold down the CONTROL and OPTION keys as you mount the problematic volume. A dialogue box will appear asking you if you are sure you want to do this. Click OK, and proceed. It might take several minutes. If for some reason that doesn't work, use the AppleShare volume screen to configure the volume to be mounted at system startup. Then restart your Macintosh and hold down the CONTROL and OPTION keys as your Macintosh comes to life.

The server's connection unexpectedly shuts down

You'll know when this happens because you and your users will recieve an error message. This often happens because network packets are being lost, dropped, or are taking too long to get their destination (server or client).

This problem can be caused by bad cables, bad interface cards, AppleTalk routing problems, or overloaded networks. This is probably not a server operating system problem. Use Inter · Poll or other AppleTalk network analyzing tools to diagnose the cause of the problem.

Without the aid of these tools, you still might be able to apply some common sense to fix the problem as long as it's not caused by bad packets coming from a bad interface card. Make sure you don't have more nodes on any network section than the recommended maximums of your cabling system permit. If your network has a fairly large number of clients and you are not using AppleTalk routers, perhaps you need one to segregate network traffic into different interconnected networks.

Conversely, if your network has a large number of routers, it could be that some users are required to travel through too many network "hops", or that you have conflicting entries in some of the router configuration tables. Macintosh computers on the other side of the router that has incorrect table entries might loose their connection to the server while the router is negotiating its conflict with other routers. If some users are experiencing attenuated signals due to too many router hops, then reconfiguration might be the best solution.

The file server is busy or the password in incorrect

This is an error messages that could be given to a Macintosh client for several different problems that manifest themselves in similar ways. In cases where users get this message, they generally see the server and its volumes, but in both cases, they are prevented from logging in.

For these problems, you should definately concentrate on the file server, because it controls who will be allowed to log in. There is nothing in the AppleTalk protocol, or the Macintosh clients AppleShare workstation software that can cause these syptoms.

One possible explanation for these messages is that the server has reached its user limit. Both NetWare v2.X and v3.X operating systems have limits on the number of users that they support, and there is an additional limit on the number of Macintosh users that can be supported in NetWare for Macintosh. The default for the number of Macintosh users supported by NetWare for Macintosh v2.X is 80, and in NetWare for Macintosh v3.X, there are configurations for 20 or 100. You can see now many users are supported by the version of operating system you are running by giving the VER command at the server console.

If user limits are not the problem, it could be overutilization. This is more likely to inhibit NetWare and NetWare for Macintosh v2.X than it is v3.X. Use the server's console, or FCONSOLE's statistics summaries from a DOS workstation to check on the servers utilization. If the numbers are consistently high it might be neccessary to add more memory to the server, or move one server's burdens to another server. One way to do that might be to transfer some of its users to another server.

Of course, don't overlook the obvious. The message might be telling you that the password is incorrect because it has expired. Passwords can be given time limits, and when these limits expire, the passwords are automatically made invalid. Use SYSCON to check the time restrictions and other similar restrictions on passwords.

The servers performance is slow, or erratic

Like login problems, slow server performance is often the result of a level of server use that is too high, or the bandwidth of the network cabling system. Many times, the condition results from both problems happening simultaneously.

The only way to conclusively trace the problem to one or the other is to analyze statisticical measurements of their utilization. NetWare makes it relatively easy to track a server utilization through the statistical measurements performed by its server console and FCONSOLE utilities. NetWare v3.X displays some of these statistics in its default console screen. FCONSOLE must be run from a DOS workstation.

Server CPU utilization is caused by user access, and the operating systems transactions with the servers disks and other resources. Server CPU utilization statistics vary from minute to minute in the course of network activity, but dedicated servers shouldn't stay higher than 30 to 40% for any significant period of time. If it appears that a large amount of this utilization is occuring from disk intensive applications, it might be possible to reduce it by adding memory and disk buffers. Otherwise, you will need to transfer some of that server's burden to another server, as previously discussed.

If server utilization is not the problem, or if that has been corrected, performance still will not improve if there is a significant problem with saturation of the cabling system's bandwidth. Network Analyzing tools, such as the NetWare LANAlyzer, have self-running statistical tests that measure a cabling system's utilization. A consistent level of 40 to 50% utilization is typically considered the maximum usage that any given cabling system can support without having performance problems.

Where to go for additional help

There is some pretty detailed troubleshooting information in the NetWare for Macintosh Installation and Maintenance manuals for NetWare for Macintosh. If you can't get enough information to help you there, however, you might get some very good assistance from Novell sponsored user organizations or independent user groups.

Perhaps the best source of information might be a local Novell user's group. Most major metropolitan areas have them. You might be able to find a phone number for the one nearest you in your local phone book or yellow pages. If you don't succeed there, try calling the nearest Novell office. They might know the phone number. Users groups are often great ways for people to run their problems by other users in a search for a solution. Many times other users have experienced the same or similar problems and can be of assistance.

Another possible source of information is an organization called NetWare Users International, which is an independent, Novell subsidized group that has information about a number of publications and references that could be very useful to you. Even if you don't need their help, it might be a good idea for you to contact NetWare Users International so that you can be recorded in their database. Novell frequently uses that database as a mailing list to keep in contact with customers about new developments and product updates for NetWare.

Glossary

accounting NetWare's accounting option lets network owners charge customers who use their network server. Owners can charge for five different network server services:

Blocks read from server hard disks

Blocks written to server hard disks

Amount of time the user is logged in to the server

Amount of data stored on server hard disks

Number of requests serviced by the server

adapters Hardware installed in a PC or other computer and used to connect the computer to other hardware.

American Standard Code for Information Interchange (ASCII) A 7-bit code intended as a U.S. standard for the interchange of information among communications devices.

AppleShare Apple Computer's networking solution, which requires a dedicated Macintosh as a network server and includes both server and workstation software. It uses AppleTalk Filing Protocol (AFP).

Novell's Macintosh connectivity solution teams NetWare for Macintosh server software with AppleShare workstation software.

Macintosh II servers can support up to 50 workstations; a Macintosh Plus or Macintosh SE is limited to 32.

AppleTalk A family of protocols developed by Apple Computer and implemented on the Macintosh and on other computers and peripherals. The protocols defined by AppleTalk might run on a number of physical media, including shielded or unshielded twisted pair (LocalTalk, PhoneNET), and thin and standard Ethernet cable (EtherTalk).

Based on the OSI model, AppleTalk is comparable to NetWare communications protocols; both specify communications that range from application interfaces to media access.

AppleTalk Filing Protocol (AFP) Allows distributed file sharing across an AppleTalk network.

application A task to which a computer or computer network is applied to solve a problem or perform a service.

application program A software program or program package that makes calls to the operating system and manipulates data files, thus allowing a user to perform a specific job (such as accounting or word processing).

application interface A set of software routines and associated conventions that permits application programmers to use that interface as a part of any application.

In general, an application interface is used to access system or networking services that would otherwise require significant development effort to create from scratch.

For example, the Btrieve application interface lets a programmer use Btrieve file structures and services within an application. See also API.

application programming interface (API) A means by which an application gains access to system resources, usually for the purpose of communication (the sending and receiving of data), data retrieval or other system services.

In the specific area of terminal emulation, an API provides for the simulation of keystrokes and for writing into and reading from the presentation space (device buffer).

It might also provide for the sending and receiving of structured fields.

archive To create a redundant copy of computer file data, typically to create a backup copy of that data to protect it if the original copy is damaged or otherwise irretrievable.

By some definitions, an archive is required to contain copies of every version of a particular file.

In this case, to archive means to save a copy of every object in a file system with a separate copy of all changes made to that file.

In addition to protecting files from loss, this approach also permits any previous versions of a file to be restored, typically by date and time.

arcnet (attached resource computing network) A proprietary token-bus networking architecture developed by Datapoint Corporation in the mid-1970s.

Currently, Arcnet is widely licensed by third-party vendors and is a popular networking architecture, especially in smaller installations.

It is relatively fast (2.5 Mbit/s) and reliable; it supports coaxial, twisted pair, and fiber optic cable-based implementations.

asynchronous A data transmission method in which each character is sent one bit at a time.

Each character has a start and stop bit to synchronize signals between the sending device and receiving device.

This allows a character to be sent at random after the preceding character has been sent.

attributes A technique for describing access to and properties of files and directories within a filing system.

For NetWare files, attributes include Read, Write, Create, Delete and Execute Only (prevents files from being deleted or copied).

For NetWare directories, attributes include Read, Write, Create, Execute and Hidden (hides information about the directory from file listings, preventing unauthorized access, deletion or copying).

AUX Apple ComputerUs implementation of AT&T UNIX System V, Version 2, Release 2.

bad block table A list kept on a hard disk of storage locations on the disk that are damaged or physically unable to hold data reliably.

The bad block table is usually duplicated on a label on the outside of the disk housing. Also called media defect list.

See also Hot Fix, read-after-write verification.

bandwidth When describing the information capacity of a network, the amount of information that can be handled at one time.

baud rate The rate at which data is transferred over a serial interface.

bridge An interface between two cabling segments of a network. Bridges are often inserted at intervals to extend the length of a network and boost, amplify, or regenerate the signal being transmitted.

coaxial A type of cable that uses two conductors: a central, solid wire core, surrounded by insulation, which is then surrounded by a braided wire conductor sheath.

This cable is particularly well suited for networking because it can accommodate high bandwidth but is relatively resistant to interference.

client In general, an entity on a network that requests some service of another entity on the network. Entities could be computers, printers or other devices.

code A particular representation of a computer program.

console The monitor and keyboard from which you actually view and control server or host activity.

dedicated A device that has only one function. For example, a dedicated server cannot be used as a workstation. See also nondedicated.

dedicated line Leased or private communications line.

device driver Software or firmware that translates operating system requests (such as input/output requests) into a format that is recognizable by specific hardware, such as adapters.

dial-up line Communications line accessible via dial-up facilities, typically the public telephone network.

directory The DOS, OS/2, and UNIX equivalents of folders.

directory caching NetWare feature to improve performance.

In directory caching, a copy of the file allocation table and the directory entry table are written into the network server's memory.

A file's location can then be read from memory, which is faster than reading it from a disk.

directory hashing NetWare feature to improve performance. Directory hashing is a method of indexing file locations on a disk, so the time needed to locate a file is reduced.

directory rights Restrictions specific to a particular directory.

disk duplexing NetWare feature that protects data from failures in network hardware.

In disk duplexing, all data on one hard disk is duplicated on a second hard disk on a separate channel.

Disk writes made to the original disk are also made to the second disk.

If the original disk or channel fails, the duplicate disk takes over automatically.

disk mirroring NetWare feature that protects data from failures in network hardware.

In disk mirroring, all data on one hard disk is duplicated on a second hard disk on the same channel.

Disk writes to the original hard disk are also written to the second hard disk.

If the original disk fails, the duplicate disk takes over automatically.

distributed processing The process in which the workload of a particular application is shared across a network. A technique to enable multiple computers to cooperate in the completion of tasks, typically in a networked environment.

Each computer that contributes to the completion of the total task actually does so by completing one or more individual subtasks independently of its peers, reporting the results from its subtasks as they are completed.

elevator seeking NetWare feature to improve performance. Elevator seeking allows the disk read-write head to pick up files in the direction it is traveling across the disk rather than picking them up in the order they were requested.

E-mail (electronic mail) A method of file transfer and message sending among workstations.

Ethernet A local area network standard defining a physical medium and its method of placing data, or packet signaling, on that medium.

EtherTalk AppleTalk packets encapsulated to run on Ethernet cables.

FCONSOLE NetWare utility used to access information from the network server and fine tune its performance.

It is a virtual console utility that allows the operator to control a server from any station on the network.

Fibre Optic A data transmission medium consisting of glass fibers that is able to carry enormous quantities of data and provide protection from eavesdropping, electromagnetic interference and radioactivity.

file allocation table (FAT) A FAT keeps track of file locations in a particular volume.

NetWare divides each volume into blocks. NetWare stores files on the volume in these blocks.

If the file consists of one or more blocks, the file might be stored in blocks that are not adjacent.

The FAT keeps track of the block numbers where different parts of the file are located.

To retrieve a file, NetWare searches through the FAT until it finds the FAT entries and corresponding block numbers for the requested file.

file sharing An important feature of networking that allows more than one user to access the same file at the same time.

frame The basic data transmission unit used in bit-oriented protocols that contains information for addressing and error checking.

gateway A program or device that resides on two or more dissimilar networks and provides a means for communications among devices on those networks.

gigabyte (GB) A unit of measure for memory or disk storage capacity. Ten to the ninth power (one billion) bytes.

host A computer, attached to a network, that provides services to another computer beyond simply storing and forwarding information.

Usually refers to mainframes and minicomputers.

Hot Fix NetWare feature that protects data from failures in network hardware.

When the Hot Fix feature is activated, a small portion of a hard disk's storage space is set aside as a Hot Fix redirection area.

When read-after-write verification determines that there is a bad data block on the disk, Hot Fix redirects data that was to be stored in the bad block to the Hot Fix redirection area.

Hot Fix marks the defective block as bad and the server will not attempt to store data there again.

internetwork Two or more networks connected by an internal or external router.

Internetwork Packet Exchange (IPX) A protocol that allows the exchange of message packets on an internetwork.

kernel The basic part of an operating system that allows application software to talk to hardware available to the computer (the disk, the Ethernet driver, the printer, etc.).

kilobits per second (kbit/s) Unit of measure commonly used for transfer rates to and from peripheral devices.

kilobyte (KB) A unit of measure for memory or disk storage capacity; two to the 10th power (1,024) bytes.

Local area network (LAN) A system that links computers together to form a network, usually with a wiring-based cabling scheme.

LANs connect personal computers and electronic office equipment, enabling users to communicate, share resources, such as data storage and printers, and to access remote hosts or other networks.

LocalTalk Shielded twisted pair cable introduced by Apple that connects Macintoshes, LaserWriters and other computers and devices on an AppleTalk network.

megabyte (MB) A unit of measure for memory or disk storage capacity. Two to the 20th power (1,048,576) bytes.

multitasking Refers to the ability of a computer to execute more than one program simultaneously.

multiuser Refers to a system that can provide service to more than one user simultaneously.

MVS (Multiple Virtual Storage) IBM operating system for large host systems.

NetView IBM network monitoring software for SNA networks.

NetWare Loadable Module (NLM) A software module that can be added to the NetWare 386 v3.x operating system to add functionality to a network server.

NLMs can be dynamically loaded on or unloaded from the NetWare 386 server without having to down the server.

NetWare operating system The operating system developed by Novell, Inc.

The NetWare operating system is loaded on the server when the server is booted; it controls all system resources and the way information is processed on the entire network or internetwork.

NetWare shell The NetWare program loaded into the memory of each workstation.

It builds itself around DOS and intercepts the workstation's network requests, rerouting them to a NetWare server.

network A system that sends and receives data and messages, typically over a cable.

A network enables a group of computers to communicate with each other, share peripherals (such as hard disks and printers) and access remote hosts or other networks.

network address The uniquely defined destination of a message sent through a communications system.

network interface card The hardware installed in workstations and servers that enables them to communicate on a network.

See also adapter.

Network File System (NFS) A distributed file system network protocol developed by Sun Microsystems, commonly used for file sharing among UNIX computer systems.

node A point in a network where one or more communicating devices are linked to the network and where information can be sent, received, or forwarded.

nondedicated A device that performs multiple simultaneous functions.

For example, a nondedicated network server runs the network functions and performs as a workstation.

OSI (Open System Interconnection) reference model A model for network communications consisting of seven layers that describe what happens when computers communicate with one another.

packet The unit of information by which the network communicates.

Each packet contains the identities of the sending and receiving stations, error-control information, a request for services, information on how to handle the request and any necessary data that must be transferred.

passwords NetWare security feature.

Supervisors of NetWare networks have the option of requiring users to use a password when they log in to the network.

If passwords are required, all users must have unique passwords.

Passwords in NetWare are encrypted; that is, they are stored on the server in a format only the server can decode.

print spooler Software that allows print jobs to be taken away from the individual computer or workstation and put into a queue while waiting to print, giving the user full use of the computer during actual printing.

protocol A set of rules relating to format and timing of data transmission between two entities on a network and which each device must accept and use in order to understand one another.

protocol suite A collection of networking protocols that provides the communications and services needed to enable computers to exchange messages and other information, typically by managing physical connections, communications services and application support.

read-after-write verification NetWare feature that protects data from failures in network hardware.

When NetWare writes data to a block on the hard disk, it reads back the data and compares it to the original data still in memory.

If the data from the disk matches the data in memory, the data in memory is released.

If the data does not match, Hot Fix marks that block on the disk as bad and redirects the data to another location on the hard disk.

record locking This feature on the network operating system prevents two users from writing simultaneously to the same record.

real-time Refers to no perceived delay in the transmission of messages in a computer system. Real-time applications perform tasks at the time they are requested.

remote access Retrieving files or using resources located on a distant computer from a local computer.

rights NetWare security feature. Rights control which directories and files a user can access and what the user is allowed to do with those directories and files.

router A software and hardware connection between two or more networks, usually of similar design, that permits traffic to be routed from one network to another on the basis of the intended destinations of that traffic.

A NetWare Router, formerly known as an internal or external bridge, can connect networks that use different network adapters or transmission media as long as both sides of the connection use the same protocols.

If a router is located in a server, it is called an internal router; if located in a workstation, it is called an external router.

Sequenced Packet Exchange (SPX) A protocol by which two workstations or applications communicate across the network.

SPX uses NetWare IPX to deliver the messages, but SPX guarantees delivery of the messages and maintains the order of messages on the packet stream.

server A computer on the network capable of recognizing and responding to client requests for services.

These services can range from basic file and print services to support for complex, distributed applications.

For example, a distributed database management system can create a single logical database across multiple servers.

supervisor The person responsible for the administration and maintenance of a network or database.

A supervisor has all access rights to all volumes, directories and files.

System Fault Tolerance (SFT) Duplicating data on multiple storage devices so that if one storage device fails, the data is available from another device.

There are several levels of hardware and software system fault tolerance.

Each level of redundancy (duplication) decreases the possibility of data loss.

System Application Architecture (SAA) A set of IBM-defined standards designed to provide a consistent environment for programmers and users across a broad range of IBM equipment including microcomputers, minicomputers, and mainframes.

System Network Architecture (SNA) IBM network architecture, defined in terms of its functions, formats and protocols.

TCP/IP (Transmission Control Protocol/Internet Protocol) A protocol suite and related applications developed for the U.S. Department of Defense in the 1970s and 1980s specifically to permit different types of computers to communicate and exchange information with one another.

TCP/IP is currently mandated as an official Department of Defense protocol and is also widely used in the UNIX community.

TCP/IP is vendor-independent; its purpose is to connect widely differing computers while providing for data errors, security and line failure.

terminal A device, usually equipped with a keyboard and display, capable of sending and receiving data over a communications link.

throughput Net data transfer rate between an information source and an information destination.

Token Ring A cabling and media access method in which each device on a LAN receives and passes the right to use the single LAN channel. This access method is usually used with the ring network topology.

TokenTalk AppleTalk implemented via Token Ring.

Token-Ring Interface Coupler (TIC) Device on IBM 3725 or 3745 allowing the use of Token-Ring topology for communication with local terminal emulation devices.

topology The physical layout of network components (cable, stations, gateways, hubs and so on).

There are three basic interconnection topologies: star, ring and bus networks.

Transaction Tracking System (TTS) NetWare feature that protects data from failures in network hardware.

TTS protects the integrity of databases by backing out incomplete transactions that result from a failure in a network component.

transparent Describes the operation of a network such that a user is unaware that a service is being provided by the network; rather, the service appears to be provided by resources local to the workstation.

twinaxial cable A cable similar to coaxial cable except that there are two center conductors.

twisted pair Cabling that consists of two insulated wires wrapped around each other, and sometimes surrounded by a shield, jacket, or other insulation, or by similar pairs of wires. Phone wire is the most common type of twisted pair cable. Apple ComputerUs LocalTalk, Farallon ComputingUs PhoneNET and SynOptics Communications' implementation of Ethernet are examples of twisted pair cabling.

Uninterruptible power supply (UPS) A backup power unit that provides continuous power even when the normal power supply is interrupted.

UNIX Operating system developed by AT&T Bell Laboratories. Allows a computer to handle multiple users and programs simultaneously.

UPS monitoring NetWare feature that protects data from failures in network hardware.

A third-party uninterruptible power supply (UPS) provides power to the server during power fluctuations and outages.

NetWare's UPS monitoring feature monitors the status of the UPS attached to the server.

user Any person who attaches to a server or host.

user accounts NetWare security feature. Each user on a NetWare network has a user account.

This account determines what name the user uses to log in to the network, the groups the user belongs to and what trustee assignments the users has.

User accounts are maintained by the network supervisor.

value-added process (VAP) An application that runs on top of 286-based network operating systems.

VAPs tie in with the network operating system so that print servers, archive servers and database servers can provide services without interfering with the network's normal operation.

Volume A volume is the highest level in the NetWare directory structure—it is the same level as a DOS root directory.

A volume represents a physical amount of hard disk storage space.

wide area network (WAN) A WAN is two or more LANs in separate geographic locations connected by a remote link.

workgroup manager A user classification in NetWare v3.X.

Workgroup managers have supervisory control over any user or user group they create on the network.

workstation Any individual personal computer that is connected to a network.

A
APPENDIX

A technical description of AppleTalk

AppleTalk is a network system whose components have in common a set of protocols, or rules for exchanging information on a network. An AppleTalk network system consists of products that support these protocols and that work together to deliver network services to its users.

The AppleTalk protocol architecture

The AppleTalk protocol architecture consists of protocol modules designed to send and receive information across a network. In order for two devices to communicate with each other over an AppleTalk internet, both devices must support AppleTalk protocols. One way to better understand the structure of the AppleTalk protocol suite is to compare its architecure to a reference model developed by the International Standards Organization, called the Open Systems Interconnection model (OSI). The OSI model is divided into seven layers for sending and receiving information across a network. Each of the AppleTalk protocols provides the services of one or more of these layers and interfaces with other protocols in neighboring layers. The diagram on Figure A-1 represents the standard AppleTalk protocols in comparison to the OSI model.

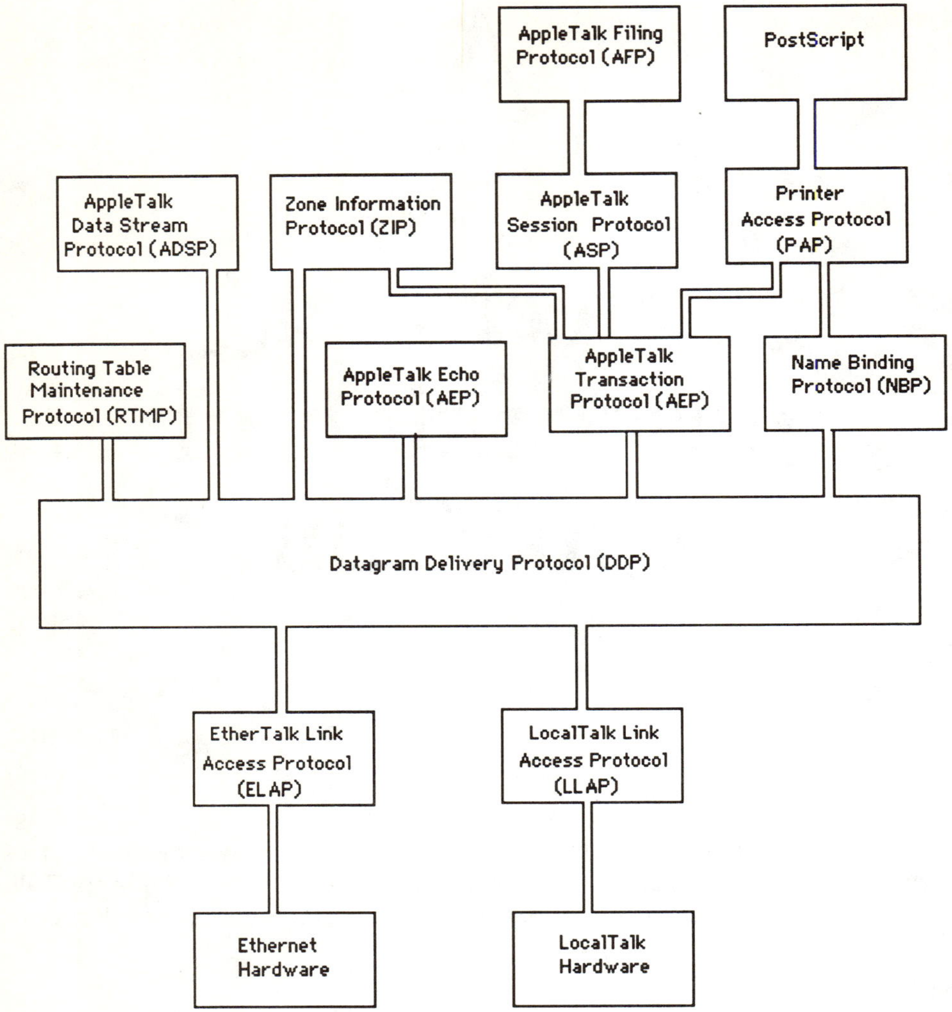

A-1 Comparison between standard AppleTalk protocols and the OSI model.

The *physical layer* establishes the physical connection between a computer and the network and controls the transmission of information. This layer includes the physical hardware, such as Token Ring, Ethernet, and LocalTalk hardware.

The *data link layer* is responsible for the transmission of data across the physical link and ensures data integrity on this link. This layer includes link access protocols, such as TokenTalk (TLAP), EtherTalk (ELAP) and LocalTalk (LLAP). The link access protocol encapsulates data into frames and permits nodes to access transmission lines for sending and receiving frames.

The *network layer* determines which route data will take through the network. The *Datagram Delivery Protocol* is the network layer protocol responsible for socket-to-socket delivery of datagrams over an AppleTalk internet.

The *transport layer* controls the quality of transmission. This layer consists of the following AppleTalk protocol modules: *Routing Table Maintenance Protocol* (RTMP), *AppleTalk Echo Protocol* (AEP), *AppleTalk Transaction Protocol* (ATP), and *Name Binding Protocol* (NBP). (Note: Both RTMP and NBP are not actually part of the transport layer but are closest to the transport layer when comparing them to the OSI model.)

The Routing Table Maintenance Protocol is used to establish and maintain the routing information required by internet routers in order to route datagrams from any source socket to any destination socket in the internet. This is used by internet routers to dynamically maintain and reflect changes in the internet topology. This is implemented in the router portion of the AppleTalk module in NetWare for Macintosh v3.0.

The AppleTalk Echo Protocol is a simple protocol that allows a node to send a packet to any other node in an AppleTalk internet and to receive an echoed copy of that packet in return. This is useful for determining whether a node on the network is alive. In NetWare for Macintosh v3.0, the Echo protocol is functionally implemented in the stack and router.

The AppleTalk Transaction Protocol provides a loss-free transaction service between sockets. This service allows exchanges between two socket clients in which one client requests the other to perform a particular task and to report the results. ATP binds the request and response together to ensure the reliable exchange of request-response pairs. This is used by both file and print services. ATP and ASP is used for client/server type communication.

The Name Binding Protocol translates a character string name into the internet address of the corresponding socket client. NBP enables AppleTalk protocols to understand user-defined zones and device names by providing and maintaining translation tables that map these names to corresponding network addresses. NBP allows users to identify devices and services (ie. network servers and printers) on an AppleTalk internet by name and not by the internet address.

For example, when a node looks for an AppleTalk service (such as a printer), a NBP request for that service is either sent to a router or, if no routers are present, a broadcast or multicast is sent directly to all nodes on the local network. In the case where routers are present (on an internet), the routers are responsible for seeing that the appropriate request is broadcast or multicast on all the networks in the zone for which the request is being made. All nodes providing the service then send responses back to the original requesting node. This is the way that printers, servers, and other AppleTalk network entities advertise themselves in response to requests from the Apple Chooser.

The *session layer* establishes and manages the dialogue between users and systems by setting up and terminating communications on the network. The session layer consists of the following AppleTalk protocol modules: *AppleTalk Data Stream Protocol* (ADSP), *Zone Information Protocol* (ZIP), *AppleTalk Session Protocol* (ASP), and *Printer Access Protocol* (PAP). (Note: ZIP actually falls closer to the transport layer; but it is closer to the session layer when comparing it to the OSI model.)

The AppleTalk Data Stream Protocol provides a reliable, full-duplex, byte-stream service between any two sockets in an AppleTalk internet. ADSP ensures insequence, duplicate-free delivery of data over its connections. Novell's NetWare for SAA uses ADSP for terminal emulation support.

The Zone Information Protocol is used to maintain and discover the internet-wide mapping of network numbers to zone names. It acquires the zone information from routers and propagates that information on the internet.

A zone is a logical grouping of devices that allows users to easily locate and access network services in the Chooser. A zone name is a logical name associated with a network or a set of networks within an internet. Zones also can be used to group networks together to alleviate network traffic on the internet.

For example, when a router gets an RTMP message indicating the presence of a new network on the internet, the router sends a ZIP Request packet to the router that sent the RTMP packet. This router sends back a ZIP Reply packet containing the zone name for the network. For extended networks (see section on AppleTalk Phase 2), ZIP extensions obtain zone multicast addresses and verify valid zone names for a given node. ZIP is also used by NBP to determine which networks belong to a zone. This protocol is almost entirely implemented in the router portion of the AppleTalk module.

The AppleTalk Session Protocol is a general purpose protocol that uses the services of ATP to provide session establishment, maintenance, and teardown, along with request sequencing.

The Printer Access Protocol manages interaction between workstations and print servers. PAP handles connection setup, maintenance, and termination, as well as data transfer over the connection. For the LaserWriter printer, commands and data sent through the PAP connection are PostScript.

The *presentation layer* performs code conversions and formats translation of messages. This layer consists of the *AppleTalk Filing Protocol* (AFP) and *PostScript.*

The AppleTalk Filing Protocol allows workstation users to share data files and application programs by interacting directly with the NetWare file system, at the same level as NCP interaction. This protocol is implemented as a separate NLM and is not included in the AppleTalk stack/router.

PostScript is the document representation/page description protocol used for communication with LaserWriter printer.

The *application layer* consists of software drivers that interact with the users' application programs. This layer consists of AFP file servers (ie. AppleShare and NetWare servers) and print servers.

When sending data from one device to another device on the network, the data on the sending device moves from the application layer down to the phyical layer where data is transmitted on the wire. As the data is moved from one layer down to the next, header and addressing information is added on as needed to transmit the data to the specified device across the network. When receiving data, the data moves through the layers in the reverse order in the receiving device. Each layer reads and strips out the appropriate header information before passing the data up to the next layer. This process is repeated until the data reaches the application where the data is processed.

AppleTalk Phase 1

AppleTalk Phase 1 is the original release of Apple's protocol suite. It aquired its Phase 1 nomenclature with the release of an update called AppleTalk Phase 2, which added some new features and characteristics to the protocol. AppleTalk Phase 1 works on LocalTalk and Ethernet networks but not on Token Ring networks.

An AppleTalk node operating on an AppleTalk Phase 1 network is identified by an 8-bit node number. Thus, the maximum number of AppleTalk nodes on one physical cable is 254. The AppleTalk node number is dynamically determined at boot time. Each AppleTalk node will either use a number stored in parameter RAM (pRAM) or generate a random number. The node number cannot be assigned explicitly. An AARP probe is sent out on the local network with an AppleTalk node number to determine if the node number is already being used. If there is no response for this node number, the node number can be used. If there is a response for this node number, the node number is already being used and a new node number must be randomly generated. This process is repeated until a unique AppleTalk node number is generated for the device on the local network.

AppleTalk Phase 2

AppleTalk Phase 2 is an extension of the AppleTalk network system that can support larger networks. The principal changes in AppleTalk Phase 2 include an extended network addressing scheme to support more nodes per network, and zone lists to support multiple zones per network. Networks that support these addressing extensions are called *extended networks*.

AppleTalk Phase 2 operates on Ethernet, Token Ring and LocalTalk networks. However, LocalTalk networks operating under AppleTalk Phase 2 cannot participate in the extended network addressing scheme.

On an extended network, the node address is comprised of the node's 16-bit network number and its 8-bit node number. The node's network number is compared with the router's range of network numbers. If the node's network number is not within the range, the node selects a different network number that is within the range. If there are no routers on the network, the node uses the initial network number determined during boot time from a startup range.

With the extended network addressing scheme, AppleTalk Phase 2 networks allow for more than 65,000 logical networks. Each logical network has a unique network number and a limit of 254 AppleTalk nodes. This increases the maximum number of AppleTalk nodes allowed on the network from 254 to more than 16 million nodes.

AppleTalk Phase 2 currently operates on Ethernet (802.3) and Token Ring (802.2) network systems. In NetWare for Macintosh v3.0, EtherTalk 2.0 (AppleTalk Phase 2 operating on an Ethernet network) and TokenTalk (AppleTalk operating on a Token Ring network) are extended Phase 2 networks. Extended networks use a range of network numbers (or *network range*) on a single physical cable. You can associate each number in a network range with up to 253 nodes. The size of the network range determines the maximum number of AppleTalk devices on the physical cable. For example, an extended network with the range 1-10 could support up to 10 x 253, or 2,530 nodes.

LocalTalk networks are unchanged under AppleTalk Phase 2, because LocalTalk does not require (and cannot support) the AppleTalk Phase 2 addressing or multiple zone extensions. All Phase 2 networks that are not configured to support these extensions are called nonextended networks.

The network number or network range must be unique to a physical network and consistent for all routers connected to that network. All routers connected to the same network must have the same network number or the same network range. None of the network numbers in the range can conflict with any other network number in the AppleTalk internet. For example, if a network is configured with range 3-6, it is illegal to have another network configured with range 3-4, range 3-8, range 5-7, net 3, or net 5 (or any combination of the numbers 3, 4, 5, and 6, because they are already used).

AppleTalk zones

A *zone* is a logical gouping of devices that make it easier for users to locate and access network services in the Macintosh Chooser. For example, file services, printers, and print queues are listed in the Chooser, grouped by zone name.

Zones are defined in the AppleTalk router configuration. One zone name is required for each network. If you wish, the same zone name can be associated with more than one network.

Each nonextended network must have exactly one zone name assigned to it. Each extended network must have at least one zone name and could have up to 16 zone names assigned to it. A *zone list* is a list of up to 16 zone names. The *default zone* is the first name you enter in the zone list.

Individual nodes connected to an extended network are placed in the default zone unless the user chooses another zone. Although a node can belong to only one zone, the user can still view and access the services in all zones. An AppleTalk zone name or zone list can be repeated on multiple networks, but this information must be consistent for all routers connected to a network. All routers connected to the same network must have the same zone name or zone list for that network.

Multiple zones within an extended network

Each extended network can support as many as 255 zone names allowing for multiple zones on a network. Any node on an extended network can belong to any zone supported in the network's zone list. Two adjacent nodes on the same physical network cable can belong to two different zones. Similarily, two nodes on two different physical network cable can belong to the same zone. Administrators can group devices according to work group requirements alone, without any regard for the physical location of the devices.

Multicasting

Multicast is a form of restricted broadcasting. If a node wants to see packets sent to a certain multicast address, it must arrange for that internally by registering on the particular multicast address in order to receive those packets. With an Ethernet chip, you can tell the chip which multicast addresses you would like to receive packets from. This is done in the software drivers by the LAN adapter manufacturers. Apple Computer has a list of multicast addresses that can be used. These multicast addresses must be well known, so that all nodes will register for the same address. AppleTalk nodes determine their multicast address, along with their network number and zone name at boot time.

AppleTalk Phase 2 uses multicasting rather than broadcasting on the Ethernet. There are two types of multicast; zone multicast and broadcast multicast. For zone broadcasts, such as NBP LkUp packets, the packet is multicast to a multicast address for a particular zone. Each zone name corresponds to one and only one multicast address. A node then can register for the multicast address and receive any zone specific broadcasts for its zone.

For broadcast multicast, such as RTMP packets, the packet is sent to a multicast address (multicast broadcast address). Each AppleTalk node on the Ethernet should register for this address in order to receive AppleTalk broadcast packets on this network. Non-AppleTalk nodes would not register on this address and therefore would not see any AppleTalk traffic.

Split Horizon

Split Horizon is another feature defined in Apple's AppleTalk Phase 2 specification. It reduces the amount of RTMP traffic on the network by routing only those RTMP packets that are neccessary to the particular router. For example, if a router is connected to network A and network B, the router is intelligent enough to route only the RTMP packets regarding network B to the router on network A. This would decrease the amount of RTMP traffic on the network because the router will not route RTMP packets regarding network A to the router on network A. Likewise, the router will not route RTMP packets regarding network B to the router on network B. The router will only route RTMP packets regarding network A to the router on network B. Split Horizon is implemented in the router in NetWare for Macintosh v3.0.

AppleTalk routing

An AppleTalk network connects one or more Macintosh workstations and printers, allowing them to communicate with each other and to access services on the network. An AppleTalk router connects multiple AppleTalk networks allowing all nodes on the multiple networks to communicate and access services on each other's networks, as well as their own "local" network. An AppleTalk internet is a group of interconnected networks.

The function of a router

A router manages the delivery of packets between any of the networks it connects. Each router on an AppleTalk internet maintains a routing table that lists all networks in the internet, their distance in number of routes (or hops), the zones associated with them, and the port and router through which they can be reached. The information in the table enables routers to determine where to send a packet as well as the most efficient route to send it. This is done by using the Routing Table Maintenance Protocol (RTMP). To keep track of all routes to all AppleTalk networks on the internet, every AppleTalk router sends RTMP packets every 10 seconds to other routers on its interfaces, updating their own and each other's routing tables, so that eventually a complete picture of the internet is propagated to all routers.

Broadcasting RTMP packets every 10 seconds to other routers on the network is part of the AppleTalk specification by Apple Computer. This can cause more traffic on your network than you want. This congestion on your network can be alleivated by running AppleTalk Phase 2 on your network. AppleTalk Phase 2 provides multicast capabilities, allowing you to send packets to only AppleTalk nodes. (See section on Multicasting.)

AppleTalk packets are units of information that have been broken down and formatted with a source and destination address for transmission on an AppleTalk network. If the source and destination addresses are not on the same network, the packet must be forwarded to the destination network by an AppleTalk router.

How zone information is maintained by routers

When an AppleTalk router is brought up on a network, it is initialized with its own zones and network numbers. It then begins to receive and send RTMP packets with every other router on the internet.

When other routers receive RTMP packets informing them of a new network on the internet, those routers send a query to the router, asking for the zone name or zone list associated with the network. The new router responds with its zone information. Eventually, all routers on the internet have an updated global list of all zones on the entire internet. This global list helps to make visible all AppleTalk services in all the AppleTalk zones on the internet; thereby, giving Macintosh users access to all AppleTalk services on the internet.

Once one router has acquired zone information from another router, it does not query for zone information related to that particular network again. As long as the network has a good entry in the router's RTMP tables, there is no way to force a router to query for its zone information again.

One of the side effects of this situation is that routers are not automatically informed about changes to zone configurations. For example, if you delete a zone name from a router configuration table for one AppleTalk network, routers connected to other networks still have the deleted zone name in their lists, so it continues to be visible in the Chooser. In addition, those routers are now inconsistent with the reconfigured router, because they are still maintaining the old zone information. This inconsistency can cause a zone name to show up in the Macintosh Chooser for some time after you have deleted it, and can even cause users to see zone names appearing and disappearing in the Chooser.

The only way to update zone information in all routers is to wait long enough for the RTMP tables in all routers to recognize that the relevant network is down. This usually takes between ten and twenty minutes, but it can take longer on a large internet. (Alternatively, you can down all routers on the internet and bring them up again. This will force an update of the RTMP tables.)

Transition mode routing

Transition Mode Routing is required on an internet that supports both Phase 1 and Phase 2 routers. An internet that supports both Phase 1 and Phase 2 without any routers will not require Transition Mode routing. Phase 1 routers only can be connected to nonextended networks (EtherTalk 1.0 or LocalTalk), because Phase 1 does not support extended networks. However, the fact that there are nonextended networks on an internet does not imply that a Phase 1 router is present.

If the internet supports Phase 1 routers, you can either upgrade them to Phase 2 or keep them installed and configured as Phase 1 routers and configure all Phase 2 routers on the internet in Transition Mode. When an AppleTalk router is configured for Transition Mode, the Phase 2 router modifies its behavior to operate with a Phase 1 router on the internet.

In Transition Mode, all Phase 2 networks must be nonextended. All Phase 2 routers must observe the following addressing constraints to avoid extended ranges and zone lists incomprehensible to a Phase 1 router:

- On extended networks, the first number in the network range is equal to the last number in the range, as in 10-10.
- On extended networks, the zone list has only one name.

The addressing contraints in Transition Mode mean that extended networks are limited to 253 devices. If you must support more than 253 EtherTalk 2.0 (Phase 2) or TokenTalk devices, you cannot use Transition Mode. Your alternative is to upgrade the Phase 1 routers to AppleTalk Phase 2.

If you need more than 253 AppleTalk nodes, regardless of whether they are Phase 1 or Phase 2 nodes, you can have a Phase 1 network with 253 Phase 1 nodes and a Phase 2 network with 253 Phase 2 nodes for a total of 506 AppleTalk nodes.

See NetWare for Macintosh v3.0 Installation and Maintenance guide for details on how to configure a router in Transition Mode.

What does a router do in Transition Mode?

When you configure a router in Transition Mode, the router is prepared to send out Phase 1 compatible RTMP packets on its nonextended interfaces. When the Phase 2 router is not in Transition Mode, it always sends out Phase 2 RTMP packets. Phase 2 RTMPs are different from Phase 1 RTMPs, and can contain information about extended networks. A Phase 1 router cannot read the Phase 2 packets and cannot incorporate the Phase 2 information into its routing table.

When the Phase 2 router is in Transition Mode and it receives a Phase 1 RTMP packet on one of its nonextended interfaces, it sends out Phase 1 compatible RTMP packets on that network. The network information contained in these packets cannot include extended ranges and zone lists, which means all extended networks (EtherTalk 2.0 or TokenTalk) on the entire AppleTalk internet must be configured with a network range of one (for example, 10-10), and a zone list of one (for example, "My zone").

List of References

The Advantages of AppleTalk® Phase 2, Apple Computer, Inc., Cupertino, CA, 1990.

Inside AppleTalk, Second Edition, Addison-Wesley Publishing Company, Inc., Menlo Park, CA, 1989.

NetWare for Macintosh, Installation and Maintenance v3.0, Novell, Inc., Provo, UT, 1991.

Index

O

P

R

S

T

U

V

W

Z